SERVICE RECORD

OF

KING EDWARD'S SCHOOL

BIRMINGHAM

DURING THE WAR 1914-1919

CORNISH BROTHERS, LIMITED

39 NEW STREET

BIRMINGHAM

1920

TO THE MEMORY OF

THE FALLEN

A TRIBUTE FROM THEIR OLD SCHOOL

CONTENTS

INTRODUCTION

WHEN the magnitude of the call which would be made upon the manhood of the British Commonwealth became apparent in the early autumn of 1914, every Public School and many other institutions took steps to compile a list of present or past members taking their part in the War. It may probably be said that had this desire not existed the War itself could never have been fought and won, for it is characteristic of our race to form strong local patriotisms first, and only on second thoughts or the occurrence of a crisis merge them in the great tide of national enthusiasm. The compilation proved a difficult task. In our own case it was originally undertaken by Captain Kirkby, the Commanding Officer of the School Contingent of the O.T.C., and when his military duties came to absorb the whole of his time, was passed on to the present Editor, Mr. Heath, of whose indefatigable zeal and unrivalled knowledge and memory of Old Edwardians I desire to express my grateful admiration. Taken as a whole the record is one which it is impossible for me, and for many others, to read without tears ; but we should be unworthy of our sons, brothers, or schoolfellows if we could not also read it with profound thankfulness and pride. Inheritors of a great tradition, it has fallen to the Edwardians whose names are inscribed in this volume to outstrip the Past and endow their School with its most precious and most inspiring memory.

R. CARY GILSON.

KING EDWARD'S SCHOOL,
  BIRMINGHAM. *July* 1919.

PREFACE

In presenting this Record, the Editor is only too well aware of its numerous shortcomings and errors alike of omission and of commission. That this was inevitable is obvious; but no pains have been spared to make the list as complete as possible. The system adopted was to enter the name of each man on a card, and build up the record by careful and systematic examination of all official documents, Gazettes, Army, Navy, and Air Force Lists (so far as they were available), newspapers, School Lists, Blue Books, and Admission Registers, often by personal inquiry and letters, and by advertisement in the newspapers. The latter two sources have sometimes proved disappointing, owing partly to changes of address, partly to the modesty of those approached, and the replies received have varied greatly in fullness. The Editor wishes to emphasize this point, to explain the apparent discrepancy in aim between the paragraphs: the fuller records, with a few modifications, have invariably been inserted when received from those concerned, subject to the general rule decided on by the Editorial Sub-committee of the War Memorial only to mention localities in the case of service abroad. He gratefully acknowledges the generous help he has received from many past and present members of the School, from the Head Master, who has placed all his information at his disposal, from Capt. W. H. Kirkby, and from Lt.-Col. G. W. Craig, who has given much valuable assistance in finishing off the Record.

The list is obviously far from complete, but it was felt that a definite date must be fixed for sending it to press. The Editor will be glad to receive corrections of mistakes and any further information, especially of names or services unfortunately omitted. Should there be a demand and the additional information justify it, it may be possible to publish a Supplement uniform with this volume, and so to make the record as definitive as possible.

I gratefully acknowledge the invaluable assistance I have received from the Controller of the Oxford University Press during the printing of the book.

CHARLES H. HEATH.
Editor.

KING EDWARD'S SCHOOL,
BIRMINGHAM.

SERVICE RECORD

OF

KING EDWARD'S SCHOOL
BIRMINGHAM

DURING THE WAR 1914-1919

ADDITIONS AND
CORRECTIONS
1931

NOTE

IN the Service Record issued in 1920 there were inevitably some names omitted, and some errors.

The following corrections are now issued on information since received. Copies of this supplement may be obtained from the Editor, Charles H. Heath, at King Edward's School, Birmingham, who will gladly receive any further information which should be included in the record.

N.B. The dates of Honours are those of the issues of the *London Gazette* in which they were published.

ADDITIONAL NAMES

CARDEW, J. H., M.C. (1895–6)
Cpl., Punjab L.H. 1915 Sec. Lt., R.F.A., S.R. Oct. 1915 France,
Ypres. 1916 Somme. Lt. M.C. for gallantry and devotion to duty
while under fire as F O.O., Aug. 1916. 1917 Capt. Passchendaele.
Died, Oct. 5, 1917, of wounds received the previous day.

†CONNOLLY, J. N. (1908–9, g)
Dec. 1915 Pte., 14 R. War. R. Mar.–June 1916 France (1). Mar.
1917 France (2). Killed May 7, 1917, east of Vimy Ridge.

DARE, W. H. (1910–16, g)
Cdt., Art. Rif. Nov. 1918 attd. 4 K.R. Rif.

EAGER, G. C. (1895–9)
Capt., R.A.M.C. Mesopotamia.

†ELDRIDGE, J. T. (1906–7, b)
Pte., B'hm City Bn., R. War. R. Jan. 1918 Sec. Lt., Worc. R.
France. Killed Sept. 18, 1918.

GLANVILLE, H. (1905–8, y)
Jan. 1914 Payr. Asst. Clk., H.M.S. Crescent. Jan. 1915 Payr. Clk.
July 1917 Payr. Sub-Lt. H.M.S. Alsatian, 4th Cruiser Sqdn. Nov.
1918 H.M.S. Carlisle.

GUISE, E. S. (1910–11, b)

HANDS, F. B., M.M. (1896)

HARRISON, F. C. (1891)
1915–1916 (Public Schools') B., Midd'x R.

HOWLETT, E. N. (1904–8, y)
Aug. 1914 Lt., S. Nigerian Vols., Camerun E.F. Wounded Nov.
1914.

JACKSON, B. W. (1903, y)
1915 R.N.R. Straits of Messina (blown up). H.M.S. London,
Dardanelles. Eng.-Lt. Dover Patrol.

JENKINS, FREDERICK (1902–5, *r*)
1909–13 Pte., R.A.M.C., 1 S. Mid. F.A. 1915 Gnr., R.G.A., 143 Siege By. 1915 transfd. Anti-Aircraft Home Defence. He was one of the gun-team which, in 1916, took part in bringing down a Zeppelin during the bombardment of Hartlepool. 1916 London A.-A. Defences.

KERBY, W. M. (1892–9)
Aug. 1917–Jan. 1919 Pte., Midd'x R.

†MILLER, NEVILLE (1892–4)
Sept. 1914 Pte., 14 R. War. R. Aug. 1915 L.-Cpl. Nov. 1915 France (1): wounded, Somme, July 1916. Jan. 1917 Sec. Lt., 1/5 S. Staff. R., T.F. Apr. 1917 France (2). Killed June 28, 1917, nr. R. Scarpe.

MILLS, F. L., M.C. (1908–9, *r*)

NICOL, W. P. (1885–90)
M.O., Military Hospital, Pretoria. M.O. for pensions Maj., S.A.M.C.

NORTON, H. R. (1903–5, *b*)
1915–19 R.E.

OXLEY, R. R. (1910–13, *g*)
Gnr., R.H.A., W By. Meerut. July 1917–Jan. 1920 Mesopotamia

RASTON, BERTRAND (1913–14, *y*)
Sept. 1914 Pte., R.A.M.C. Nov. 1915 Sec. Lt., Midd'x R. July 1916 France, Somme: Ypres. Wounded Sept. 1916.

†SCHWABEN, C. W. (1902)
Pte., 13 Cty. of London R. Died o.a.s., Alexandria, Dec. 23, 1917.

SHIMWELL, A. G. (1912–14, *g*)
S.A.M.T. S. Africa.

†TALBOT, E. F. (1893–7)
Nov. 1915 Pte., 26 (Bankers') Bn., R. Fus. Apr 1916 France. Killed Sept. 16, 1916, nr. Flers, Somme.

WATSON, E. E., M.M. (1912–15, *g*)
1917 Tr. Res. May 1918 Pte., 1/7 Lan. Fus., xlii Div., France, Bucquoy-Achiet. Aug. 23 onwards, final advance of 3rd Army Sept. 1918 wounded, M.M.

ADDITIONS AND CORRECTIONS

ALCOCK, A. B. F. *at end* Capt., R.M.L.I.

ARNOLD, STANLEY (1910–13, *r*)

AUSTER, Rev. W. W.

†BACHE, J. E. K. (1898–1904, *r*)
Died Jan. 21, 1931, from effects of war injuries.

BALL, J. F. A. Gen. List. *for* Actg. A.P.M. *read* D.A.P.M. *add* 1918–19 A.P.M., Charleroi.

BANTOCK, J. R. G. Nov. 1919 Lt.

BARK, G. M. 15 Inf. Bde. Bombing Officer.

BARKER, C. H. 1915 raised a batty. of arty., and served in command 'through all the opns. at Ypres, Somme, Arras, Messines, and Passchendaele'. 1918, in the retreat, Amiens: in the advances, Amiens and farther S. Served with the French Army in the big (south) counter-attack; with the Belgian Army in the 2nd push N. of Ypres. Later, Afghan War, commanded a batty. throughout, and assisted in covering retreat of 1st Div. from Dakka.

†BARNSLEY, T. K. 3 Bn. transfd. to 1st Bn. after Loos.

BARTLEET, E. J. *for* J.

BENNITT, Rev. F. W. *not* BENNETT

BENSON, C. R. Apr. 1919 Lt.

†BOURNE, R. B. Oct. 1916 France. 860 hours' flying. Aug. 1919 Fl. Off. Killed in flying accident, o.a.s., at Baldonnell Aerodrome, Co. Dublin, Nov. 6, 1919.

BRADFIELD, E. W. C. 1914 Adjt., Hosp. Ship Madras. 1916–19 Mesopot. E.F. 1916 O.C. Troops, Hosp. Ship Sikkim. 1917–19 O.C. 40 C.F.A., Actg. Lt.-Col. At captures of Basra, Baghdad, Mosul. Mentd. Jan. 1919.

†BREARLY, N. B. (1910–12, *b*)

BRINDLEY, P. S. *line 2* 10 Bde. (*not* 11). *line 7* Staff Course. *line 9* Sen. Offrs. Course, Aldershot. Order of the Nile, Cl. 4.

BROWN, P. W. 1919 Actg. Capt.

BULLOCKE, J. G. (1907–16, *g*)
July–Aug. 1919 Actg. Capt. and Adjt,

CADDICK, R. V. *line 2 for* behind *read* in front of

CHASE, R. G. B. *line 2* Actg. Capt., cdg. a Section.

CLARKE, H. 1919–20 Thrace.

CLAYTON, A. C. B. (1916–17, *y*)

†COKE, L. S. Killed at Zandvoorde, Oct. 31, 1914.

COLEMAN, H. D. Mentd. Nov. 1918 for Retreat, Mar. 1918.

COLLETT, J. R. W. *line 2* 2nd By., 9 Bde.

CORSER, C. H. June 1919 Lt.-Cdr., R.I.M.

CRESWELL, P. T. Attd. R.N.A.S., Meteorological Branch.

†CRICHTON, G. E. Killed in Gallipoli, Lone Pine.

CRONIN, R. H. 1918 France: Somme.

CURLE, G. 1918 Capt.

CURLE, Victor. Mentd. War Services.

†CURTIS, K. S. Killed at Polderhoek.

DAVIS, S. A. Nov. 1915 France, T.M., xxi Div.

DAVISS, L. Vincent (*for* L. F.) Sec. Lt. (*del.* Cpl.)

†DISTURNAL, F. L. France, 49 Bn. Killed Aug. 8, 1918, nr. Amiens.

DONOVAN, E. T. G. (1911–16, *b*)

DOWNING, A. M. *add* Dec. 1918 Adjt. and Q.-M., Actg. Capt.

†EHRHARDT, W. H. Died, after 8th operation on his wound, June 17, 1923.

EVANS, E. A. Actg. Capt. May 1919 Capt.

FAWDRY, J. W. Sept. 1919–May 1920 Staff Capt., 29 Inf. Bde., Alexandria.

FIFE, D. MacD. Aug. 1919 Lt.

FISHER, L. G. Dec. 1919 Lt.

FITZPATRICK, B. P. S. Jan. 1920 Lt.

FORREST, H. Wounded July 1, 1916. Oct. 1917 O.C. Coy.

GODFREY, C. B. Aug. 1919 R.A.F. permanent commission.

GOODE, T. F. June 1920 Maj.

GRANT, K. W. 1920 British Military Mission, attd. Greek Army of Smyrna, Brusa. June 1920 Greek M.C. 3rd Cl. June 1920 1st Cl. Agent.

†HARROWER, A. P. *line 2 read* Jan. 1917 France (2). Lt., 11–12 Bn. Apr. Hénin, Héninal. Wounded (2). Dec. France (3). . . .

HAYWOOD, N. A. *add* Cpl., Actg. S.S.-M., ½ Coy. Mentd. (1) July 1917.

HEMMING, F. J. (1903–11, *r*)

HENDERSON, R. B. France 1916, 117 Siege By.: 1917–18, 155 S. By. 1918 Maj., 2nd Army Calibration. Mentd. 1918.

†HILL, B. G. Killed, reported missing Sept. 25, 1915.

†HIPKINS, N. *del.* 14 Lan. R. *read* N. Staff. R. July 1917 Lt. Sept. 1917 Actg. Capt. Killed Sept. 28, 1918.

HOLDEN, H. F. 1915 Lt. Actg. Capt. (*not* Temp.) Wounded July 19, 1917.

HOLDING, B. C. C. Oct. 1918 France.

HOLMES, J. L. (1901–6, *t*) *Corrected notice.*
Aug. 1914 Pte. A.S.C., M.T., Aldershot. Oct. Sgt. Drill Instructor. Feb. 1915 W.O. Dec. 1915–Jan. 1918 Whitchurch, Salop. Jan. 1918 France: Doullens to Namur.

HOPKINS, E. L. Actg. Maj. July 1919 2nd i.c. of Bn.

HORSLEY, N. A. May 1919 Lt.

HORTON, W. CECIL (1895–9). *Substitute for* Horton, C.
1907 Eng.-Lt., R.N. Aug. 1914 (from R.N. Coll., Dartmouth) H.M.S. Argonaut, prot'd. cruiser, Plymouth: Atlantic Coasts of Spain and Portugal, Madeira, &c. Oct. 1914–Dec. 1915 at Gibraltar, H.M.S. Leviathan, armd. cruiser: N. Sea, N. America, and W. Indies Station. Oct. 1915 Eng.-Lt.-Cdr. Courses at Portsmouth. Mar. 1916 Chatham, H.M.S. Llewellyn, destroyer, Harwich Force, Dover Patrol. Mar. 18, 1917, torpedoed in action with German destroyers in Straits of Dover; ship towed back to Dover. Dec. 4, 1916, depth-charged and sank German submarine U.C. 19 in Straits of Dover. May 1917 joined H.M.S. Vortigern, destroyer, building at Cowes, I. of W. July–Aug. 1917, temporarily, H.M.S. Monaco, destroyer, N. Sea and Scandinavian Convoy. Aug. 1917 rejd. H.M.S. Vortigern, commd. Jan. 1918, 11th Flotilla: in N. Sea with Grand Fleet; searched German destr. Ship transfd. to 1st Flotilla: in Baltic 1918–19. Dec. 26–7, 1918, in action with Bolshevik destrs. off Reval, capturing and bringing in Spartak on 26th and Avtroll on 27th.

†HUDSON, J. W. W. Oct. 1914. Mar. 1915 France.

HUGHES, H. W. France.

†HUGHES, W. B. *read* P.F.O. *for* Air Mech.

HYDE, C. W. Maj. R.A.F. (*del.* R.F.A.)

HYDE, G. L. 1918 Actg. Capt. and Adjt. *add at end* 2/91 Punjabis, Egypt. May 1918 Capt.

INGALL, D. H. (1900–9, *y*)

JENSON, A. G. (*for* Jensen)

JERVIS, B. A., M.C. (1900). M.C. 1919.

JONES, C. C. July–Dec. 1919 Actg. Maj.

JONES, W. R. LLOYD. Apr. 1920 Capt. I.A.

KEMP, T. C. *add* France, Belgium, Italy.

†KING, N. T. Killed at Noreuil.

LAMB, F. B. *add* July 1919–Aug. 1920 1st Asst. Superintendent.

LAMPLUGH, A. G. ·*del.* Oct. 1919, &c.

LANDON, J. W. *at end of line 1 add* ,T.F. *line 3* Gen. List. (*del.* Spec.)

†LAWRENCE, R. R. France 5 Bn. Missing Delville Wood, Battle of the Somme.

LYCETT, C. V. L., O.B.E. O.B.E. Jan. 1921 for services with British Army of the Black Sea. Mentd. (2) (Milne) Oct. 1920.

†LYTHGOE, J. W. Killed Somme.

†MALINS, E. F. *del.* B.U.O.T.C. Wounded Doulieu, N.E. of Neuf Berquin. Died Apr. 12, 1918.

†MANN, HORACE *line 1 add* S.R.

MARKS, C.S.I. (1913–16, *r*)

MATTHEWS, H. J. (1901–4, *b*). *Corrected notice.*
Nov. 1914 Pte. O.T.C. Pte. R.A.M.C., 3/1 S. Mid. Bde. Nov. 1915 Palestine. Died Nov. 17, 1917, of wounds recd. bet. Gaza and Hebron.

†MOULD, C. W. Killed Railway Wood, nr. Ypres.

MOULE, E. S. R.G.A., S.R.

†MURRAY-BROWNE, G. Lt.-Cdr.

†NICHOLL, O. J. Died, the result of war-wounds, at Karoola, Tasmania, Nov. 25, 1923.

OLD, R. E. *last line del.* Afghanistan. *add* June 1919 Delhi, 1/81 Pioneers. Sept. 1919 Actg. Capt. At Thal, bridging Kurram River.

OLDLAND, O. W. (1914–15, *b*)

PARKES, L. F. Dec. 1919 temp. Capt.

POLLARD, S. July 1919 Lt.

PRIEST, T. S. (1903–4, *g*)

PROSSER, C. K. K. (1911–16, *y*). Lt.

RAVENHILL, T. H. *last line but one del.* Mentd.

RAYNER, O. T., M.B.E. Capt., Gen. List. M.B.E.

READE, T. H. Capt.

†RICHARDSON, F. H. (1910–12, *g*).   *Corrected notice.*
1914 Pte 7 Bn., 1st Canadian Cont. Mar. 1915 France. Killed Apr. 23, 1915, in the first gas attack, Ypres.

RICHARDSON, S. H. *line 4 del.* Volunteered. Sept. 1918 Actg. Capt. and Adjt., attd. R.G.A.

ROBINSON, G.E., M.C. (1897–1900).   *Corrected notice.*
June 1915 Sec. Lt., R.F.A., T.F., 1/3 S. Mid. Bde. May 1916 France, xii Div. May 1917 attd. xvii Div. T.M. By. Sept. 1916 Actg. Capt. 1917 Divl. T.M. Offr. July 1917 Lt. Mentd. May, 1918. Wounded Oct. 26, 1918. M.C. Feb. 1919.* Bar to M.C. Jan. 1919.

ROSE, N. F. Capt.

SAMSON, G. W. *add* Nov. 1919 Lt., Actg. Capt., A.D.C., Asst. Embarkation Staff Offr.

SAUNDERS, B. R. *line 2* Actg. Lt., Signal Section. *line 4 del.* Actg. *and read* Dec. 1917 Capt.

SAWYER, A. W. (1914–16, *r*)

SEARLS, T. H. *line 2* France 1st Bn.

SLIM, W. J. wd. (1) Gallipoli. Mesopotamia, wd. (2) Mar. 1917. Nov. 1918 Actg. Maj., while holding appt. in India, 6 Gurkha Rif. May 1919 Capt., I.A.

SPENCER, C. L. (1901–6, *y*)

STIFF, C. L. June 1915 Sec. Lt. June 1916 Lt. Aug. 1916 attd. R.E. Dec. 1916 Actg. Capt., attd. G.H.Q. France 1916, 1917.

TAYLOR, E. A. (1913–16, *g*)

†TREGLOWN, R. C. France. Killed, Somme, . ., 1916.
UNDERWOOD, M. J. F. R.F.C. Egypt, Italy, Greece, Mesopotamia.
USHER, J. M. 1/1 W. Riding By.
VAUGHTON, S. J. J., M.C. M.C. Nov. 1919, Finland and Baltic States.
VOKES, F. C. (1899–1902)
WALKER, E. G. S., M.C. M.C. Sept. 1920,* S. Russia.
WALTON, F. W. 1915 Sec. Lt.
WARDEN, S. H. Oct. 1917 Maj., Inspector O.M., 1st Class.
†WARWOOD, F. J. D. Killed at Delville Wood.
WEBB, J. G. June 1918 Sec. Lt., 4 The King's (Shrops. L.I.)
WEBBE, W. H., C.B.E.
WHITE, A. H. S. Jan. 1919 Lt.
†WOOD, E. H. Killed at Lesboeufs.
WOOD, T. S. *line 2 for* behind *read* in front of
WYNNE, H. 1915–16 attd. R.E. as Asst. Director, Army Postal
    Services, British Army in Greece (Salonika E.F.): then Asst. Dir.,
    A.P.S., W. Frontier of Egypt.

TWO CASES OF CIVILIAN SERVICE

JOLLY, C. N. (1909–12)
    1916 Y.M.C.A. France: Mt. Kemmel, Regent Street dugouts,
    Sailly, Wytschaete. 1917 Italy: Taranto; 1918 Ganezza.
MILWARD, C. A. (1872)
    British Consul of Punta Arenas in early part of the War; was useful
    in the catching of S.M.S. Dresden. He received a gold chronometer
    'presented by the Lords Commissioners of the Admiralty in recogni-
    tion'.

ROLL OF HONOUR

    John Edward Kenneth Bache.
    Richard Balfour Bourne.
    John Henry Cardew.
    John Newman Connolly.
    Frederic Lynn Disturnal.
    William Hereward Ehrhardt.

John Thomas Eldridge.
Neville Miller.
Oswald James Nicholl.
Charles William Schwaben.
Edgar Francis Talbot.
Robert Cecil Treglown.

HONOURS

O.B.E. (*Mil.*)

E. W. C. Bradfield.
C. V. L. Lycett.

M.B.E. (*Mil.*)

O. T. Rayner.

M.C. and Bar

E. G. Robinson.

M.C.

†J. H. Cardew.
B. A. Jervis.
F. L. Mills.
S. J. J. Vaughton.
E. G. S. Walker.
del. J. L. Holmes.

T.D.

J. Barnsley.

M.M.

F. E. Hands.
E. E. Watson.

Egypt. Order of the Nile. 4th Class.
P. S Brindley.

Greece. M.C. 3rd Class.
K. W. Grant.

MENTIONED IN DISPATCHES
E. W. C. Bradfield.
H. D. Coleman.
N. A. Haywood (2).
C. V. L. Lycett.
F. R. Phipps.

Distinguished War Services
V. Curle.

DEEDS OF GALLANTRY

ROBINSON, G. E., Temp. Lt., Actg. Capt., R.F.A., attd. 17th
T.M. Batty.—*M.C.* (July 30, 1919).
At Neuvilly on the morning of October 20th, 1918, he displayed
great gallantry in handling a mobile trench mortar. From one of
the houses a machine gun was giving trouble to the advance of the
infantry. He made a personal reconnaissance of the spot, located
the machine gun, and ran his piece into the open and wrecked the
house. He was heavily sniped while making the reconnaissance, and
the later accomplishment of the task was full of danger, but he
carried it through with great coolness and courage.

WALKER, E. G. S., Capt., General List.—*M.C.* (Sept. 27,
1920, South Russia).
For gallantry at Ushun on March 8 and 10, 1920. He attached himself to the Police Regiment and remained with them throughout
the two days' counter-attacks, during which they sustained heavy
casualties. By his personal example and coolness, under heavy
machine-gun fire, he was largely responsible for the decisive success
gained.

SAUNDERS, B. R. *read* 2/6 R. War. R., T.F.
del. Holmes, J. L. (p. 189).

SUMMARY
M.C. and Bar, 9.   M.C., 101.   M.M., 10.

Total serving   1,412
Total Killed or Died 254

NOTES AND ABBREVIATIONS

† before a name signifies killed in action or died of wounds or from other causes after entering His Majesty's service and before the conclusion of peace.

* signifies that the deed for which the honour so marked was given will be found described among the Deeds of Gallantry taken from the *London Gazette*.

Dates in brackets after the names give the years spent at King Edward's School. The letters following those dates give the House to which its bearer belonged (the Houses were started in January 1904) :

b=1904–July 1910, Mr. Manton's ; Sept. 1910 onwards, Mr. Langley's.

g=1904–July 1906, Mr. A. H. Reynolds' ; Sept. 1906 onwards, Mr. Richards'.

r=Mr. Measures'.

y=Mr. Heath's.

The dates given for honours are those of the issues of the *Gazette* in which they were published ; those of commissions and promotions are taken mainly from the *Gazette* or official lists ; those of casualties are either privately supplied or taken from personal notices in the Press.

The abbreviations used are mainly those of the Army List or such as are in general use.

ROLL OF SERVICE

ABBOTT, A. N. (1910–13, *r*)
Nov. 1917 Sec. Lt., R.F.C. Apr. 1918 Sec. Lt. (A.), R.A.F.,
E. Coast of Yorkshire.

ABBOTT, J. J. (1914–18, *r*)
Dec. 1918 Cdt., R.M.C., Sandhurst.

ABBOTT, W. R. (1911–13, *r*)
1916 Obs. Sub-Lt., R.N.A.S. Mudros. Lt., Hon. Capt. Sept.
1918 Capt. (T.), R.A.F.

ABBOTT-GREENWOOD, W. E. W. (=Abbott, W. E. W.,
1913, *r*)
Jan. 1918 Artists Rif. Mar. 1919 Sec. Lt., Herts. R., T.F.

ABRAHAM, T. H. (1909–12, *r*)
Air Mech., R.N.A.S.

ABRAHAMS, R. G. (1902–9, *g*)
Sept. 1914 Lt., R.A.M.C. No. 10 Stationary Hosp., France.
Sept. 1915 Capt.

ACHURCH, G. P., M.B.E. (1899–1900)
May 1916 Sec. Lt., R.F.C. June 1916 France : Asst. Equipment
Offr., 2nd Army Aircraft Park, Hazebrouck ; Jan. 1917 Equipmt.
Offr., 3rd Cl., 20 Sqn., near St. Omer. Aug. 1917 Lt. Jan. 1918
Equipmt. Offr., 2nd Cl., Home Establishment : Wing Equipmt.
Offr., 37 Wing. Sept. 1918 Actg. Capt. (T.), R.A.F. M.B.E. Jan.
1919.

ADAMS, A. E. (1899–1903)
1915 Pte., H.A.C.

ADAMS, A. J. (1909–14, *g*)
1916 B.U.O.T.C. 1917 Wireless Operator, H.M. Trawler, Lord
Annandale. 1918 Telegraphist, H.M.S. P. 25.

B

†ADAMS, A. W. H. (1893–6)
1914 Spr., Can. Eng. France. Died of pneumonia in hospital,
Feb. 22, 1915.

ADAMS, D. (1901–3)
Sept. 1914 Driver, Motor Amb. Unit, B.R.C. Feb. 1915 France,
No. 2 M.A.C., nr. Armentières ; Graves Commission, Ypres
district ; drove for H.Q., from Dunkirk all the way down the
lines : 1916 to Verdun, with the French ; Section leader. June
1917 Sec. Lt., R.F.C., pilot. Nov. 1917 France, 82 Sqn., close to
Arras. Early 1918 Lt. Jan. 1918 Goulencourt, working the lines
from St. Quentin, South. Wounded Mar. 22, 1918 (at 7,000 ft.
in fight with nine enemy planes). Apr. 1918 Lt. (A.), R.A.F.

ADAMS, G. W. (1901–3)
1914 Pte., Sea. Highrs., 29 Can. Inf., Vancouver, 2nd Cont.
Sept. 1915 France, N.C.O. Ypres, St. Eloi. 1916 Sec. Lt., com-
missioned in the field at St. Eloi. Aug. 1917–19 Instr., Bombing
School, Pernes, nr. Béthune. Dec. 1917 Capt.

ADAMS, JAMES B. (1899–1900)
Apr. 1917 Pte., Lond. Scottish. Aug. 1917 transfd. to M.G.C.
Oct. 1917 France, 20 M.G.C. Nov. 1917 Italy. Actg. Cpl. Taken
prisoner by Austrians at Battle of Asiago, June 15, 1918 (gassed) :
in Austrian Hosp. at Trento six weeks. Nov.–Dec. 1918 three
weeks in Bohemia, during the Revolution. Dec. 12, 1918 escaped
with ten others from Prague to Genoa, and thence home.

ADAMS, JOHN (1897–1903)
Aug. 1914 Capt., R.A.M.C., S.R., No. 7 Fd. Amb. Aug. 1914
France, 3 Div. Mar. 1916 temp. Maj., cdg. No. 7 Fd. Amb.
Aug. 1916, invalided home. Jan. 1917 France (2) 1. No. 101
Fd. Amb. ; 2. attd. Glasgow Highrs., Somme. Feb. 1917 invalided
home : Regl. M.O., 3 Res. Oxf. and Bucks. L.I. Oct. 1918–
Jan. 1919 France (3). Mentd., 1915, for services during 2nd
Battle of Ypres.

†ADAMS, JOSEPH (1897–1902)

1915 Pte., H.A.C. France, July 1915. Wounded Oct. 1916. Dec. England. July 1915 29 Lond. R., T.F., attd. S. Wales Bord., France. Captured by Germans May 1918 : Friedrichsfeld Camp. Died, a prisoner, in hosp. at Worms-am-Rhein, Oct. 3, 1918.

ADAMS, L. E. (1912–14, g)

1917 B.U.O.T.C. 1918 Cdt., 8 O.C.B., Lichfield. Sept. 1918 Sec. Lt., 3 R. Highrs. Ireland.

†ADAMS, R., M.C. and bar (1904–10, r)

Aug. 1914 Sec. Lt., 1/8 R. War. R., T.F. Mar. 1915 France. Lt., June 1915. Mentd. in Disp. Dec. 1915. M.C. Jan. 1916 ; bar, Sept. 1916.* Wounded. Killed (repd. wounded and missing) July 1, 1916, nr. Beaumont-Hamel.

ADAMS, W. S. (1906–15, g)

July 1916 Surg. Sub-Lt., R.N.V.R., H.M.S. Moresby. July 1919 Surg. Lt., to R. N. Hosp., Haslar. H.M.S. Bee, Aug. 1919.

ALABASTER, A. S., M.C. (1898–1902)

Apr. 1910 Lt., 5 R. War. R., T.F. Aug. 5, 1914 mobilized. Oct. 1914 temp. Capt. June 1915 Capt. July, France, with reinforcements for Bn. No. 1 Entrenching Bn., nr. Poperinghe (3 months) constructing strong points to cover the rear of Northern line. Nov. 1915–Apr. 1916 1/5 R. War. R. at Fonquevillers, opp. Gommecourt Wood. June, Sailly-au-Bois : June 22, trenches at Hébuterne, just S. of Hébuterne–Puisieux-au-Mont Road, garrisoned during the great attack. July 13 La Boisselle ; July 16 from a position 700 yds. S.W. of Pozières, immediately N. of Albert, advanced due W. and captured enemy positions N.E. of Ovillers-la-Boisselle, causing the evacuation of that village, with heavy casualties. July 24 nr. Pozières. Aug. 18 attacked due north of Ovillers, advanced 500 yds., capturing 2 M.G.s and 250 prisoners. (Received the M.C., gazetted * Oct. 1916.) Sept. temp. Maj., 2nd in cd. of Bn. Oct., road construction, Mametz Wood. Nov.–Dec. N. and N.E. of Le Sars, or in reserve about Martinpuich and Contalmaison. Feb. 1917 relieved the French in sector nr. Biaches. Mar. 17–18 followed retreating enemy, occupied Péronne. Apr. 1

capture of Epéhy. Apr.–June Sen. Officers' course, Aldershot. July 1 France (2), in temp. cd. of 1/7 Bn. Vlamertinghe, 2nd in cd. of 1/7 Bn. : attd. H.Q., 48 Div. Aug. 17–27 local attacks, on blockhouses and strong points bet. the Stroombeek, N. of St. Julien, and the Langemarck line N.E. of St. Julien ; bad weather and mud. Oct. 14–17 east of Vimy. Nov. 24–30 to Italy. Dec., reconnoitred positions on foothills N. of Marostica. Mar., Piave. Apr. Asiago Plateau ; support positions on M. Kaberlaba. June 15–16 in command on the left of successful counter-attack after the Austrians had penetrated our line. Aug. 9–10 in command of successful raid with 1/7 Bn., on Asiago Plateau, reaching outskirts of Asiago, 1 mile behind the enemy's line. Croce di Guerra (gazetted Sept. 1918). July 1919 Maj., T.F. Res.

ALABASTER, E. B. (1906–11, g)

Oct. 1914 Dresser, Lady Paget's combined Serbian Relief Fund and St. John's Amb. Unit, Serbia. Nov. 1914–Apr. 1915 3 Res. Mil. Hosp., Uskub. Mar. 1915 Cross of Serbian Red Cross Soc. Hon. Lt., Serbian Army. Aug. 1916 to Apr. 1919 Lt., R.A.M.C., Mesopotamia E.F. Sept 1916 Basrah : Oct. River Sick Convoy Unit, embarkation duty. Dec. Sub-Medical Charge of Paddle Steamer 55 ; P.S. 1 ; Jan. 1917 Medical Charge, P.S. 35, attd. 7 Ind. Div. ; May, Downstream from Baghdad, i.c. of P.S. 53 ; Basrah, 3 British Gen. Hosp. ; Jan. 1918 Upstream, 15 Div. ; Feb. attd. No. 1 Combd. Fd. Amb., Uqbah ; Mar. Unit marches to Hit, to serve as C.C.S. ; Apr. via Baghdad, to take over Hillah Area ; May, Kufa, Hosp. and Sub. Area. Feb. 1919 Mentd.

†ALABASTER, F. C. (1899–1905, g)

July 1915 Sec. Lt., 1/5 R. War. R., T.F. France, Jan. 1916. Severely wounded, Hébuterne (Alsace Trench), June 25, 1916. Died of wounds, in London, Aug. 25, 1916.

ALABASTER, G. H. (1902–7, g)

June 1915 Lt., R.A.M.C. France, 83 Fd. Amb., 27 Div., attd. 19 Bde., R.F.A. 1916 Aldershot. 1916–18 36 Gen. Hosp., Salonica F., Vertekop. June 1916 Capt.

ALABASTER, J. W. (1904–8, *y*)

Aug. 1914 Pte., 2 Oxf. and Bucks. L.I. France 2 Bn., 2 Div. Nov. 1914–Feb. 1915. Invalided home. May 1915 Sec. Lt., 13 R. War. R. 11 Bn., France, 37 Div., 112 Bde. Wounded (1) Somme, July 1916. France. Wounded (2) Apr. 10, 1917, Monchy-le-Preux. Oct. 1916 Lt. Empd. Min. of Munitions, A.D.M.A. ; June 1918 Sectl. D.M.A.

ALCOCK, A. B. F., D.S.C. (1909–14, *b*)

1914 Sec. Lt., R.M.L.I. Mar. 1915 Actg. Lt. Gallipoli. Wounded, 1915. Mentd. D.S.C., Sept. 1915.* Dec. 1916–19 H.M.S. Hyacinth, light cruiser, Cape Station. Lt. Aug. 1918 Capt.

ALCOCK, A. E. G. (1911–16, *b*)

June 1918 Cdt., R.A.F.

ALLDAY, G. J. (1903–7, *y*)

1914–16 Driver, Br. Red Cross Soc., France ; Transport Officer. June 1917 Sec. Lt., R.F.C. (Equip.), Res. Sqn., France, in charge of aero-engine tests). 1918 Actg. Lt. (T.), R.A.F., Equipment Off., 2nd Cl. Nov. 1918 Invalided home.

ALLDAY, H. R. (1898–1902)

3 Cl. Air Mech., R.F.C. Records Dept.

ALLDAY, P. G. (1910–15, *b*)

Dec. 1915 Sec. Lt., R.F.A., T.F., 3/3 S. Mid. Bde. Feb.–Nov. 1917 France, 48 Div., C 241 Bde. : Feb.–Mar. Somme (Péronne) ; Apr.–June, Beaumetz (E. of Bapaume) ; July–Oct., Ypres ; Nov. Vimy Ridge. July 1917 Lt. Nov. 1917–July 1918 Italy : Nov.–Feb., N. Italy ; Feb.–Mar., Piave ; Mar.–July, Asiago Plateau. July 1918 transfd. to R.A.F. Nov. 1918 Sec. Lt. (O.), Hon. Lt., R.A.F. : Nov. 1918–Apr. 1919 Italy : Flying Observer, 34 Sqn., Villaverla.

ALLDAY, R. P. (1905–11, *b*)

Sept. 1914 Cpl., 14 R. War. R. Feb. 1915 Sec. Lt., 6 The King's (Shrops. L.I.), T.F. France July 1916 The Somme. Wounded, Delville Wood. Oct.–Nov. 1917 France (2) ; Ypres. July 1917

Lt. Nov. 1917 transfd. R.F.C. Apr. 1918 Sec. Lt. (O.), Hon. Lt.
R.A.F. Mar. 1918 Italy; 42 Sqn., Piave. Apr.–July 1918
France, Merville Sector. Reading, Instr. in Aeronautics.

ALLDRIDGE, W. H. (1900–4)
Tpr., Staff. Yeo.

ALLEN, ARTHUR, M.C. (1898)
May 1915 Inns of Court O.T.C. Dec. 1915 Sec. Lt., 3/7 Worc. R.,
T.F. Feb. 1916 France, 1/7 Bn. : Battle of the Somme, La
Boisselle, Martinpuich, Péronne ; Passchendaele Ridge. July
1917 Lt. Nov. 1917 Italy. Mentd. Apr. 1918. Italian Bronze
Medal, Nov. 1918, for raid on Austrian lines Aug. 8–9. M.C.
Jan. 1919.

ALLEN, C. G. L. (1898–9)
1916 Sec. Lt., R.E.

†ALLEN, F. R. (1910–12, y)
End of 1914 Mid., R.N.R., H.M.S. Ebro. Seriously wounded,
Oct. 16, 1915, in North Sea ; died of wounds at Lerwick Naval
Hosp., Oct. 19, 1915.

ALLEN, J. (1913–14, y)
1914 Cdt., R.M.C., Sandhurst. Apr. 1915 Sec. Lt., A.S.C. France.
Wounded, Somme, Sept. 11, 1916. July 1917 Lt. M.G.C., Cav.
Secd. Tank Corps. Wounded (2) Oct. 8, 1917. Nov. 1917 France (2).
Apr. 1918 Capt. Mar. 1918, in the retreat, with old large Tanks ;
May 1918, Whippets ; Aug., Amiens to Bohain.

ALLEN, J. G. (1910–12, y)
Aug. 1914 H.M. Transport Service, S.S. Majestic. Nov. 1917
P.F.O., R.N.A.S. ; Sec. Lt. (O.), R.A.F. Aug. 1918–Apr. 1919,
back at sea, Engineer Officer.

ALLEN, P. (1904–10, y)
Cyclist, 64 Divl. Coy., A. Cycl. C.

ALLEN, SIDNEY (1896–9)
Aug. 1914–Oct. 1915 Hon. Sec., Duchess of Westminster's Hosp.
Nov. 1915–Oct. 1916 Director of Finance in France and Belgium

for B.R.C.S. Dec. 1916–Apr. 1918 Lt., R.N.V.R. Apr.–Dec.
1918 Cost Investigation Dept. of Acct. Gen. of the Admiralty.

ALLKINS, A. W., M.C. (1909–11, *b*)
1915 Pte., 6 Oxf. and Bucks L.I. June 1915 Sec. Lt., 12 Worc. R.
Apr. 1916 M.G.C., France. Nov. 1916 Lt. M.C. Oct. 1917.*
Severely wounded Dec. 1917.

†ALLKINS, W. S. (1905–8, *g*)
L.-Cpl., R.M.L.I. Killed, Gallipoli, 1915.

AMBLER, C. A. (1912–13, *r*)
Jan. 1917 Sec. Lt., Aust. L.I. Apr. 1918 Lt.

†ANDERTON, S. (1905–9, *r*)
Pte., 14 R. War. R. France. Missing, presumed killed, July 23, 1916.

ANDREWS, C. E. A. (1908–16, *g*)
Aug. 1916 1 Cl. Air Mech., R.N. Naval Experimental Station,
Stratford (Submarine Defence; smoke screens); later, Jan. 1919,
Chemist, R.N. Anti-gas Dept., Stamford Hill.

ANDREWS, W. H. (1889–98)
Gnr., R.H.A., O.C.U., Woolwich. Nov. 1917 Sec. Lt., R.G.A.
Empd. Min. of Labour.

†ARBUTHNOT, G. C. (1903–10, *g*)
Dec. 1914 Sec. Lt., 7 N. Staff. R. Gallipoli. Killed (repd. wounded
and missing) Aug. 7, 1915.

ARCHER, DAVID (1909–11, *r*)
L.-Cpl., 5 Oxf. and Bucks L.I. France, 1915. Feb. 1918 Sec. Lt.,
2/4 Bn., 61st Div.

ARGYLE, E. P., D.S.O. (1889–92)
Jan. 1909 Capt., A.V.C. July 1915 Maj., Asst. Dir. of Vet.
Services. Aug. 1917 Actg. Lt.-Col., D.D.V.S. Mentd. 3 times.
D.S.O. Croix de Guerre. June 1919 Bt. Lt.-Col., G.H.Q., Egypt.

ARNOLD, STANLEY (1910–13, *r*)
Jan. 1915 Pte., 15 R. War. R. France. 1916 Sgt. Oct. 1917
Sec. Lt., 6 Rif. Brig. France. Prisoner in Germany, Mar. 21, 1918.

†ARNOTT, David W. (1893–1903)
Mar. 1915 Inns of Court O.T.C. Apr. 1915 Sec. Lt., 12 R. War. R. France, attd. 2 Bn. Killed at Ginchy (repd. wounded and missing) Sept. 3, 1916.

ASH, E. B. (1904–12, b)
B.U.O.T.C. Feb. 1918 Lt., R.A.M.C. Feb. 1919 Capt. 79 Gen. Hosp., Taranto, Italy.

ASH, L. (1908–11, b)
Cdt., R.A.F.

ASSINDER, A. Clive (1891–4)
1917 Sec. Lt., A.S.C. June 1918 Lt., R.A.S.C.

ASSINDER, E. W. (1899–1905, b)
Mar. 1915 Capt., R.A.M.C., T.F., 1st S. Gen. Hosp.

ASSINDER, G. E. G. (1897–1902)
May 1915 Sec. Lt., R.F.A., T.F., 3 S. Mid. Bde. June 1916 Lt., Adjt., D.A.C., France. Sept. 1917 Actg. Capt., 2nd in cd. of By., A/241, S. Mid. Bde. Nov. 1917 Italy. Mentd. Jan 6, 1919. Croce di Guerra.

ASTBURY, Rev. H. S., M.C. (1901–9, b)
Jan. 1915 C.F., 4th Class, attd. 5 Bord. R., 151 Inf. Bde. M.C. 1916. Invalided home 1918.

ASTBURY, R. H. (1892–9)
Mar. 1913 Lt., 6 R. War. R., T.F. Mentd. 1915. Four months with Salonica F. Mar. 1916 Actg. Capt. June 1916 secd. Lt., R.A.M.C. June 1917 Capt., R.A.M.C., attd. 2/22 Lond. R., T.F. Egyptian E.F. Two years in Palestine ; mentd. (2) for period Mar. to Sept. 1918.

†ASTBURY, T. L. (1901–5, b)
1914 Pte., 14 R. War. R. Sept. 1915 Sec. Lt., 2/6 S. Staff. R., T.F. 1/6 Bn., France. Feb.–June 1916 Actg. Lt. Lt. Dec. 1917 Actg. Capt. Killed (repd. missing) Mar. 21, 1918.

ASTON, A. (1902–10, b)
Sept. 1914 Sec. Lt., 7 N. Staff R. Feb. 1915 Lt., attd. 3 Bn., home service.

ASTON, A. J. G. (1899–1902)
Sept. 1916 Sec. Lt., 5 Glouc. R., T.F. France. Wounded 1916.
Mar. 1918 Lt.

ASTON, L. (1904–10, *b*)
1914 Sec. Lt., 16 R. War. R. Jan. 1915 Lt. France. Dec. 1915
Capt. Wounded July 1916. France. Army of Occupn., Germany.

ATKINS, F. G. L. (1893–5)
1915 Pte., A.S.C., M.T. 1916 Sec. Lt. Apr. 1918 Lt.

ATKINSON, D. (1895–1905, *r*)
1918 Gnr., R.G.A., 2/1 S.M. By.

ATTLEE, C. M. (1907–12, *y*)
1917 P.F.O. and P.O.O., R.N.A.S. Jan. 1918 Sub-Lt., R.N.V.R.
1918 Lt. (T.), R.A.F., 54 Wing, France.

AUCOTT, B. (1914–16, *b*)
1917 Cdt., R.M.A., Woolwich. Jan. 1918 Sec. Lt., R.G.A. July
1919 Lt.

AUSTER, W. W. (1880–7)   Pte., R.A.M.C., 35 Lond. Coy.

BACHE, A. R. (1892–9)
June 1915 Sec. Lt., Worc. Yeo., T.F. Oct. 1917 Capt. 1 Sqn.
Palestine.

BACHE, C. S. (1890–7)   Lt., Appeal Mil. Repres. July 1917 Capt.

BACHE, F. E. L., M.C. (1893–1900)
1914 Pte., 10 S. Staff. R. Nov. 1914 Sec. Lt., 5 Bn., T.F. Nov.
1914 10 Bn. ; 3 Bn. : 1 Bn., France. Feb. 1916 Capt. Wounded
1918. M.C. July 1918.

†BACHE, H. G. (1898–1908, *g*)
Oct. 1914 Sec. Lt., 10 Lan. Fus., France ; Bombing Offr. Ypres
salient ; Sanctuary Wood. Killed Feb. 15, 1916, by a sniper,
just after returning from an attempt to regain lost trench.

BACHE, Rev. H. NORMAN (1887–95) 1918 Pte., 2/28 Artists Rif.

BACHE, J. E. K. (1888–1904, *r*)
1914 Pte., Linc. R. Dec. 1914 Sec. Lt., 2/5 S. Staff. R., T.F.
1915 France, 1/5 Bn. Lt. Wounded (1). Dec. 1916 Capt., Bde.
Bombing Off. 1918 Wounded (2). Aug. 1918 Capt., T.F. Res.
Empd. Min. of Munitions.

BACKHOUSE, S. R. (1908–13, *r*)
Pte., R.A.M.C., Imtarfa Mil. Hosp., Malta. 1916 St. Paul's Mil.
Hosp., Malta.

BAILEY, G. T. (1911–14, *g*)
May 1916 Pte., 29 R. Fus. (P.S.). Aug. 1916 France. Oct. 1917
5 Bn.

BAKER, B. (1908–14, *r*)
Nov. 1915 Gnr., R.F.A., 14 Res. Bn. Aug. 1916 Cdt. and Cdt.
Cpl., 18 Res. By. Oct. 1916 Sec. Lt., R.F.A., S.R., 53 Res. By.
Jan. 1917 France, D/175 Bde., Army Field Artillery. Nov. 1917
Italy. Mar. 1918 France. Wounded (1) Apr. 21, 1918. Apr. 1918
Lt. July rejoined By. Wounded (2) Oct. 31. Mar. 1919 A/5
Res. Bde.

BAKER, E. W. (1909–17, *r*)
1917 Cdt., 12 O.C.B., Newmarket. Dec. 1917 Sec. Lt., 3 Norf. R.,
attd. Ind. Army (E.E.F.), 2nd Guides R., 60th Div., nr. Alexandria.

†BAKER, F. F. (1896–1903)
Pte., Artists Rif. O.T.C. France. Artists Rif. Nov. 1917
Killed (reported missing) Passchendaele.

BAKER, SIDNEY (1905–7, *r*)
Ind. Army.

BAKER, S. F. (1893–9)
Leading Seaman, R.N. Dépôt. Instructor. 1918 Petty Off.,
R.N.D., Otranto, Italy.

BAKER, W. F. (1897–1902)
Able Seaman, R.N. Dépôt. 1918 Instructor.

BALL, G. H., D.S.O., M.C. (1908–14, *b*)
Oct. 1915 Sec. Lt., 3/5 S. Staff. R., T.F. France, 1/5 Bn. July 1, 1916 Gommecourt. Mar. 13/14, 1917 Bucquoy (Ancre). Mentd. Apr. 1917. June 1917 in front of Lens. July 1917 Lt. Aug. 1917, May 1918 Actg. Capt. Sept. 27/28, N.W. of Bellenglise (St. Quentin Canal) : repelled counter-attacks for 18 hours, with heavy losses ; reorganized the front next day, after the great attack. D.S.O. Mar. 1919.* Oct. 3, N. of Sequehart. Oct. 12, attack on Riquerval Wood, E. of Bohain, under heavy fire. M.C. Mar. 1919.* Mentd. (2) Dec. 1918, (3) July 1919. 1919 Murman coast.

BALL, J. F. A. (1906–11, *b*)
Oct. 1914 Cpl., 14 R. War. R. Dec. 1914 Sec. Lt., 14 R. War. R. 1915 32nd Div. Cycl. Coy. France. Dec. 1915 Lt., 7th Corps Cycl. Bn. Mil. Traff. Control Coy. Sept. 1917 Actg. Capt., 2nd in *Gen. List* command. (Actg. A.P.M., 1st Div., on the march into Germany.)

BALL, L., M.C. (1895–1902)
Nov. 1914 Lt., R.A.M.C., T.F., S. Mid. Div. Cas. Clearing Statn. 1915–16 with 56 C.C.S. in France. 1916 with 1 S. Mid. F.A., on the Somme. 1917–19 attd. 1/4 R. Berks. R. on the Somme, at Ypres, and in Italy. Wounded Aug. 1917. Mentd. May 1918. M.C. June 1919.

BANCROFT, W. G. (1900–1)
1914 R.A.M.C.

BANKS, F. W. R. (1910–12, *y*)
1915 R.N.A.S. Flt. Sub-Lt.

†BANKS, J. H. (1904–6, *y*)
Aug. 1914 Pte., 10 R. Fus. Dec. 1914 Sec. Lt., 13 R. War. R. Aug. 1915 Lt. 1916 Actg. Capt., M.G.C. France, July 1917. Died of wounds Aug. 15, 1917.

BANTOCK, J. R. G. (1913–16, *r*)
Inns of Court O.T.C. Cdt., 14 O.C.B. May 1918 Sec. Lt., 3 Cam'n. Highrs., S.R., Ireland. Aug. 1918 France, attd. 11 Bn. Army of Occupn., Germany. *Le.*

BARAGWANATH, G. J. (1914–16, *y*)
B.U.O.T.C. 1918 Flt.-Cdt. (O.), R.A.F. Nov. 1918 Sec. Lt. (O.).

BARBER, W. M. (1886–90)
1918 Inns of Court O.T.C.

BARK, E. G. (1888–94)
Feb. 1917 Lt., R.A.M.C. Feb.-Dec. 1918 Capt., 10 Statry. Hosp., France.

BARK, G. M. (1892–1901)   *15 Inf. Bde., Barnby · Of.*
1915 Sec. Lt., 4 R. War. R., S.R. 16 Bn., France. Wounded Apr. 1917. July 1917 Lt. Empd. at War Office. Jan. 1919 retd. list.

BARKER, C. H. (1893–8)
Sept. 1907 Capt., R.G.A. Mar. 1915 Maj. France. Wounded (1) June 1917. 135 Heavy By. Wounded (2) Aug. 1917.

BARKER, E. A., M.C. (1890–2)
1910 Sec. Lt., 1/5 York and Lanc. R., T.F. 1915 Lt. Mar. 1915 France. Aug. 1915 secd. R.E., Sign. Serv., Adjt., Wireless, G.H.Q. June 1916 transfd. R.E. Mentd. 1917. June 1916 Capt. and Adjt., Wireless Coy. M.C. June 1917. July 1917 Capt., Gen. List, T.F., Empd. R.E. Q.M. and Hon. Lt., R.E., T.F. Aug. 1918 to June 1919 Actg. Maj.

†BARKER, G. (1895–1901)
1914 Capt., R.M.L.I. Maj. Killed 1915.

†BARKER, H. B. (1896–9)
Dec. 1915 Sec. Lt., R.G.A., S.R. Lt. Killed Aug. 15, 1917.

BARKER, H. N. D. (1895–1905, *y*)
1917 Lt., R.A.S.C.

BARKER, W. A. J., D.S.O. (1893–7)
Feb. 1915 Capt., 8 S. Staff. R. France. Feb. 1916 Lt.-Col., 8 Bn. D.S.O. 1916. Croix de Guerre, July 1917. Mentd. in Disp. Dec. 1917. Wounded : (1) 1916, (2) 1917, (3) (severely) Oct. 12, 1917.

BARNES, S. E. (1908, *r*)
May 1918 Sgt.-Instr., 9 Res. Lond. R., T.F.

BARNSLEY, A. (1909–15, *r*)
Apr. 1915 Sec. Lt., 2/5 Glouc. R., T.F. May 1916 France. Sept.
1916 invalided home. Dec. 1916 Lt. Feb. 1917–Mar. 1918
4 Res. Bn. Mar. 1919 52 Notts and Derby. R., Army of the
Rhine.

BARNSLEY, SIR JOHN, Knt., V.D. (1872–3)
Oct. 1914 Lt.-Col., 14 R. War. R. Col. Jan. 1915 Actg. Brig.
Gen., cdg. Bde., 61 Div., T.F. Hon. Brig.-Gen., T.F. Res. Empd.
in France. Nov. 1918 retd.

†BARNSLEY, T. K. (1908–11, *r*)
Oct. 1914 Sec. Lt., 14 R. War. R. Dec., Capt. May 1915 Sec. Lt.,
1 C. Gds., S.R. Lt. Sept. 1915 France. Wounded, Somme, Aug.
1916. Jan. 1917 France (2). Actg. Capt. Feb. 1917 Capt.
Killed, near Ypres, July 31, 1917, while consolidating a captured
position. Buried, near Poperinghe, in the Guards' Cemetery,
Canada Farm. Mentd. Dec. 1917.

BARROW, GEOFFREY (1910–17, *g*)
1917 Cdt., R.N. (Keyham). Feb. 1918–19 Mid., H.M.S. Superb,
H.M.S. Collingwood.

BARROWCLOUGH, S. (1905–13, *r*)
Dec. 1914 Sec. Lt., R.F.A. Sept. 1915 France (1), Somme,
C 115 Bde., 26 Div. Dec. 1915–July 1916 Salonica. Jan. 1916
Lt. Invalided home. Mar.–May 1917 France (2). Wounded
May 1917. June 1917–Jan. 1919 Home Service.

BARTLEET, E. J. (1906–7, *y*)
Sept. 1915 Sec. Lt., North'd Fus. France, attd. 13 Bn., 23 Div.
July 1917 Lt., Lab. Corps.

BARTLETT, A. C. (1907–12, *b*)
1915 Spr., R.E., Wireless Section. Feb. 1916 Egypt ; Salonica.

BARTLEY, E. O. (1911–14, *y*)
1914 Pte., 16 R. War R. 1916 Discharged. Passed R.M.C., Sandhurst, rejected medically. Cdt., 22 O.C.B., Christ's Coll., Camb. June 1918 Sec. Lt., Lab. Corps.

†BARTLEY, W. R. (1912–13, *y*)
Pte., 24 Midd'x R. France. Killed, before Messines, July 31, 1917.

BARTON, C. H. (1909–16, *r*)
Apr. 1918 to Jan. 1919 Pte., 1 S. Staff. R. Italy.

BARTON, M. G. W. (1906–10, *r*)
1914 Pte., 15 R. War. R. France.

BARWELL, J. H. (1914–17, *y*)
Cdt., R.A.F., Ch.Ch., Oxford. Flt. Cdt., Uxbridge. Aug. 1919 Sec. Lt. (Hon Commn.)

BARWISE, S. (1875–80)
Jan. 1909 Maj., R.A.M.C., Sanit. Service.

BASFORD, W. (1903–4)
1914 Pte., A.O.D.

BATE, L. (1912–14, *b*)
1914 Pte., R.A.M.C., 1 S. Gen. Hosp. Oct. 1918 69 Fd. Amb., Italy.

†BAYLISS, P. B. (1910–16, *y*)
Nov. 1916 Sec. Lt., Tank Corps. France. Sept. 19–23, 1917 in action at Triangle Farm after a 9-mile run from Oesthoek to Bochcastel; and again, with 20 Div., at Langemarck after driving 16 miles and ditching for 67 hrs. under shell-fire. Mentd. Dec. 1917. 1918 Lt., 9 Sectn., 15 Coy., 5 Bn. Aug. 1918 Actg. Capt., cdg. a section in great attack. Inter-allied Tank School, Paris. Killed (reptd. missing), Manniquin Hill, nr. Ramicourt, Oct. 3, 1918.

BEACHCROFT, E. A. (1892–4) R.N.

BEDINGTON, S. J. (1889–92) Pte., 28 R. Fus.

BEDINGTON, W. P. (1888)
Jan. 1915 Sec. Lt., R.F.A., T.F., 3 S. Mid. Amm. Col. May 1915 Capt., 3 S. Mid. Bde.

BEDWORTH, R. G. (1912-15, g)
1918 Cdt., 8 O.C.B., Lichfield. Feb. 1919 Sec. Lt., Worc. R., T.F.

†BEECH, E. W. (1887-9)
Capt., R.E., T.F., 1 N. Mid. Fd. Coy. Killed, the result of an accident, on mobilization, Aug. 11, 1914.

BELL, E. D. RYAN (1904-11, y)
1917 Spr., R.E., I.W.T.R.C., Mesopotamia.

†BELL, HUGH R. RYAN (1897-1904, y)
1914 Pte., 14 R. War. R. Aug. 1915 Sec. Lt., 1/8 Worc. R., T.F. Lt. France. Died Aug. 29, 1917, of wounds received Aug. 27 : he did splendid work, Aug. 16-17 and 26-7, in capturing a strong point at Springfield Farm, about 1 mile N.E. of St. Julien, falling in the moment of victory.

BELL, R. J. RYAN, M.M. (1899-1903)
1915 Tpr., Worc. Yeo., T.F. 1917 Gnr. R.G.A. M.M.

BENNETT, Rev. F. W. (1888-92)
June 1918-Apr. 1919 Pte., R.A.M.C. : Salonica.

BENOY, Rev. J (1878-84)
July 1913 C. F., 1st Cl., D.A.C.G. Aug. 1918 Retd. pay.

BENSLYN, W. T. (1897-1901)
Spr., R.E., 10 Sig. Coy. Salonica Force, H.Q., 30 Inf. Bde. Sec. Lt. Feb. 1919 Lt.

BENSON, C. R. (1910-17, b)
Apr. 1917 Cdt. R.M.C., Sandhurst. Attd. 52 Hamps. R. Apr. 1918 Sec. Lt., Unattd. List, Ind. Army. India.

†BERESFORD, H., M.C. (1909-15, y)
Nov. 1915 Sec. Lt., R.F.A., T.F., 3 N. Mid. Bde. Amm. Col. Anti-aircraft K.A.A. By. Lt. A/64 Bde., France. M.C. May 1918.* Died of wounds May 24, 1918.

BERESFORD, J. H. A. (1912–17, *y*)
1917 Cdt., R.M.C., Sandhurst. Aug. 1918 Sec. Lt., R.A.S.C.
Archangel.

BERLYN, J. A. (1881–2)
Lt., R.A.M.C. Nov. 1918 Capt.

BERLYN, R. C. (1909–16, *b*)
P.F.O., R.N.A.S. Vendôme. Flt.-Sub-Lt. Lt., R.A.F. Dunkirk. Wounded Apr. 1918. Sept. 1918 Instr., Vendôme.

BERMEJO, V. T. (1896–1900)
Cpl., Can. Inf., 15 Res. Bn.

BERNSTEIN, H. (1895–6)
Pioneer, R.E.

BERRY, A. B. (1911–14, *b*)
B.U.O.T.C. 1918 Gnr., R.G.A.

BERTELS, G. (1915–16, *y*)
Aug. 1917 joined Belgian Army, Infantry Centre ; Nov., Artillery
Centre ; Jan. to Sept. 1918 2/III 16 Artillery, 6″ battery, at the
front ; Sept. 1918 to Jan. 1919 Centre Instruction Sous-Lieut.,
Auxillaire Artillerie.

BEST, G. (1912–14, *y*)
Artists Rif. Sept. 1916 Sec. Lt., 1/4 Glouc. R., T.F. France.
Wounded and gassed Aug. 1917. Mar. 1918 Lt. July 1918 Sec.
Lt. (Obs.), Hon. Lt., R.A.F. Rendcomb.

†BEST, N. A. (1908–15, *y*)
Dec. 1915 Sec. Lt., R.F.A., T.F., 3/3 S. Mid. Bde. Sept. 1916
France, 2 Sectn., 8 Div. Amm. Col. 33 By., 8 Div. Killed near
Ypres July 19, 1917. Buried at Vlammertinghe.

BILL, C. G. (1910–13, *y*)
1915 Pte., 6 N. Staff. R., T.F. France. Wounded May 1918.

BILL, Rev. S. A. (1896–1901)
C.F. (Allahabad, India).

BIRCH, G. D. B. (1902–4, *r*)
Aug. 1914 Sec. Lt., 5 R. War. R., T.F. Dec. 1914 48th Divl. Cycl. Coy. Secd. A.C.C. 1915 Lt. France. June 1916 Capt. Bde. Physical and Bayonet Training Instn. Off., Sutton Cold-field.

BIRD, OLIVER, M.C. (1890–8)
Sec. Lt., W. Gds., S.R. Apr. 1917 Lt. Anti-gas Instr. Aug. 1918 Actg. Capt., Divl. Gas Off. M.C. June 1919.

BISHOP, H. O. (1900–1)
1914 Cpl., Duke of Lancaster's Own Impl. Yeo. July 1915 Sec. Lt., 2/7 Manch. R., T.F. July 1917 Lt. Nov. 1916 secd. K.A.R.

†BISSEKER, A. V. (1897–1900)
Oct. 1914 Sec. Lt., 6 R. War. R., T.F. Secd. Bde. M.G. Coy. France. Lt. Capt. May 1917 Restd. to Estabt. Killed in action Oct. 4, 1917.

BISSEKER, E. G. (1895–7)
Sept. 1916 Sec. Lt., R. W. Fus., S.R. Mar. 1918 Lt.

†BISSEKER, J. W. (1894–6)
1916 Inns of Court O.T.C. Sec. Lt., 6 R. War. R., T.F., France. Killed in action Apr. 1, 1917.

BLADON, T. W. (1904–9, *r*)
Dec. 1914 Sec. Lt., 10 R. War. R. June 1915 A.S.C., M.T., S.R. Nov. 1917 Lt. 39 Divl. Amm. Sub-Park. Mentd. in Disp. July 1918. Aug. 1918–Jan. 1919 Actg. Capt.

BLAKE, S. B. (1903–4, *g*)
R.A.M.C.

BLAKSTAD, E. (1914–17, *y*)
L.-Cpl., 52 R. War. R. Cdt., O.C.B.

BLEBY, W. H. (1903–4, *b*)
Mar. 1919 Sec. Lt., R. War. R., S. Bn.

D

18   OLD EDWARDIANS

†BLEWITT, J. H. (1912–15, *r*)
1915 Cdt., I.A. 1916 Sec. Lt., attd. 54 Sikhs. Apr. 1917 Actg.
Lt. and Adj. Lt. Mentd. in Disp. Aug. 1917. Died of wounds in
Mesopotamia Apr. 22, 1917.

BLOOD, J. H. (1891–2)
Oct. 1914 Lt., A.O.D. Oct. 1915 Secd. to 178 Tunnelling Coy.,
R.E.

BLOOMFIELD, E. R. (1909–10, *y*)   Spr., R.E.

†BODDINGTON, R. T. (1894–1902)
1915 Sec. Lt. Lt., 1/10 Lond. R., T.F. Killed in Palestine Nov. 2
1917, while leading his men in an attack on Turkish trenches.
Buried at Gaza.

BOEDDICKER, H. F. W. (1890–4)
Jan. 1913 Capt., R.A.M.C., T.F., 1 S. Mid. Fd. Amb. 1915 Capt.,
Actg. Maj. Nov. 1914–Dec. 1918. 1918 Italy. Dec. 1918 Capt.,
T.F. Res. Registrar, No. 1 Birmingham War Hosp.

†BONNER, A. (1907–12, *g*)
1914 Pte., 14 R. War. R. Feb. 1915 Sec. Lt., 2 S. Staff. R. Attd.
7 Bn., France. 1916 Wounded. Attd. R.F.C. Flying Off., Obs.
Killed in France Apr. 29, 1917, in an attack by five enemy machines.

BONNER, G. H. (1905–14, *g*)
Nov. 1914 Sec. Lt., 7 S. Staff. R. July 1915 R.F.A. 1916 France,
Lt., 25 Auto-A.-A. By. Invalided home Nov. 1916.

BOOKER, C. A. E. (1914–15, *g*)
1918 Nott. Univ. O.T.C.

BOOME, E. J. (1897–9)
Aug. 1913 Capt., R.A.M.C., T.F., 1 S. Mid. Fd. Amb. Actg.
Maj., spec. empd. Italy ; France. Mentd. July 1919.

BOOTH, C. S. (1910–15, *b*)
July 1915 Sec. Lt., R. Mon. R.E., S.R. Feb. 1916 No. 1 Siege
Coy., R.E., France. Mar. 1917 Lt. Nov. 1918 Actg. Capt. and
Adjt. Adjt. to C.R.E., 8th Corps troops. Apr. 1919 Adjt. to

C.R.E., Douai–Valenciennes Sub-Area, British troops in France and Flanders. Temp. Maj., Staff Offr. to C.R.E., No. 1 Area. Mentd. July 1919.

BOSLEY, E. R. (1909–12, *y*)

1914 Pte., 16 R. War. R., France. Wounded. 1916, 3 Bn. 1917 A.S.C., M.T.

BOULGER, J. C. (1894–5)

Aug. 1914 Cpl., D.R., R.E. Aug. 20 landed in France : through the great retreat and subsequent advance—at battles of Landrecies, the Marne, the Aisne, 1st battle of Ypres. Dec. 1914 Sgt. : 2nd battle of Ypres : Messines, Passchendaele : on that front till Nov. 1917. Italy. Mar. 1918 France. At Roubaix at the Armistice : then right through Belgium, to Cologne, remaining there till Mar. 1919. Mentd. Nov. 1918.

BOULGER, P. I. K. (1894–5)

Aug. 1914 Pte., R.A.M.C. Sept., Staff Sgt. Feb. 1915 Sec. Lt., R. Fus. July 1915 France. Nov., transfd. A.S.C., M.T. May 1916 — *Dec.* France (2). 1916 attd. R.G.A., Battle of the Somme : May 1917 Actg. Capt. Last battle of Ypres : Messines Ridge, Passchendaele : retreat of 5th army. Mar. 1918 : Villers Bretonneux. May 1918 Invalided home. Empd. Min. of Munitions.

BOULTBEE-WHALL, G. H. B. B. (1902)

Jan. 1917 Lt., Spec. List, empd. with Inland Water Transport.

BOULTON, N. S. (1913–18, *b*)   1918 Cdt., R.F.A.

·BOURNE, R. B. (1909–12, *y*)   *Oct. 1916 France.*

July, Oct. 1916 Sec. Lt., R.F.C., S.R., Apr. 1918 Lt., Actg. Capt. (A.), R.A.F. *Aug. 1919 H. Qr. Killed, o.a.s., in flying accident, at Baldonnell Aerodrome, Co. Dublin, Nov. 6. 1919.*

BOWATER, W., M.C. (1893–9)

Aug. 1914 Lt., R.A.M.C., T.F., 1 S. Mid. Fd. Amb. Mar. 1915 France. Apr. 1915 Capt. M.C. 1917. Italy. Jan. 1918 Actg. Maj., cdg. a Fd. Amb.

BOWATER, Sir W. H. (1868–70)

1914 Hon. Col., 14 R. War. R.

†BOWEN, L. H. (1900–2)

1914 Cpl., 9 Qn. Victoria's Own (City of Lond.) R., T.F. Dec. 1915 Lt., 3 Linc. R. 1 Bn., France. Killed in action Dec. 22, 1915, Armentières ; buried at Louin, nr. Lille.

BOWEN, T. O. (1899–1901)

1917 Cdt., O.C.B., Cambridge. Aug. 1917 Sec. Lt., Lan. Fus., France. Prisoner of war in Germany (Mainz), Mar. 21, 1918 to Dec. 2, 1918.

†BOYTON, V. H. T. (1910–16, r)

1916 Cdt., R.G.A. Nov. 1916 Sec. Lt., R.G.A. Mar. 1917 France. 289 Siege By. Killed in France May 30, 1917.

BRACEY, H. C. H. (1897–9)

Nov. 1915 Capt., R.A.M.C., T.F., 1 S. Gen. Hosp.

BRADFIELD, E. W. C., O.B.E. (1892–8)

Aug. 1906 Capt., I.M.S., attd. 31 Duke of Connaught's Own Lancers. Feb. 1915 Maj.

BRADLEY, R. H. (1905–7, y)

1917 R.N.V.R., H.M.S. Orlanza.

BRADSWORTH, C. C. (1906–14, y)

1915 R.N. Hosp., Chatham. 1916 Sick Berth Res., H.M.S. Plassey. July 1917 Surg. Sub-Lt., R.N.V.R., H.M. Sloop Valerian (Mediterranean).

BRADSWORTH, N. H. (1910–14, y)

Pte., A.S.C., M.T. 1916 France. Wounded Aug. 1916. Discharged Oct. 1917.

BRAITHWAITE, R. G. (1911–14, b)

1917 Air Mech., R.F.C.

†BRAME, J. R. (1895–1902)

Pte., 26 R. Fus. Killed Sept. 10, 1916, at Flers. Buried at Rouen.

BRAND, S. H. (1902–5, b)

1915 Dispatch Rider, R.E. Oct. 1916 Lt., A.S.C., M.T., 33 Aux. M.T. Coy. France.

BRAWN, H. E. (1891–5)
    June 1915 Lt., R.A.M C.   Dec. 1916 Capt., S. Afr. Med. Corps.

BRAY, H. H. (1911–12, y)
    Apr. 1915 Sec. Lt., 13 R. War. R.   July 1916 Lt., M.G.C.   155 M.G.
    Coy., 55 Div., France.   Wounded Oct. 1917.

†BREARLEY, A. J. (1902–9, b)
    Apr. 1914 Lt. 7 Devon R., T.F.   May 1915 Actg. Capt.   July 1916
    secd. Spec. Bde., R.E., France.   Killed June 20, 1917.

†BREARLEY, N. B. (1910–12)
    B.U.O.T.C.   Nov. 1914 Sec. Lt., 12 R. War. R.   1916 9 Bn.
    Killed in Mescpotamia (reported missing) Apr. 17, 1916.

BREEDEN, F. J., M.C. (1901–6, b)
    Nov. 1914 Sec. Lt., 5 R. War. R., T.F.   1915 Lt.   1916 Capt.
    France.   Attd. 11 Bn., 2/5 Bn., 1/5 Bn., 2/6 Bn.   M.C. Apr.
    1918.*   Captured in German attack on Portuguese lines, Apr. 9,
    1918.   Prisoner in Germany (Mainz), Apr. to Dec. 1918.

BREWER, O. T. (1908–10, g)
    1915 Pte., 16 R. War. R.

BRINDLEY, P. S., M.C. (1907–11, y)
    (June 1914) Sec. Lt., 3 R. War. R., S.R.   Aug. 22, France, 1 Bn.,
    10 Bde., 4 Div. : Le Cateau, Marne, Aisne, Flanders.   Wounded (1)
    Meteren, Oct. 13, 1914.   Jan. 1915 France (2), 2 Bn., 22 Bde.,
    7 Div.   Mar., Neuve Chapelle, Liaison Officer, 22 Bde. ;   Apr.,
    Festubert.   Sept., attd., Adjt., 9 Devon. R. :   battle of Loos :
    Wounded (2).   Oct. 1915 Capt.   Mentd. in Disp.   M.C. Fricourt,
    till Mar. 1916.   Camp Commandant, 6 Army Corps.   ~~Sen. Offr.~~ Staff
    Course, Cambridge.   G.S.O.₃, 72 Div.   June 1917 France (3),
    2 R. War. R.   Aug. 1917, secd. Asst. Instr., 3rd Army School.   *Sen. Offrs' Course Aldershot*
    Feb. 1918, attd., Bimbashi, Egyptian Army.   1st Egyptian Bn.,
    Palestine.   13 Sudanese Bn., Omdurman.   Aug. 1918 El Fasher.
    1919 Camel Corps, El Obeid, Kordofan.   *Order of the Nile 4th Cl.*

BRINTON, A. G. (1888–94)
    1914 Capt., S. Afr. Med. Corps.

BRODERICK, R. A., D.S.O., M.C. (1900–2)
Aug. 1914 Lt., R.A.M.C., T.F., 1/2 S. Mid. Fd. Amb. Mar. 1915
France. Apr. 1915 Capt. Mar.–June 1917 Actg. Lt.-Col. M.C.,
Somme, June 1917. Sept. 1917–Apr. 1919, Actg. Lt.-Col., cdg
1/2 Fd. Amb. Nov. 1917 Italy. D.S.O. Jan. 1919. Mentd. (1)
Dec. 1917, (2) Jan. 1919. Croce di Guerra May 1919.

BROMAGE, J. C. (1901–6, *b*) R.F.C.

BROOKE, W. R. (1905–7, *y*)
Feb. 1915 Sec. Lt., 16 R. Fus. July 1917 Lt., 20 Bn.

BROOKES, H. S. (1900–8, *y*)
1917 Cpl., A.S.C., Adjt.'s office, No. 3 Base Supply Dépôt, Rouen.

BROOKS, A. E. F. (1903–4, *b*)
June 1916 Sec. Lt., R.F.C.: Aero-engines, supply and production
of spares at Air Ministry. Jan. 1918–Ap. 1919 Technical officer,
R.A.F. Capt., 2 in cd. of machine and fitting shops, Sch. of
Technical Training, Halton Camp, Bucks.

BROOKS, L. (1903–7, *b*)
Sept. 1914 Pte., 14 R. War. R. L.-Cpl. Nov. 1915 France
(observer and sniper): Carnoy, on Somme; Arras; Somme.
Wounded, in attack near Longueval, July 27, 1916. S. Command
Dépôt till end of the war.

BROWN, A. C. (1914, *y*)
1915 Pte., A.S.C., M.T. Apr. 1917 Sec. Lt., R.F.A., 3c Res. Bde.

BROWN, A. W. (1906–9, *y*)
Pte., Worc. R. L.-Cpl., 4 Worc. R., Bn. H.Q., France.

BROWN, D. McD. (1908–15, *y*)
1915 Sec. Lt., 3 Arg. and Suth'd. Highrs. Oct. 1916–June 1918
1 Bn., Salonica F., Struma front. July 1917 Lt. attd. R.A.F.
June 1918 to May 1919, Egypt: Ismailia. Nov. 1918 Sec. Lt.,
Actg. Lt. (Admin.). Mar.–Apr. 1919, up the Nile, bombing, as
far as Assiout. Batoum; Constantinople; home.

BROWN, E. J. (1900–2) 1917 Pte., A.S.C.

†BROWN, H. H. W. (1904–6, *y*)
Cpl., 14 R. War. R. 1917 Sec. Lt., R.N.T.S. Died in hospital abroad, Mar. 22, 1917.

†BROWN, H. N. (1897–1900)
1915 Pte., 5 R. War. R., T.F., France. Italy. Killed 1918.

BROWN, J. R. (1907–11, *y*)
Jan. 1916–May 1919 2nd Writer, R.N. June 1916–May 1919, H.M.S. Benbow, Grand Fleet, N. Sea. Battle of Jutland.

BROWN, P. B. (1904–8, *y*)
Sept. 1914 Sec. Lt., 8 S. Staff. R. 1915 Sec. Lt., R.F.C.

BROWN, P. W. (1910–12, *y*)
1914 Cpl., 14 R. War. R. Feb. 1915 Sec. Lt., 14 R. War. R. July 1917 Actg. Lt. 92 Tr. Res. Bn. 52 Tr. Res. Bn. Jan. 1918 Lt. 3 Bn. 1919 Actg. Capt. 52 R. War. R., Army of the Rhine.

BROWN, W. A. (1896–9) 1915 Cpl., R.E., Sig. Coy.

BROWN, W. K. (1902–5, *r*)
1915 Pte., 3/14 Lond. R. (Lond. Scott.), T.F. Nov. 1918 Sec. Lt., R.G.A., T.F., 6 How. By., France.

BROWN, W. R. F. (1908–11, *y*)
Air Mech., R.F.C. Mesopotamia. Wounded. In hospital in India. Egypt. Salonica. July 1917 Cdt., O.T.C., Lee Grove Bank. Nov. 1917 Sec. Lt., A.S.C. E. Africa. Feb. 1919 Lt., R.A.S.C.

BROWNE, R. F. H. (1911–15, *y*)
1915 Cdt., R.M.C., Sandhurst. Aug. 1915 Sec. Lt., 6 Worc. R. 1st Bn., France. 1916 Invalided home from the Somme. Actg. Lt., Tr. Res. Oct. 1916 Lt. Lab. Bn. to Nov. 1917. Wounded in France, May 1918.

BRYANT, R. J. T. (Asst. Master, 1913–   )
Apr. 1917 Sec. Lt., A.S.C. May–June 1917 Offr. in ch. of Supplies, Dublin. July 1917–Mar. 1918 Asst. to O.C., A.S.C., Southern District, Ireland. Mar. 1918 France. Apr.–June 1918 Havre, Audruicq, Vendroux. May–Nov. 1918 Asst. to O.C., D.I.S., Calais. Oct. 1918 Lt., R.A.S.C. Nov. 1918–Feb. 1919 O.C., D.I.S., Dunkirk.

BUCHANAN, N. (1887–92)   1915 Sub.-Lt., R.N.V.R.

BULL, G. G. (1906–15, *y*)
Feb. 1915 Sec. Lt., R.F.A., T.F., 3 S. Mid. Bde.   France, B/307 Bde.   Attd. D/306.   V/61 T.M.B.   June 1916 Lt.   1917 invalided home.   Mar. 1918 Italy, A/103 Bde.

BULLIVANT, A. (1907–12, *y*)
1914 Pte., 14 R. War. R., France.   Discharged after wounds recd. on active service, July 1916.

BULLIVANT, F. B. (1908–12, *y*)
1915 Pte., 5 R. War. R., T.F.   Sgt.

BULLOCKE, J. G. (1907–15, *g*)
1915 Pte., H.A.C.   1917 Cdt., 5 O.C.B., Cambridge.   1918 Sec. Lt., Ind. Army, R. of O.   Jan. 1918 (Aug. 1917) 2/81 Pioneers. N.W. Frontier six mths.   Invalided.   Aug. 1918 Lt.   July 1919 Afghan Frontier.

BURLEIGH, L. G. (1909–12, *b*)
1914 Pte., 14 R. War. R.   Cpl.   May 1915 Sec. Lt., 4 High. L. I., S.R.   May 1916 secd. M.G.C.   Dec. 1916 Lt.   Egyptian E.F. Palestine.   Mentd. in Disp. Jan. 1918.   Nov. 1917 Capt.   Grantham. June 1918 France.   Severely wounded, near Tournai, Nov. 1918.

BURLEIGH, W. H. (1908–10, *b*)
Aug. 1914 Sec. Lt., A.S.C., M.T.   Mar. 1915 Lt.   Feb. 1917 Capt. Italy.   1918 France.   Mar. 1918 attd. R.A.F., blimps.   Aug. 1918 Restd. R.A.S.C.   France.

BURNETT, R. P. (1915–18, *b*)
1918 Pte., Inns of Court O.T.C.   Nov. 1918 Pte., 6 Res. Bn., M.G.C.

BURNS, S. H. (1907–11, *r*)
1914 Pte., 15 Lond. R. (Civil Serv. Rif.), T.F.   1915 Sec. Lt., 15 North'd Fus.   7 Bn.   Dec. 1916 Lt.   Secd. M.G.C., 47 Bn.

BURT, P. H. (1910–11, *g*)   Sec. Lt., R.F.C.

BURTON, W. L. (1910–12, *y*)
1914–19 Pte., 14 R. War. R., Italy, France.

†BUSBY, E. W. (1909–13, *b*)

1916 Sub-Lt., R.N.A.S. Apr. 1917 France. Killed in action at Pervyse, July 10, 1917, while engaging four Albatross scouts, after bringing down one of his assailants. (' Was responsible for bringing down 1 kite balloon, and 4 enemy machines, driving down 2 and assisting in destroying 2.')

†BUSBY, V. E. G. (1905–10, *b*)

Aug. 1914 Cpl. Dispatch Rider, R.E. Aug. 1914 France. Injured. Nov. 1914 Sec. Lt., R.E., S.R., Motor Cycl. Sect. Res. Sig. Coy. 1915 Lt., R.F.C., France, till Dec. 1916. Capt., Flt.-Cdr., R.A.F. 1917 Employed at Air Ministry. Killed in flying accident at Hendon, June 9, 1918. Buried at Lodge Hill Cemetery.

BUTLER, A. A. P. (1888–9)

Mar. 1912 Maj., Staff Paymaster, A.P.D. Mar. 1917 Lt.-Col.

BUTLER, C. P. (1904–6, *r*)

1914 Pte., 14 R. War. R. 1915 Sec. Lt., 6 Worc. R.

BUTLER, J. W. (1913–15, *b*)

1918 Cdt., 8 O.C.B., Lichfield. Sept. 1918 Sec. Lt., 3 R. War. R., S.R.

†BUTLER, L. S. L. (1913, *b*)

1914 Pte., 14 R. War. R., France. Killed in action 1916.

BUTLER, L. W. (1900–4, *r*)

1915 Cpl., N.S.W. Defence Force.

BUTTLER, F. L. (1910–15, *b*)

Apr. 1917 Sec. Lt., 3 R. War. R., S.R. 1 Bn., France. Mar. 1918 Secd. R.F.C. Sept. 1918 Restd. 1 R. War. R., France. Oct. 1918 Lt. Valenciennes.

BYWATER, F. J., M.C. and bar (1893–7)

Sept. 1914 Lt., R.E., T.F., 2 Lond. Fd. Coy. Dec. 1915 to Feb. 19 Actg. Maj. June 1916 Lt. (confirmed). M.C. Jan. 1918.* Bar to M.C. July 1918.

E

CADDICK, R. V. (1898–1902)

May 1915 Sec. Lt., R.F.A., T.F., 2/3 S. Mid. Bde. June 1916 Lt., France, A/307 Bde., 61st Div. Aug.–Sept. 1917 behind Ypres. Wounded (1) (gas) Sept. 1917 ; (2) Nov. 1917. Aug. 1918 recapture of Merville. Final advance, Cambrai to Maubeuge.

CAIRNS, J. W. (1907–12, g)

Pte., R. Fus. (Publ. Sch.). Sec. Lt., R.F.C. (Fl. Off.) Sept. 1917 Lt., temp. Capt. 1918 Lt. R.A.F., Equipment Off., 2nd Cl., Coy.-Cdr., Sch. of Tech. Training.

CALDICOTT, C. H., O.B.E. (1884–9)

Aug. 5, 1914–1919 Capt., R.A.M.C., T.F., attd. 5 Queen's (R. W. Surr. R.). Aug. 1914 S.E. Mounted Bde. Fd. Amb. O.B.E. (Mil.) June 1919.

CARLIER, S. E. WACE (1913–17, y)

Jan. 1918 Cdt., 12 O.C.B., Newmarket. June 1918 Sec. Lt., 5 R. War. R., T.F. France, 16th Bn. Beaucamp Ridge. 4th Corps School (Abbeville).

CARPENTER, N. (1910–13, g) Gnr., R.F.A. Wounded June 1917.

CARR, A. N. (1914–16, b) 1918 Inns of Court O.T.C.

CARR, E. DE G. (1911–13, b)

Mar. 1915 Sec. Lt., 8 Linc. R. Mar. 1916 Lt., 7th Bn., France. Wounded. Mentd. in Disp. May 1917 Actg. Capt. Prisoner of war (Germany) Aug. 1918.

CARR, J. S. (1911–13, b)

Aug. 1915 Sec. Lt. 9 Linc. R. 1st Bn. France. Wounded (1) Sept. 1916. July 1917 Lt. Wounded (2), Cap Martin, France, Nov. 19, 1917. Attd. 80 T.M.B., 80 Inf. Bde., Salonica F. Wounded (3) Jan. 1918. Feb. 1919 Actg. Capt.

CARR, S. A. (1906–14, b)

Aug. 1914 B.U.O.T.C. Dec. 1914 Sec. Lt., 8 Leic. R. June 1915 10 Bn. Jan. 1916 Egypt. Salonica, attd. 2 K. Shrops. L.I. till Dec. 1916. Oct.–Dec. 1916 Actg. Lt. Feb. 1917 Lt. 1917 2nd in cd., 80 T.M.B. Invalided home Mar. 1918. Jan. 1919 Actg. Capt., cdg. Coy., 52 Leic. R. Discharged unfit, as Capt., May 1919.

† CARDEW, J. H., M.C. (1895–96)

Capt., Punjab L.H. 1915 Sec. Lt., R.F.A., S.R. Oct. 1915 France, Ypres Sector, thro' winter. 1916 Somme Sector. Lt. M.C., Aug. 1916. 1917 Capt. Died Oct. 5, 1917 of wounds recd. prev. day.

†CASHMORE, E. L. (1890–6)
L.-Cpl., Can. Eng. Died of pneumonia at Étaples Jan. 22, 1919.

CASTIGLIONE, V. S. (1900–4, *b*)
1915 Pte., 31 Inf. Bn., Can. Cont. 1916 9th Res. Bn.

CATHERALL, J. E., M.B.E. (1911–15, *g*)
1915 R.M.C., Sandhurst. Aug. 1915 Sec. Lt., R. War. R. Nov. 1915 Attd. R.F.C. 1915–17 France: Loos and Somme battles. July 1916 Pilot R.F.C. 1917 Lt. Apr. 1918 Actg. Capt., R.A.F. (Admin. Br.) Home Service first in connexion with R.F.C. (Air Ministry); subsequently from 1918, with R.A.F. (Adjt. at Winchester, July). M.B.E. (Mil. Div.) Jan. 1919.

CAVE-MOYLES, Rev. G. E. P. (1888–94)
July 1915 C.F., 4th Cl.

CAVE-MOYLES, Rev. T. H. (1883–90)
Nov. 1915 C.F., 4th Cl. (till Oct. 1918).

CHAMBERLAIN, J. H. (1904–9, *b*)   1916 O.S., 6 Bn., R.N.D.

CHAMP, G. H. (1906–9, *y*)   1914 Trumpeter, War. Yeo., T.F.

CHANDLER, J. L. C. (1906–7, *r*)   Pte., W. Kent Cycl. Corps.

CHANTRILL, A. L. (1894–8)
1914 Pte., 17 R. Fus. 1915 Sec. Lt., R.F.A. Nov. 1915 Lt. Sept. 1917 Actg. Capt., 41 By. 42 Bde., France. Actg. Maj. Missing May 27–31, 1918. Prisoner in Germany.

CHANTRILL, G. M., M.C. (1900–2)
1918 Sec. Lt., Spec. Appt. (N. Russia). M.C. Feb. 1919.* Mentd. (Archangel) June 1919. June 1919 Capt. Croix de Guerre Oct. 1919.

CHANTRILL, H. H. (1902–6, *y*)
1917 2 Artists Rif. O.T.C. Sec. Lt. 26 Midd'x. R. 26 Bn. May 1917 5 Bn. Salonica F. Nov. 1918 Lt.

†CHANTRILL, R. P. (1892–5)
July 1915 Sec. Lt., R.F.A. Lt. B/78 Bde., France. Killed in action Oct. 26, 1917.

CHARRINGTON-KNOWLES, A. (1892-4)
1915-Apr. 1918 France : Sgt. Maj., (1) A.S.C., (2) Intell. Corps.

CHASE, R. G. B. (1892-1900)
Nov. 1915 Sec. Lt., R.F.A., T.F., 3/3 S. Mid. Bde. July 1917 Lt. France. S. Mid. Divl. Amm. Col. Feb. 1918 Actg. Capt. Mentd. July 1919.

CHATWIN, N. J. (1898-1901)
Chief Motor Mech., R.N.V.R. Instr. on Patrol Boats, Southampton.

CHATWIN, R. B. (1902-4, g)
Dec. 1914 Sec. Lt., A.S.C., M.T. Jan. 1918 Capt. Inspr., M.T., 2nd Cl., Aug. 1918-Feb. 1919.

CHAWNER, J. S. (1903-4, g)
1914 Pte., 16 R. War. R. Feb. 1915 Sec. Lt., 16 R. War. R., France. Jan. 1916 attd. 13 T.M.B. July 1917 Lt. Aug. 1916 Actg. Capt. Nov. 1918 Lt., Lab. Corps.

CHECKLAND, L. W. (1910-12, b)
Oct. 1914 Lt., A.S.C., T.F., 1 S. Mid. Mtd. Bde., Trans. and Supp. Col. Egypt. Salonica F. July 1916 Capt. Mar. 1918 Secd. 4 Devon. R., T.F. France : at 1st Army Inf. Sch. May 1918. Severely wounded Aug. 1918.

CHESHIRE, H. T. (1905-8, g)
Nov. 1915 Sec. Lt., 12 R. War. R. 10th Bn., France. July 1917 Lt. Nov. 1917 Wounded (gas). 1918 attd. O.U.T.T.C., Sch. of Russian Studies, Liverpool. Empd. School of Aeronautics.

†CHESHIRE, R. R. (1914-15, g)
B.U.O.T.C. 1917 Sec. Lt., 1/8 R. War. R., T.F., France. Killed Oct. 4, 1917. Buried near where he fell, on banks of R. Strombeke, nr. St. Julien.

CHILD, C. G. (1892-5) 1915 Tpr., War. Yeo., T.F.

CHILDS, G. E. (1913-16, r)
1917 Tpr., Worc. Yeo., T.F. Mar. 1918 Sec. Lt., 12 N. Staff. R., France. Severely wounded Oct. 1918.

CHOVIL, A. W. (1904–10, *r*)
Apr. 1915 Sec. Lt., 1/6 R. War. R., T.F. July 1917 Lt. France.
Nov. 1916, June to Aug. 1917 Actg. Capt. Wounded Aug. 22, 1917.

CLARE, T. C. (1892–1900)
Aug. 1914 Capt., R.A.M.C., T.F., 5 N. Gen. Hosp. 1918 Empd.
Gen. Hosp.

CLARKE, E. C. G. (1902–7, *b*)
1914 Pte., 15 R. War. R. Nov. 1914 Sec. Lt., 6 Worc. R. Jan.
1915–July 1916 France. Dec. 1915 Lt. Severely wounded, on
R. Somme, July 1916.

CLARKE, F., M.C. (1904–9, *b*)
Oct. 1914, 14 R. War. R. June 1915 Sec. Lt., 3 N. Staff. R., S.R.
8th Bn., France. Attd. 8 Leic. R. Wounded (1) Somme, Sept.
1916. 8 N. Staff. R. France (2). Wounded (2) June 1917 ; (3)
(severely) Jan. 1918. May 1917 Lt. M.C. Jan. 1918. 1918
Empd. Min. of Labour.

CLARKE, G., M C. (1902–9, *b*)
1914 Pte., 14 R. War. R. 1915 Sec. Lt., 3 N. Staff. R., S.R.
Dec. 1915 Lt. Attd. 2 North'd Fus. Salonica F. July 1917
Actg. Capt. Wounded Nov. 1917. M.C. Apr. 1918.* 1918
Empd. Min. of Labour.

CLARKE, H., M.B.E. (1900–7, *b*)
1915 Pte., Can. A.S.C. Nov. 1915 Sec. Lt., 3 N. Staff. R., S.R.
Attd. 9 Leic. R. Wounded severely, Somme, Sept. 1916. 1918
temp. Hon. Lt., Spec. Appt., Asst. Intr., G.S.I., E.E.F. Palestine,
Egypt. July 1917 Lt.

CLARKSON, R. N. M. (1900–8, *g*)
A.S.C., M.T. France.

CLAY, E. L. (1890–6)
Aug. 1918 Capt., R.A.M.C.

CLAYTON, A. C. B. (1914–17, *y*)
Nov. 1918 Cdt., Scott. Eng. Corps. Sec. Lt.

†CLAYTON, C. C. T. (1912–16, y)
1917 Cdt., R.M.C., Sandhurst. Sec. Lt., 3, attd. 1 Glouc. R. France. Guards Div. Called North suddenly from Bapaume district. Died of wounds at Nieuport, July 19, 1917. Buried at Coxyde, Belgium.

CLAYTON, J. R. H. (1909–13, y)
Sept. 1914 Lt., R.E., T.F. N. Egypt. Gallipoli. Instr. Signal Sch. (Egypt). Restd. to Estabt., July 1918.

CLEASE, A. G. D. (1902–9, g)
1915 Sous-Lieut., Corps Automobile, French Army Red Cross. 1918 Empd. under Air Board.

CLEASE, E. K. J. (1908–16, g)
1917 Cdt., R.M.C., Sandhurst. Dec. 1917 Sec. Lt., Unattd. List, Ind. Army, 53 Sikhs. Actg. Capt., Adjt. of Dépôt.

CLEASE, W. E. G. (1907–13, g)
1915 Sec. Lt., 9 King's (Shrops. L.I.), France. July 1917 Lt. 1918 Empd. Min. of Labour. Invalided out Feb. 1919.

CLEMENTS, G. L. (1907–8, g)
Capt., 16 R. War. R.

CLENDON, A. (1882–7)
1915 Sec. Lt., Handsworth G.S. O.T.C. Lt. Oct. 1918 Capt.

CLENDON, D. R. T. (1909–16, b)
Apr. 1916 Cdt., R.M.C., Sandhurst. Oct. 1916 Sec. Lt., S. Staff. R. Attd. R.F.C. Severely injured in flying accident, 1917. Mar. 1918 Rejoined S. Staff. R. Apr. 1918 Lt. May 1918 attd. M.G.C. Jan. 1919 ret. on retd. pay, on acc. of injuries recd. on active service.

CLIFT, S. W. (1902–4, r)
Apr. 1915 Sec. Lt., R.F.A., T.F., 3 S. Mid. Bde. Sept. 1915 temp. Lt. Nov. 1915 transfd. R.G.A., T.F., S. Mid. H. B. Jan. 1916 Actg. Capt., Staff Capt., Artillery. May 1916 Secd. R.A. (Reg. F.), as

Actg. Capt. June 1916 Lt. Oct. 1917 Secd. R.F.C., as Actg. Capt. Apr. 1918 R.A.F. June 1918 Mentd. and promoted Capt. Jan. 1919 Mentd. (2).

CLIVE, B. F. (1885–8)
Spr., Aust. Imp. Force.

CLULEE, E. N. (1908–12, b)
1914 Pte., 16 R. War. R. Jan. 1915 Sec. Lt., 16 R. War. R., 17 Bn. Aug. 1916 Lt., M.G.C. Inf. Wounded 1916. Cdg. Bde. Lewis Gun Coy., 222 Inf. Bde. Instr. Invalided out Oct. 1918.

CLUTTERBUCK, R. I. (1909–12, b)
1915 Cdt., R.N. Sept. 1917 Sub-Lt. H.M.S. Ajax. Apr. 1918 H.M.S. Vidette.

COHEN, H. (1893–6)
Sgt.-Maj., 119 Lab. Coy. Queen's (R. W. Surr. R.).

COHEN, M. M. (1888–93)
R. Sc. Fus.

COKE, J. D'E. Fitz E. (1888–95)
1914 Capt., A.S.C., Staff Capt., W.O. Aug. 1914 Maj. Bt. Lt.-Col., Asst. Q.M.G. Asst. Dir. Transport, W.O. Dec. 1917 temp. Col., temp. Dep. Dir. Mentd. in Disp. Twice mentd. Dist. War Services. Legion of Honour (Croix de Chevalier).

†COKE, L. S. (1893)
1914 Lt., I. Gds. Killed in action 1914 *Oct. 31 at Zandvoorde.*

†COLDICOTT, A. C., M.C. (1909–15, g)
May 1915 Sec. Lt., 3 R. War. R., S.R. May 1916 France (1), 2 Bn. : Battle of the Somme, 3 July, Mametz Wood ; wounded by sniper in attack N. of Bazentin-le-Grand Wood, July 16, 1916. Oct. 1916 France (2), 15 Bn. Wounded (2), slightly, and won the M.C.* (Gazetted Sept. 1917) at Fresnoy, July 16, 1917 : 3rd Battle of Ypres ; Polderhoek Chateau. Nov. 1917 Italy : Piave. Apr. 1918 *Capt.* back to France. Wounded, near Merville, and taken prisoner, June 28 ; in hospital at Lille and later at Dortmund, where he died of his wound Aug. 16, 1918.

COLDICOTT, C. U. (1910–18, g)
1918 Cdt., Ind. Army. Hipswell Camp, Catterick. Sept. 1918–
Apr. 1919 R.M.C., Quetta. 1919 Sec. Lt., 2/8 Gurkha Rifles :
B.O., Rewat Camp, Murree Hills : Hanga, 30 miles from Rohat.

COLEMAN, H. D. (1904–12, g)
1915 Sec. Lt., R.F.A., T.F., 2/3 N. Mid. Bde., 59 Divl. A.C. June
1916, Lt. Mar. 1917 Actg. Capt., R.G.A., 270 Siege By. Injured.
Actg. Maj., June–July 1917, Mar. 1918. Menḥd Nov·1918.

COLEMAN, P. N. (1908–10, g)
1915 Pte., 15 R. War. R. Sept. 1917 Sec. Lt., Worc. R. Mar. 1919
Lt.

COLEY, Colin (1903–9, b)
1914 Pte., 14 R. War. R. L.-Cpl. 1915 Sec. Lt., 11 Suff. R.
1916 Actg. Lt., Tr. Res. July 1917 Lt. Oct. 1917 Actg. Capt.,
Adjt. 1918 France, 1 Suff. R., 3 Div. Wounded Aug. 1918.

COLGRAVE, B. (1906, r)
1917 Sec. Lt., Merchiston Coll. O.T.C.

COLLETT, J. R. W. (1909–14, g)
1918 Cdt., R.F.A., Topsham Bks., Exeter. Aug. 1918 Sec. Lt.,
R.F.A.

†COLLIER, F. H. D. (1904–5, g)
1915 Pte., 14 R. War. R., France. Wounded July 22, 1916.
Killed Apr. 11, 1917.

COLLINGE, E. H. H. (1911–15, y)
Aug. 1917 Sec. Lt., attd. Lan. Fus. Oct. 1917 Sec. Lt., R.E.
France.

†COLLINS, E. S. (1898–1902)
Inns of Court O.T.C. Dec. 1916 Sec. Lt., Worc. R. Christmas
1916 France. Killed in action Aug. 1917.

COLLINS, H. J. W. (1907–10, b)
July 1916 Sec. Lt., R.F.C., Pilot. France. Wounded, Somme,
1916. July 1917 Lt. Lt. (A.), R.A.F. Admin. Br. Nov. 1918.

COLLINS, L. K. (1902–7, *b*)
1915 Sec. Lt., Glouc. R. France. Wounded, Somme, 1916. Lt., temp. Capt., empd. under lands branch.

COMMANDER, E. N. (1908–11, *y*)
1915 Pte., R.A.M.C., 101 Fd. Amb. Nov. 1915–Mar. 1917 France. Wounded (gas). Aug. 1917 Sec. Lt., R.G.A., S.R. France (2). 1/1 Highrs. Heavy By. 498 Siege By.

†CONATY, D. G. (1908–11, *y*)
1914 Cpl., R.E., Motor-Cycle D.R. France. Seriously injured, Sept. 1915. Feb. 1918, Sec. Lt., R.F.C. Egypt. Lt. (A.), R.A.F. Pilot Instr. (abt. 2 years). Killed in flying accident at Alexandria, July 26, 1919.

†COND, A. T. (1900–4, *g*)
1916 Sub-Lt., R.N.V.R. H.M.S. Hermione : Motor Patrols. Motor Patrol flotilla, Holyhead, for Irish Channel, between Holyhead and Douglas, Isle of Man. July 1917 Lt. Milford Haven, in cd. of a trawler. Died of pneumonia at Halifax, N.S., Apr. 17, 1919.

COND, J. H. (1897–1902)
1918 Cdt., Tank Corps. Nov. 1918 Sec. Lt.

COOKE, V. S. (1903–5, *r*)
1914 L.-Cpl., 16 R. War. R. Sec. Lt., 17 Bn. France, 15 Bn. July 1917 Lt. Italy, France (2). Wounded Apr. 19, 1918.

COOKE, W. C. C. (1893–1900)
Jan. 1916 Sec. Lt., 2/4 North'n R. Sept. 1916, July 1917 Lt. Apr. 1918 France, 7 Bn. temp. Capt., while Educ'n Off., H.Q., 24 Div., France, Sept. 1918 to Mar. 1919.

COOP, R. (1912–16, *r*)
1917 Sec. Lt., R.F.C. France. (Sopwith Camels.) Severely wounded, Cambrai, Nov. 30, 1917.

COOPER, F. E. (1910–16, *r*)
1918 3rd Cl. Air Mech., R.A.F. (Clerical work.) Blandford.
F

COOPER, G. M. (1911–13, *r*)
 1914 Pte., R. Fus. (Publ. Sch.). Apr. 1916 France. Sept. 1916
 Lt., Sea. Highrs. France (2). Wounded and prisoner (in Germany)
 Apr. 1918, Rastatt, Stralsund.

COOPER, G. R. H. (1906–8, *y*)
 B.U.O.T.C. 1918 Surg. Prob., R.N.V.R.

COPE, R. K. (1914–18, *g*)
 1918 Cdt., R.E.

CORAH, R. N. (1898–1903)
 July 1916 Sec. Lt., R.F.C., Motor Transport. Apr. 1918 Lt. (T.),
 R.A.F. Sept. 1918 France, M.T. and convoys. Army of Occupn.,
 Cologne. Capt., Actg. Maj., Inspector of M.T.

CORSER, C. H. (1896–9)
 1914 Lt., R. Ind. Marines (S. Dufferin). Wounded 1914. 1919
 Lt., Ind. Army.

CORSER, R. B. (1895–9)
 Feb. 1914 Capt., 2 York R. Wounded Oct. 1914. Aug. 1918
 Staff Capt.

COTTON, A. R. (1912–17, *r*)
 1917 Cdt., R.F.C. Aug. 1918 Sec. Lt., R.A.F. (A.), East Coast.

†COTTRELL, G. F. (1904–5, *b* ; 1907–11, *g*)
 July 1913 Sec. Lt., R.G.A. 1914 France, attd. 68 Coy. A.S.C.,
 Ind. Army Amm. Pk. 108 Heavy By., 5 Div., 28 Div. Killed
 near Ypres, May 11, 1915, by shell-fire, while keeping his men
 under cover and encouraging them.

†COTTRELL, H. W. (1910–15, *g*)
 1915 R.M.C., Sandhurst. July 1916 Sec. Lt., 2 S. Lan. R., attd.
 13 King's (L'pool R.). France. Killed a few days after his arrival
 in France, at Mouquet Farm, on the Somme, Sept. 30, 1916,
 while looking after his men under heavy shell-fire ; buried near
 Pozières.

COULSON, E. J. (1900–7, *r*)
 Sec. Lt., 14 Worc. R. Injured Aug. 1916. July 1917 Lt.

COUNSELL, J. A. (1903–5, *y*)
1914 Tpr., 12 Res. Cav. Regt. Dec. 1914 Sec. Lt., 14 The King's (L'pool R.) Mar. 1916 Lt., M.G.C. Wounded Feb. 1917.

COWDY, S. C. G. (1912–14, *b*)
1914 Pte., 16 R. War. R. 1916 Cpl., R.E., 30 Sectn., 188 Coy.

†COWPER, F. N. (1908–13, *b*)
1914 Pte., 14 R. War. R. 1915 Sec. Lt., 3 Suff. R., S.R. France. Killed in action Oct. 12, 1916.

COWPER, S. G. (1906–11, *b*)
1914 L.-Cpl., 14 R. War. R. 1915 Sec. Lt., 3 Suff. R., S.R. France. Twice wounded ((2) Apr. 1917). July 1917 Lt. Attd. 2/7 Durh. L.I., Archangel.

COX, C. H. (1891–6)
Aug. 1916 Lt., R.A.M.C. Mesopotamia. San. Off., Magil. 1918 India. Capt.

COX, L. D. (1910–15, *b*)
1917 Inns of Court O.T.C. Sec. Lt., 2/7 R. War. R., T.F., May 1918. France (Aug.), 61 Div., in the advance to Préseau.

COX, W. MUNDY, M.C. (1883–6)
Apr. 1915 Lt., R.A.M.C., T.F., 48 C.C.S. Oct. 1915, Capt. Two years in France, 1/2 S. Mid. Fd. Amb. Severely wounded June 1917. Attd. Military Hosp., Devonport, Dec. 1917 to Apr. 1918. 1/2 S. Mid. Fd. Amb. Italy. M.C. Dec. 1918 (immediate award).

COZENS, C. H. (1911–12, *g*) Pte., 1/5 R. War. R., T.F.

†CRAIG, D. L. L., M.C. (1906–15, *b*)
July 1915 Sec. Lt., R.F.A., T.F., 3 S. Mid. Bde. Oct. 1916 France. 531 How. By. June 1917 Lt. Killed (repd. missing) July 31, 1917, in a trench where he was acting as forward officer for the brigade. M.C. Aug. 1917.*

CRAIG, G. W. (1890–8)
Oct. 1913 Lt.-Col., R.A.M.C., T.F., 1/2 and 2/2 S. Mid. Fd. Amb. 1917 France, 61 Div. S.M.O., Birmingham Area. Mentd. for Distd. War Services, Aug. 1919.

36 OLD EDWARDIANS

CRAIG, W. J. F. (1903–7, b)
Sept. 1915 Lt., R.A.M.C., T.F., 2 F.A., 61 Div. 1917–18 France.
1918 Italy. Mar. 1916 Capt.

†CRAWFORD, A. B. (1900–1)
Capt., W. York. R. Killed 1916.

CREESE, H. H. (1903–5, g)
Sec. Lt., A.S.C. Apr. 1916 Lt. Actg. Capt. June 1917.

CRESWELL, P. T. (1897–9)
Lt., R.N.V.R. Attd R.N.A.S. , meteorological Br.

CREW, F. A. E. (1902–4, y)
Oct. 1914 Capt., 6 Devon. R., T.F. Secd. M.G.C. Attd. R.A.M.C.
Twice wounded, Mar., Nov. 1918. Maj., R.A.M.C., Aug. 1917.

†CRICHTON, G. E. (1900–2)
1915 Pte., 4 Bn., 1 Bde., Aust. Inf. Gallipoli. Killed in Gallipoli
Aug. 6, 1915.

CRICHTON, H. T. (1898–1901)
Oct. 1906 A.P., R.N.R. 1914 H.M. Ships Victorious, Ben McCree.
Retd. 1915.

†CRICHTON, J. D. (1905–10, b)
Dec. 1914 Sec. Lt., 6 Loyal N. Lan. R., 13 Div., 38 Bde. Gallipoli.
Wounded (1) (Hill Q) Aug. 1915. 1916 Lt., attd. 9 Bn., France.
Wounded (2) Vimy Ridge, May 9, 1916. Feb. 1917 Capt. France
(2) 25 Div. Wounded (3) July 1917. Killed by a shell about
200 yds. behind the front line in front of Frémicourt, near
Bengnâtre, when leading up his Coy. to reinforce at Beaumetz-les-
Cambrai, March 22, 1918. Mentd. in Disp., May 1918.

†CRICHTON, RONALD (1901–6, b)
Dec. 1914 Pte., 20 R. Fus. (P. Sch.). 1915 L.-Cpl., M.G. sectn.
Cpl. Nov. 1915 France. Wounded (1) Apr. ; (2) July 1916.
Cdt., Bristol. Mar. 1917 Sec. Lt., 1/5 R. War. R., T.F. France,
Apr. Killed, having been already wounded, while leading his Coy.

to attack at Westhoek, Aug. 22, 1917, nr. St. Julien–Poelcapelle road.

CROCKFORD, L. C., M.C. (1896–1901)
June 1912 Lt., 6 R. War. R., T.F. Temp. Capt. France. Mentd. in Disp., 1916. M.C., Oct. 1916.* Italy. Staff Capt., 13 Bde. Bt.-Maj. June 1918. D.A.Q.M.G. Oct. 1918–Mar. 1919. Croce di Guerra, Nov. 1918.

CROFT, L. W. P. (1903–7, b)
1915 Sec. Lt., 8 Leic. R. Mesopotamia. Invalided. 1917 Lt., attd. T.M.B.

CRONIN, R. H. (1912–13, r)
Inns of Court O.T.C. May 1918 Sec. Lt., R.E. (Haynes Park). 1918 France, Somme.

CROOKE, J. W E. (1907–15, g)
Apr. 1915 Sec. Lt., R.M.L.I. Nov. 1915 Actg. Lt., H.M. Ships Orion, Emperor of India. Retd. 1918.

CROOKE-ROGERS, G. H. C. (1910–15, b)
1914 Cdt., R.M.C., Sandhurst. 1915 Sec. Lt., Worc. R. 1916 attd. R.F.C. (Fl. Off.). Nov. 1917 (sen. Oct. 1916) Lt. Dec. 1916 Equipment Off Lt., R.A.F. (T.). June 1919 Rel. Commn. June 1919 Lt., Worc. R., Gen. R. of O.

CROSBY, G. C. S. (1908–9, y)
Aug. 1914 Pte. 10 Can. Inf. France. Severely wounded 1915. 9 Res. Bn. Off. i. c. Records, Can. Rec. Office. Disch'd Aug. 1917.

CROSS, A. L. R. (1898–1900)
1914 Can. Cont. 1917 Can. R.E. Oct. 1917 Sec. Lt., R.E. Mar. 1919 Lt.

†CROSS, F. A. (1909–13, r)
1914 Pte., 21 R. Fus. (P. Sch.). 1916 Sec. Lt., 15 Glouc. R. Mesopotamia. Killed in action Feb. 26, 1917.

CROSS, H. F. (1901–2)
June 1916 Lt., R.F.A., T.F., 48 S. Mid. Div. A.C.

38   OLD EDWARDIANS

CROSS, L. F. (1911–16, *r*)
Mar. 1918 3 Cl. Air Mech., R.F.C. 1918 R.A.F. (Clerical work).

CROSS, S. T. (1894)   Bombr., R.G.A.

CROSS, W. A. (1902–3)
1914 Pte., 19 R. Fus. (P. Sch.). 1916 Sec. Lt., 1 Worc. R., S.R. 2nd Bn. France. Wounded May 1917. July 1917 Lt. Empd. M. of Munitions.

CROSSLAND, G. H. B. (1912–17, *r*)
French Red Cross. Apr. 1918 Balkans. Croix de Guerre for courage and devotion to duty in offensive of Sept. 18, 1918.

CROUCH, A. L. (1908–11, *g*)
1914 Pte., R.A.M.C., T.F., 1 Sn. Gen. Hosp. 1916 Tpr., 1 War. Yeo. Suez.

CROUCH, R. K. (1907–10, *g*)
1914 Pte., R.A.M.C., T.F., 1 Sn. Gen. Hosp. 1916 Sgt., 3 War. Yeo. Instr. Phys. Ex. 1 Res. Lancers. Feb. 1917 Sec. Lt., Res. Reg. Cav. Apr. 1918 M.G.C. (Inf.). France. Aug. 1918 Lt.

CROW, T. B. (1909–14, *b*)
1915 Sec. Lt., 11 King's Own (York. L.I.). Sept. 1916 Lt., 2 Bn. France. (Salvage Dump).

CROWTHER, H. N. (1896–1901)
1914 Pte., Cape Union Def. F. (Duke of Edinburgh's Own Rif.) to cessation of hostilities in German S.W. Africa, 1915.

CROWTHER, W. C. (1899–1904, *g*)
1914 Capt., Dulwich Coll. O.T.C. Sept.–Dec. 1918 Lt., 19 Lond. R., T.F.

CURLE, A. C. (1910–14, *r*)
Sept. 1914 L.-Cpl., 14 R. War. R. 1915 Sec. Lt., 4 High. L.I., S.R. June 1916 18 Bn., France. Through the Battle of the Somme; to June 1917, in the line from Arras to the South; invalided home after operation. Mentd. in Disp. May 1917. July 1917 Lt. Dec. 1917 France (2): 14 Bn. (Bullecourt). Taken prisoner at Laventie, near Armentières (repd. missing), Apr. 9, 1918. At

Pforzheim, Baden. Home, via Basle, Dec. 1918. Rejd. 53 Bn. till Mar. 1919.

URLE, C. L. (1906–9, *r*)
Guy's Hospital. 1914 Univ. of Lond. O.T.C.

URLE, G. (1909–12, *r*)
Sept. 1914 Sgt., 14 R. War. R. Oct. 1915 Sec. Lt., 17 Bn., Chisledon. Aug. 1916 France, 14 Bn. Severely wounded in Battle of the Somme, near Guillemont Farm, Sept. 1916. May 1917 transfd. Gen. List, New Armies, Actg. Capt. Adjt., Vol. Bn., Durh. L.I., 1917–19. *Aug 1918 Capt.*

URLE, VICTOR (1911–15, *r*)
1915 Cdt., R.M.C., Sandhurst. Aug. 1915 Sec. Lt., Unattd. List, Ind. Army. Oct. 1915 sailed for India : 81 Pioneers. 1916 attd. 64 Pioneers, Mesopotamia. Aug. 1916 Lt. July 1917 Actg. Capt. Dec. 1917 Actg. Capt. Addl. Aug. 1918 Temp. Capt. Left Persia Feb. 1919. Special Service, Knox's Mission via Bombay, Singapore, Hong Kong, Japan, Vladivostok, to Tomsk, Siberia. *ments. war service.*

URRALL, L. V. (1902–9, *b*)
Sept. 1914 Sec. Lt., 16 R. War. R. Oct. 1914 11 Bn. France. Severely wounded Sept. 1916. July 1917 Lt.

CURTIS, K. S. (1907–11, *g*)
1914 Pte., 14 R. War. R. L.-Cpl. Sec. Lt., 14 Bn. France. Wounded. Killed Oct. 26, 1917.

UTLER, H. A., D.C.M. (1903–6, *g*)
1914 Cpl., R.E., D.R. France. Wounded 1915. Motor-Cycle-Sgt., Sign. Coy., 1st Div. D.C.M. Jan. 1919.*

UTLER, W. R. (1903–4, *g*)
1914 Pte., R.A.M.C., Mtd. Div. Italy.

UXSON, J. L. D. (1908–11, *b*)
1915–19 Pte., R.A.S.C., M.T. 3½ yrs. in France.

UXSON, S. G., M.C. (1905–11, *b*)
Nov. 1914 Sec. Lt., 9 S. Staff. R. June 1915 Lt. Nov. 1915 Egypt : attd. 1 R. Innis Fus., 29 Div. 1916 France. Sept. 1916

Invalided home. Nov. 1917 Italy, 1 S. Staff. R., 7 Div. M.C.
Apr. 1918 (Gaz. Sept. 1918).* Nov.–Dec. 1918 Actg.Capt. Battles:
1916 Somme ; June 1918 Austrian Offensive ; Oct. 1918 Piave.

DALTON, R. F. (1909–14, *b*)

1914 Pte., R. Fus. (P. Sch.). 1915 Cpl., R.E., 1 Bn. Spec. Bde.
Chemists' Section. 3½ yrs. in France.

DALTON, W. P. (1907–11, *b*)

1915 Sec. Lt., 6 (Cycl.) Bn., Norf. R., T.F. Jan. 1917 Lt. France
(1 yr.). Empd. Min. of Labour.

DAMAN, T. W. A. (1879–86)

Oct. 1908 Lt.-Col., R.A.M.C., T.F., 4 Northn. Hosp.

DAMON, C. A. I., M.C. (1911–14, *y*)

1915 L.-Sgt., 3/5 R. W. Kent R. July 1916–Sept. 1919 Egypt
and Palestine. 1st and 2nd Battles of Gaza and minor operations.
Sept. 1917 Sec. Lt., Glouc. R. (Reg. F.), attd. 1/5 Bed. R., T.F.
Oct. 1918, Nov. 1918–Mar. 1919 Actg. Capt. 3rd Battle of Gaza
and final offensive, and subsequent march to a point bet. Beirut
and Tripoli. M.C. Mar. 1919.*

DANIEL, W. J. (1907–11, *b*)

1914 Pte., 14 R. War. R.

DANIELL, E. H. (1902–8, *r*)

Feb. 1915 Gnr., R.F.A., T.F., 2/3 Lond. Bde. Oct. 1915 Bmdr.
Jan. 1917 France: Battles of Arras, Bullecourt, 3rd Ypres. Re-
turned, accidentally wounded, Mar. 22, 1918. Oct. 1918 Cdt.,
R.F.A. (Topsham, Exeter). Sec. Lt., R.F.A., Apr. 1919.

DANIELL, P. J. (1900–7, *r*)

Oct. 1918 Lecturing on Aero-dynamics to U.S.A. Officers (Flt.
Cdrs.), Houston Coll., California.

†DANIELS, F., M.C. (1906, *r*)

1914 Scoutmaster on Coastguard service, nr. Reculvers, Herne Bay.
1915 C.S.-M., 5 R. War. R., T.F. Mar.–Dec. 1916 France, 2/5 Bn.,
in all their engagements. M.C. July 1916.* 1917 Sec. Lt., 5 R.
War. R., T.F. Wounded and missing (presumed killed) Dec. 3, 1917.

DANKS, H. G. (1906–9, *r*)
R.Q.-M.-S., 92 Tr. Res Bn., Chisledon. Sec. Lt., R.A.S.C., Mar. 1918.

DARLING, F. G. (1910–12, *r*)
Nov. 1915 Pte., 3 Res. H.A.C. (Inf.) Nov. 1916 France, 1 Bn. 1917, early mths., Ancre region : long period of hard fighting at Arras : esp., Apr., on Oppy Wood–Gavrelle front. Last 6 wks. of the war, final pursuit, finishing at Cologne.

DAVENPORT, E. B. (1903–6, *r*)
Sec. Lt., R. Mon. R.E., S.R. July 1917 Lt.

DAVENPORT, E. C. (1908–9, *r*)
July 1917 Lt., Rif. Brig. 1918 5 Res. Bn.

DAVIES, C. C. (1890–5)
Aug. 1914 Sec. Lt., 8 Worc. R., T.F. Lt. France. Wounded 1915. Capt., June 1916. Tr. Res. Bn.

†DAVIES, E. P. (1907–1C, *g*)
1915 Gnr., R.F.A., T.F., 3 S. Mid. Bde. France. Killed Nov. 28, 1917.

DAVIES, H., M.C. (1885–9)
Feb. 1909 Sec. Lt., R. Fus. Lt., July 1909. Capt., Dec. 1911. Nov. 1914 Capt., 8 R. War. R., T.F. O.C. B Coy. France. Mentd. in Disp., Apr. 1915, Jan. 1916. M.C. Apr. 1915.* Secd. 64 Prov. Bn., and attd. 14 Suff. R., T.F., Dec. 1916. Apr. 1917 Maj., 1/8 R. War. R. France (2), Aug. 1917. Severely wounded Oct. 1917. Rel. Commn. Feb. 1919.

DAVIES, J. B. (1901–6, *y*)
P.F.O., R.N.A.S. Sept. 1918 Sec. Lt., R.A.F. (S.) Unempd. List.

†DAVIES, T. A. M. (1908, *g*)
1916 Lt., R.F.A., T.F. 5 Staff. By. France. Killed July 1, 1916. Ypres, La Bassée, Arras.

G

DAVIES, V. W. (1903–5, *g*)
1916 Pte., R.A.M.C. Cpl.

DAVIS, L. S. (1900–6, *g*)
Sec. Lt., R.F.A., S.R., 24 Div.

DAVIS, S. A., D.S.O., O.B.E. (1900–3)
Mar. 1914 Sec. Lt. 8 S. Staff. R. Jan. 1916 Lt., Actg. Capt.,
Gen. List, T.M.B. D.S.O. 1916.* 1918 Lt., Min. of Nat. Service
(Recruiting). O.B.E. (Mil.) June 1919.

DAVISON, G. S. (1905–11, *b*)
1914 Cpl., R.E., T.F., D.R., 1 Lond. Divl. Sign. Coy. 1915 Sec.
Lt., R.E. France. Lt., Jan. 1916.

DAVISS, L.W. (1902–3)
1916 Cpl., A. Cycl. C.

DAWSON, J. B. (1893–4)
1916 Lt., R.A.M.C., 12 C.C.S. France.

DEELEY, W. J. (1905–9, *b*)
Dec. 1915 Pte., 1 Garr. Bn., Worc. R. Apr. 1916 Invalided out.
Aug. 1918 Pte., Glouc. R., Hotchkiss M.G. Coy., E. Coast Service.

DENT, H. H. C. (1891–2)
Sept. 1911 Lt.-Col., R.A.M.C., T.F. O.C. 1/3 N. Mid. Bde.
Fd. Amb. France. Neuve Chapelle, Mar. 1915. Apr. 1916
temp. Col. and A.D.M.S., 59 Div. June 1916 Col. Restd. to
Establt., France, Aug. 1917. Advanced dressing statn. 1917 to
Mar. 1919, O.C. Military Hosp., Clipstone, and senior M.O.,
Clipstone Camp, Mansfield.

DENT, J. R. C., D.S.O. and bar, M.C. (1893–9)
Sept. 1914 Capt., 1 R. Innis. Fus., India. 29 Div. Apr. 1915
Gallipoli—landing. Wounded (1) June 7, 1915. Mar. 1916
France. Wounded (2), Beaumont Hamel, July 1, 1916. Apr.
1917–Mar. 1919 France. M.C. 1916. Bourlon Wood and Cam-
brai (Nov. 1917). Wounded (3) Aug. 1918. D.S.O. Dec. 1918 *
Croix de Guerre (silver cross) Dec. 1918. Mentd. (1) (Gallipoli)

1916, (2) Dec. 1918; bar to D.S.O. Jan. 1919. O.C., 1 R. Innis. Fus. (Actg. Lt.-Col.) Mar. 18, 1918 to Mar. 1919. Jan. 1919 temp. Lt.-Col. Mentd. (3) July 1919.

D'ESTE, H. G. (1911–13, *g*)
1915 Inns of Court O.T.C. 1916 Sec. Lt., 5 R. War. R., T.F. Lt. Jan. 1918.

DE VINE, Rev. C. N., M.C. (1895–1902)
Mar. 1915 C.F. 4th Cl. Mentd. in Disp. Dec. 1917. M.C. June 1919.

†DE VINE, Rev. H. B. St. J. (1895–9)
1914 C.F., 4th Cl., attd. W. Rid. R., and later a Scottish Regt. Killed in action Apr. 27, 1916.

†DEVIS, F. (1907–10, *r*)
1914 Pte., H.A.C. Sec. Lt., 4 R. War. R., S.R. Attd. 2nd Bn., Scout Offr. France. Wounded, N. of Bazentin-le-Grand Wood, July 14, 1916. Feb. 1917 France (2), attd. 1st Bn. Killed at Fampoux, Apr. 11, 1917, by sniper, while aiding a wounded officer.

DEVIS, H. F. (1873–81)
June 1917 Lt., R.A.M.C. Nov. 1917 Capt. Mediterranean.

DIBBLE, J. (1913–15, *r*)
1918 Cdt., R.A.F.

†DICKINSON, Rev. H. (1901–3)
C.F., 4th Cl., 1 Artists Rif. France. Killed Oct. 30, 1917.

DIGGLE, Rev. R. F., M.C. (1902–3)
C.F., 4th Cl. M.C. Dec. 1918.*

†DINGLEY, P. G. (1903–7, *y*)
Sept. 1914 Pte., 14 R. War. R. France. Killed (repd. missing) July 22, 1916.

†DISTURNAL, F. L. (1905–10, *b*)
1917 Pte., Can. Inf., 9 Res. Bn. Wounded 1917. *France 49 Bn.*
Killed Aug. 8 1918, nr. Amiens.

DIX, F. H. R. (1909–17, *y*)
1917 Cdt., 13 O.C.B., Newmarket. Oct. 1917 Sec. Lt., 8 attd.
7 Notts and Derby R., T.F. Nov. 1918 France. Lt., 8 Bn.,
May 1919.

DIXON, Rev. H. H. (1903–5, *r*)
Sec. Lt., Dulwich Coll. O.T.C. Lt.

DIXON, H. J., M.C. (1908–14, *r*)
Sept. 1916 Sec. Lt., 3 R. War. R., S.R. Nov. 1916 France, 1 Bn.,
4 Div. : (Somme) Priory Farm, Pierre St. Vaast Wood, Rancourt,
Sailly-Saillisel, Bouchavesnes. Apr. 1917 (Picardy) Arras, Fam-
poux, Chemical Works, Roeux. Oct. 1917 (Flanders) Poelcapelle,
Langemarck. Nov. 1917 (Picardy) Arras, Monchy-le-Preux,
Roeux, Cambrai Road. Mar. 1918 (Picardy) Arras, Fampoux.
Mar. 1918 Lt. Apr. 1918 Actg. Capt., Intell. Offr. ; Asst. Adjt.
Apr. 1918 Pacaut Wood, Hinges, La Bassée Canal, capture of
Riez-du-Vinage. Apr. 1918–Mar. 1919 Actg. Capt., Addl., Adjt.
July 1918 (Picardy) Arras, Eterpigny, Etaing, Dury, Cambrai,
Naves, Saulzoir, Verchain, Préseau, Valenciennes. Feb. 1919
(Belgium) Binche. Mentd., Dec. 1918. M.C. June 1919.

DIXON, J. S. (1914–15, *r*)
B.U.O.T.C. 1918 Sec. Lt., R.A.F. (A.). Hormead, Yorks.

DIXON, S. F., M.C. (1909–12, *r*)
Dec. 1914 Lt., 12 R. War. R. Temp. Capt., 9 Bn. Mesopotamia.
Oct. 1916 Capt. Injured 1918. India. M.C. June 1918.

DOCKER, P. (1906–8, *r*)
1914 Sec. Lt., 8 R. War. R., T.F. France. Mentd. 1916 Lt.,
Secd. 143 Bde. M.G. Coy., attd. M.G.C. Injured Jan. 29, 1917.
Grantham. June 1916 Capt. Maj., M.G.C., Feb. 1918.

DONOVAN, A. S. (1910–12, *b*)
Cdt., R.N.C., Dartmouth. Aug. 1914 Mid., R.N., H.M.S.
Benbow. Battle of Jutland, May 31, 1916. Mar. 1918 Sub-Lt.,
H.M. Minesweeper Foxglove. Jan. 1919 H.M.S. President for
course of instn. at Camb. Univ. Aug. 1919 H.M.S. Thunderer.

DONOVAN, E. T. G. (1911–15, *b*)

Jan. 1917 Sec. Lt., R.F.A., S.R. France. Wounded (gas) Sept. 1917. France. Lt., July 1918.

DONOVAN, H. (1908–15, *b*)

1917–18 Surg. Prob., R.N.V.R., H.M.S. Plucky.

DOWNING, A. M. (1894–9)

1915 Sec. Lt., The King's (L'pool R.). July 1915 Lt. 1918 Rif. Brig. Egypt, attd. 19 (Western) Bn. P. of W. Camp, Kantara.

DRUMMOND, D. B. (1909–17, *r*)

Aug. 1917 Pte., 1/8 R. War. R., attd. Cdt., 22 O.C.B., Jesus Coll., Camb. Nov. 1917 Sec. Lt., Lab. Corps., 304 Res. Lab. Coy. France. Mar. 1918, 142 Lab. Coy. : Dec. 1918, 17 Lab. Group (Educn. Offr.). Feb. 1919 Actg. O.C. 827 Area Empt. Coy. Feb.–May 1919, 304 P. of W. Coy. (Educn. Offr.).

DUNCUFF, S. L. (1915–16, *y*)

R.A.S.C.

DUNN, P. (1901–2)

1917–18 Signlr., R.N.V.R.

DYER, E. J. R. (1897–1900)

Lt., R. Fus. Apr. 1918 Lt., R.A.F. (T.).

DYER, G. C. S. (1900)

Capt., N.Z. Staff Corps, England.

EADEN, S. P. P. (1893–8)

1917 L.-Cpl., Tr. Res. Bn.

EADIE, D. H. (1909–12, *y*)

Dec. 1914 Pte., 16 R. War. R. June 1915 discharged unfit. Sept. 1916 to June 1919 Pte., R.A.S.C.

EAGLES, K. S. (1910–14, *g*)

Sec. Lt., R.F.C. R.A.F. (Admin.). Apr. 1918 (A.).

EALES, W. H. F. (1897–1900)

June 1917 Lt., R.A.M.C. June 1918 Capt. Salonica. Italy ; Ophthalmic Specialist, 24 C.C.S., Italy.

EARLE, S. G. T. (1909–14, g)
Dec. 1914 Pte., R. War. R. Sec. Lt., 8 S. Lan. R. Wounded
July 1916. 1918 Rel. Commn.

EDEN, J. R. (1907–12, y)
1915 Pte., 12 Can. Inf. France. 2 Bde., 1 Div. M.G. Coy. Sgt.
Wounded (Passchendaele) Nov. 1917. Actg. C.-S.-M., Can. M.G.
Dépôt. June–Dec. 1916 Instr.

EDMONDS, W. G. B., M.C. (1906–11, y)
1914 Pte., R. Fus. (P. Sch.). Sec. Lt., 3 R. War. R., S.R. 15 Bn.
Lt., July 1917, 1st Bn. Sign. Off. M.C. Apr. 1918.* Fampoux,
Hinges, capture of Riez-du-Vinage ; Aug.–Nov. 1918 Cambrai,
Naves to Villers, Saulzoir ; Verchain ; Querenaing, Artres,
Préseau ; Valenciennes. Binche. Mentd. May 1918. Actg. Capt.,
Addl., June 1918–Feb. 1919.

EDMONDS-SMITH, Rev. E. (1892–9)
Oct. 1910 C.F., 4th Cl. June 1916, 3rd Cl., Malta. Mentd. in
Disp. 1918 Senior C.F., Malta.

EDMONDSTON, J. S. (1906–7, y)
1914 Pte., 14 R. War. R. Sec. Lt., 6 R. War. R., T.F. France.
Apr. 1917 Secd. M.G.C. July 1917 Lt. Wounded (1) Apr. 1917,
(2) Oct. 1917.

EDWARDS, A. S. (1910–14, r)
Aug. 1915 Sec. Lt., 12 R. W. Fus. May 1916 transfd. M.G.C.
July 1916 Lt. Nov. 1916–Mar. 1919 Mesopotamia, 40 Coy.,
M.G.C., 40 Bde., 13 Div., in every action from siege and capture
of Kut onwards (except the last expedn. to Kirkuk in the Mosul
action of Nov. 1918), with one month's leave in India, and one
month's sickness (July 1917) in hosp. Actg. Capt. Jan.–Mar. 1919.

EDWARDS, E. M. (1904–6, g)
Aug. 1914 Sec. Lt., A.S.C., T.F., H.Q. Coy., S. Mid. Div. Mar.
1916 Lt. June 1916 Capt.

EDWARDS, H. M., O.B.E. (1907–10, *r*)

Sept. 1914 Pte., 14 R. War. R.   Jan. 1915 Sec. Lt., 11 Worc. R. Sept. 21, 1915 to Sept. 1, 1919 France, Salonica, Russia.   Dec. 1916 Lt. and Adjt.   Mar. 1917 Capt.   June 1918 Maj.   Oct.–Nov. 1918, Feb. 1919 Actg. Lt.-Col. (cdg. 11 Worc. R.).   O.B.E. June 1919.   Officer of the Crown of Roumania Feb. 1919.   Mentd. June 1919.

EDWARDS, N. (1902–6, *b*)

Early in 1915 Pte., 14 R. War. R.   France.   Severely wounded in Delville Wood, July 1916.   In hospital till Sept. 1917.   Home Service, Ireland.

EGERTON, A. C. (1907–9, *b*)

1914 Pte., 14 R. War. R.

†EGLINGTON, F. (1899–1904, *r*)

Aug. 1914 Sec. Lt., 5 S. Staff. R., T.F.   Lt.   France.   Severely wounded Apr. 1915.   France (2) 1916.   Capt.   Killed (Gomme-court), July 2, 1916.

EGLINGTON, S. A. (1905–6, *r*)

1915 O.S., R.N.V.R.   July–Sept. 1915 Pte., R.N.D., Gallipoli. May–Nov. 1916 France, Lens.   Mar. 1917 Sec. Lt., 1/5 S. Staff. R., T.F.   France.   Mar.–Sept. 1917 Somme.   Twice wounded ((2) Sept. 1917).   Sept. 1918 Lt.

†EHRHARDT, J. A. (1911–16, *r*)

1916 Sec. Lt., Tank Corps, 3 Coy., 1 Bn.   France.   Killed Mar. 26, 1918 (having been twice previously wounded the same day).

† EHRHARDT, W. H. (1906–11, *r*)

Sept. 1914 Sec. Lt., 14 R. War. R.   Dec. 1914 Capt., C Coy. France.   Severely wounded Apr. 17, 1916.   Rel. Commn. Dec. 1917.   Died of wound June 17, 1923.

EITE, W. (1909–11, *b*)

Sept. 1915 2nd Cl. Mech., R.N.A.S., Chemical Research Sectn. (later, R.N. Experimental Station.   To Feb. 1919 C.P.O. in control of ' Smoke ' Section.

ELLIS, N. T., M.C. (1899–1902)
1915 Sec. Lt., R.E., 202 Fd. Coy. Lt. Sept. 1917 Capt. Dec. 1917–May 1919 Actg. Maj. M.C. Jan. 1918.

EMANUEL, J. G. (1882–90)
July 1908 Capt., R.A.M.C., T.F., 1 Sn. Gen. Hosp.

EMERSON, G. C. (1906–8, r)
1914 Pte., R.A.M.C., 1 Fd. Amb., 61 Divn. Sept. 1916 Sec. Lt., 4 R. War. R., S.R. 11 Bn. France. Wounded May 1917. Mar. 1918 Lt. Empd. Min. of Labour.

EMERSON, J. C. (1906–11, r)
1914 Cpl., R.E., D.R. Mar. 1917 Sec. Lt., N. Staff. R. Wounded Apr. 1918. Serving under Air Ministry.

ENGLISH, C. F. (1885)
1917 Cpl., R.A.M.C.

ENNALS, W. H. (1906–9, g)
Sept. 1914 Y.M.C.A. (military service). France, Feb. 1915–May 1918. Mentd. Sept. 1918. May 1918 Inns of Court O.T.C. Dec. 1918 transfd. Lond. Scottish.

ENSOR, A. H. (1904–7, y)
1916 Cpl., 7 R. Fus. Wounded 1917.

EVANS, E. A. (1906–14, y)
Aug. 1914 Sec. Lt., 2/5 R. War. R., T.F. 1915 France. Wounded May 1915. Sept. 1915 Lt. Apr. 1917 India. June 1918, 1 Garr. Bn., Oxf. and Bucks. L.I., Trimalgherry, Deccan. July 1918 transfd., Lt., Ind. Army. 40 Pathans, Campbellpur ; at Rawal Pindi, N. W. Frontier.

†EVANS, F. D. (1909–15, y)
Sept. 1915 Sec. Lt., 4 R. War. R., S.R. Attd. R.F.C. Killed in flying accident nr. Bristol, June 9, 1916.

EVANS, R. M. (1901–6, b)
1914 King Edward's Horse. Jan. 1915 Sec. Lt., 5 S. Staff. R., T.F. Feb. 1918 Lt.

EVERETT, E. G. (1911–14, *y*)
1916 R.F.A., Cadet Sch., Exeter. Feb. 1917 Sec. Lt., R.F.A., 52 By., France. Dec. 1917 to Apr. 1918 80 By., 15 Bde., 5 Div., Italy. France (2). Wounded May 20, 1918. Aug. 1918 Lt.

EVERETT, J. S. (1910–13, *y*)
1915 Tpr., N. Somerset Yeo. L.-Sgt. 1916 Sec. Lt., Suss. Yeo., attd. 10 R. Fus. France. Counter-attack, Polderhoek Chateau, Mar. 8, 1918. Oct. 1918 Lt. Actg. Capt. to Apr. 1919.

EVERETT, R. B. (1908–13, *y*)
1914 Cpl., 14 R. War. R. Sgt. France. Cadet Sch. in France. 1916 Sec. Lt., 1 D. of Corn. L.I. Severely wounded, Somme, Sept. 1916. Feb. 1918 Lt. Asst. Offr., No. 1 Record Off., Exeter, Oct. 1917. May 1918 Gen. List.

EVERTON, W. B. (1906–7, *b*)
1916 Flt.-Sgt., R.F.C., No. 1 Aircraft Dépôt. Sec. Lt. No. 2 Aircraft Dépôt. France. Apr. 1917 Lt. Equipt. Offr., 2nd Cl. R.A.F. (T.). Apr. 1918 Actg. Capt.

FATHERS, J. A. (1890–2)
1914 Pte., Can. Inf.

FAULCONBRIDGE, F. T. (1909–12, *g*)
1916 Pte., 3/7 Worc. R., T.F., D Coy.

†FAWCETT, F. A. (1911–13, *y*)
1914 Sgt., 14 R. War. R. 1915 Sec. Lt., 1/5 S. Staff. R., T.F. France: Vimy Ridge, Somme. Missing, believed to have been killed, Gommecourt, July 1, 1916.

†FAWDRY, A. G. (1910–15, *r*)
Oct. 1915 Sec. Lt., 3 R. War. R., S.R. Sept. 1916 France, 2nd Bn. Bn. Sig. Off. Killed at Bullecourt (Bn. H.Q.) May 4, 1917.

FAWDRY, J. W., M.C. (1911–15, *r*)
Feb. 1915 Sec. Lt., 3 R. War. R., S.R. France, 2 Bn. 4 Bn., Sig. Off. Mar. 1916 Lt. Feb. 1917 Actg. Capt. and Adjt., Sig. Sch., Southwick Fort, Cosham. 1/7 Bn., T.F., Italy. H.Q.,

H

143 Bde., Signals. Oct. 1917 The Great Advance through the mountains. English troops of 48 Div. were the first in Trent : Bn. captured 6,000 prisoners, 6 generals, and many guns. Dec. 1918–Jan. 1919 temp. Capt., Educ. Offr. Mentd. in Disp. Jan. 1919. Croce di Guerra, May 1919. M.C. June 1919. Egypt.

FEATHERSTONE, H. W. (1903–11, *b*)

June 1917 Lt., R.A.M.C., S.R. Salonica. Capt., 42 Fd. Amb., June 1918. France.

†FEATHERSTONE, W. D., M.C. (1906–14, *b*)

1915 Sec. Lt., R.F.A., T.F., 3/3 S. Mid. Bde. France, D/77 Army Bde. M.C. Aug. 1917.* July 1917 Lt. Killed Mar. 23, 1918.

†FELTON, H. R. (1911–14, *y*)

Dec. 1915 Pte., S. Staff. R. Oct. 1916 Sec. Lt., 7 Worc. R. Sept. 1917 France. Oct. 9, 1917, while leading his platoon in the big attack on Passchendaele he was wounded and left lying under heavy shell-fire : he is believed to have been killed then (reported missing).

FERNIE, G. H. (1911–14, *g*)

R.N.D., Crystal Palace.

FIDDIAN, E. A. (1906–11, *y*)

1915 Surg. Prob., R.N.V.R., H.M.S. Nereid. Apr. 1916 Surg. Lt., R.N., H.M.S. Glory. 1918 R.N. Dépôt, Crystal Palace.

FIELD, A. G. (1911–13, *y*)

Jan. 1918 Mid., R.N.R.

†FIELD, B. J. M. (1908–14, *b*)

1916 Pte., A. Cycl. C. Pte., North'd Fus. France. Repd. missing, 1917. Prisoner—died of wounds in German hands.

FIFE, D. McD. (1912–17, *g*)

1917 Cdt., R.M.C., Sandhurst. Cdt., Ind. Army, Wellington Coll. Aug. 1918 Sec. Lt., Ind. Army, 2/6 Rajputs.

†FINK, S. (1907–10, *r*)

1917 Lt., S. Lan. R. Killed in action 1917.

FINNEMORE, D. L. (1901–8, *r*)
1917–18 2nd Grade Field Off., B.R.C.S., Wounded and Missing
Dept., Rouen.

FIRMSTONE, H. I. (1913–14, *g*)
1915 Pioneer, R.E., T.F., 52 Airline Sectn.   Spr., Sig. Serv.
Four years in France.

FISHER, J. W., T.D. (1866–73)
Oct. 1914 Maj., 4 North'n R., Adjt., attd. 2nd Bn.   France. Bt.
Lt.-Col., 9th Bn.   Retd. Dec. 1918.

FISHER, L. G. (1906–14, *b*)
Pte., 23 R. Fus.   France.   Wounded (gas) May 1917.   Cdt.,
7 O.C.B., Fermoy, Ireland.   June 1918 Sec. Lt., 3 Res. Bn., N.
Staff. R.   Attd. 7 Leic. R., France (2).

†FITCH, P. H. B., M.C. (1911–15, *b*)
1915 Sec. Lt., R.F.A., T.F., 3/3 S. Mid. Bde.   D/177 Bde.   France.
Lt. M.C. June 1917.* Killed while engaged in night-firing, by
a shell from a field gun, July 23, 1917.

FITZPATRICK, B. P. S. (1916–18, *r*)
Aug. 1918 King's India Cadet.   12 O.C.B., Newmarket.   Dec. 1918
India, Wellington Coll.

FLEWITT, C. Y., (1886–93)
Lt., R.A.M.C. July 1916 Capt.   Salonica F.   1918 Order of St. Sava,
Serbia, 4th Cl.   Mentd. Nov. 1918, Mar., June 1919.

FLINT, C. B. B. (1911–14, *g*)
1916 2nd Cl. Air Mech., R.F.C.

FLOAT, S. E. (1907–10, *g*)
1914 Pte., 14 R. War. R.   France.   Italy.

†FOIZEY, H. E. (1901)
Sept. 1914 Pte., 15 Prince of Wales' (W. Yorks. R.).   Feb. 1915
L.-Cpl.   Mar. 1915 Sec. Lt., 18 Bn.   Dec. 1915 Egypt, 31 Div.
Spring 1916 France.   May 1916 Lt.   Wounded and missing,

subsequently reported killed, at Serre, July 1, 1916. Buried Bus-en-Artois, Somme, Sept. 1916.

†FOLEY, W. A. (1907–13, *r*)
1913 Cdt., R.M.C., Sandhurst. 1914 Sec. Lt., 2 R. Ir. F
France. Wounded (1) 1915. Attd. 4th Bn. Sept. 1915
France. Actg. Capt. Killed Nov. 1917.

FORBES, A. E. F. L. (1901–6, *r*)
Nov. 1916 Capt., R.A.M.C., Spec. List. Dental Surg. Fran⟨
Aubigny.

FORD, G. R. H. (1900–9, *r*)
Sept. 1914 Sec. Lt., 8 N. Staff. R. Lt. Capt., Jan. 1916. Wound
Somme, July 1916. Rel. Commn. Mar.–Aug. 1917. Attd. 3 1
Nov. 1918 attd. 23 R.W. Fus. Dec. 1918 52 Grad. Bn., S.W. Bo⟨
Sig. Off.

FORDRED, H. I. (1909–12, *g*)
1915 Sec. Lt., 1/3 (4/3) Lond. R., T.F. (R. Fus.), France. Woun⟨
July 1916. Apr. 1917 Lt. Oct. 1916 secd. R.F.C. Obsr. J⟨
1918 Sec. Lt., Hon. Lt., R.A.F. (T.).

FORGHAM, E. V. S. (1908–15, *b*)
Rfn., Q. West. Rif., B Coy. Four times wounded ((4) (gas) Se
1918).

FORREST, H., M.C. (1904–13, *g*)
1915 Sec. Lt., 10 S. Staff. R. Nov. 1915 France (1), T.M.B., 9 Di
Ypres (Hill 60). Transfd. to 21 Div., Armentières : end of M⟨
Fricourt on the Somme ; wounded in Battle of the Som⟨
July ⟨1, 1916. Apr. 1917 France (2) ; Lt., 7 S. Staff. R., 11 Di
near Bapaume (the line running by Demicourt and Hermie⟨
June, Wytschaete attack. July 1917 Capt. Ypres, 2nd in cd.
Coy. ∧ Till Jan. 1918, Loos, St. Pierre, and Hill 70. Jan. 1⟨
Hulluch. Aug., Arras front, just before Biache St. Vaast. ⟨
left of Canadians, well to the North, in Cambrai advance. In l⟨
advance to Mons and Maubeuge. M.C. Oct. 1918.* Supernumera
2nd in cd. of Bn., Oisy and Épinoy.

Oct. O.C. Coy.

FOSTER, F. LE N. (1899–1902)
> 1916 Lt., Inns of Court O.T.C. Mentd., Distd. War Services.
> June 1916 Capt. Dec. 1918 secd., Inns of Court Regtl. Assocn.

FOSTER, P. A. (1906–10, *b*)
> Sept. 1914 Sec. Lt., R.E., T.F., 1 N. Mid. Fd. Coy. France.
> Severely wounded June 2, 1915. May 1915 Lt. Empd. Min. of
> Munitions.

FOWLER, A. S., M.C., M.M. (1899–1901)
> 1914 Cpl., 1 King's Own (3 Hussars). France. Retreat from
> Mons. Wounded 1914. Q.-M.-S., attd. H.Q., 4 Cav. Bde.
> M.M. 1917. Dec. 1917 Sec. Lt., R.F.A., T.F. M.C. Nov. 1918.*
> Apr. 1919 Adjt. June 1919 Lt.

FOY, F. B. (1912–16, *g*)
> 1917 Cdt., R.M.C., Sandhurst. Aug. 1918 Sec. Lt., Dorset. R.

FRANCIS, L. B. (1914–16, *r*)
> 1917 Cdt., R.M.A., Woolwich. Sept. 1917 Sec. Lt., R.G.A.,
> 509 Siege By. Codfcrd, Aldershot, Lydd. Aug. 1918 France,
> 218 Siege By. Beuvry, nr. Béthune : Hindenburg line (tunnel) :
> bombarding Auchy : advanced to Annequin : Sept. 20 went
> South ; by Ronssy ; Escaufort ; St. Souplet, across R. Selle,
> to Mazinghien ; Nov. 5 out of action. Mar. 1919 Lt.

†FRANKLIN, F. C. (1911–15, *r*)
> Jan. 1916 L.-Cpl., 2/5 R. War. R., T.F., France. Killed (in a raid,
> for which he had volunteered), Somme, July 1916.

FRANKLIN, T. R. (1904–9, *y*)
> 1914 Bombay Volunteer Art. 1915 Sec. Lt., Notts and Derby R.
> Lt., M.G.C., Jan. 1917.

FRASER, M. F. K., M.C. (1911–13, *b*)
> 1914 Pte., 14 R. War. R. 1915 Sec. Lt., 2 York. and Lanc. R.,
> attd. 8th Bn., France. Intell. Off. M.C. Aug. 1917.* Feb. 1917
> Lt. July 1918 Actg. Capt. Wounded Oct. 1918.

FRAZIER, G. S. (1904–8, *g*)

Sept. 1914 Pte., 14 R. War. R. July 1915 L.-Cpl. Aug. 17 Bn.
Feb. 1916 Cpl. July Sgt., Actg. C.Q.-M.-S. Transfd. 92 T.R. Bn.
Dec. 1916 Cdt., 13 O.C.B. Mar. 1917 Sec. Lt., 3 S. Staff. R.
June 8 Bn. France: Arras, Langemarck. Oct. 12, 1917 severely
wounded. Sept. 1918 Rejd. 3 Bn.: Lt. Oct. 1918 transfd. 1/6 Bn.,
T.F. France (2): Bohain, Mormal Forest; at Armistice, in front line
at Sains du Nord.

FRAZIER, R. W. (1899–1907, *g*)

Sept. 1914 O.S., R.N.V.R., Crystal Palace. Mar.–Jan. 1916
Signalman, H.M.S. Pembroke; H.M. trawlers King Emperor,
Empyrean; H.M.S. Actaeon. Feb. 1916 Sub-Lt., for R.N.A.S.
Oct. 1916 Obs. Off., H.M.S. Ark Royal, E. Medit. Sqn. R.N. Air
Stn., Thasos. Prisoner in Bulgaria Dec. 1, 1916–Oct. 11, 1918.
Oct. 1917 Obs. Lt., R.N. Apr. 1918 Capt., R.A.F.

FREEMAN-SMITH, H. E. (1896–1903)

Feb. 1915 Sec. Lt., 11 R. War. R., bef. the Bn. went to France.

FRITZ, G. G. (1893–7)

1916 Pte., A.S.C., M.T.

FROST, A. M. B. (1909–13, *y*)

1914 Pte., 14 R. War. R. France. Twice wounded ((2) severely,
1918).

†FROST, C. C. (1908–12, *y*)

Aug.–Nov. 1914 Sec. Lt., Church Lads Bde., guarding bridges.
Aug. 1915 Gnr., B By. H.A.C. Sept. 1916 Egypt. Went through
the whole Palestine Campaign, including the fall of Jerusalem,
till Oct. 1918, when he was invalided to Alexandria. Accidentally
killed in Palestine, Jan. 24, 1919.

FRYER, A. H. (1905–9, *b*)

Gnr., R.G.A.

FULLWOOD, J. H. (1904–7, *g*)

1914 Lt., R.A.M.C., Anglo-Belgian Amb. Corps.

FURSE, C. H. S. (1913–16, *g*)
B.U.O.T.C.

FUSSELL, H. S. (1903–6, *b*)
Jan. 1915 Sec. Lt., 9 S. Staff. R. July 1915 Lt. Capt. Actg. Maj.
1917 Sec. Lt., Ind. Army. July 1917 to May 1918 Lt. Actg. Capt.,
Ind. Inf. Base Dépôt. Apr. 1918 Lt., 111 Mahars, Actg. Capt.

GAMGEE, L. P. (1882–8)
July 1908 Capt., R.A.M.C., T.F. 1914 1 Sn. Gen. Hosp. June
1915 Maj.

†GAMMELL, B. E. (1903–4, *g*)
Lt., R.A.F. (A.). France. While he was working with the French
on the Marne, his machine caught fire. He extinguished the
flames and, after landing, carried his wounded observer 2½ miles
to the Ambulance Station. Killed in action (at first repd. missing),
Sept. 4, 1918.

GARDNER, L. F. B. (1905–10, *g*)
1914 Pte., R.A.M.C. Sec. Lt., R.F.A. A/84 Army Bde. France.

†GARRATT, H. W. (1906–13, *g*)
Pte., 14 R. War. R. France. Missing July 1916, posted as
killed.

GATHERAL, GODFREY MORGAN (1894–6)
1916 Pte., Lond. Scott. L.-Cpl. Palestine. Taken prisoner (at
first repd. missing) Mar. 8, 1918 : in Cilicia.

GATHERAL, R. O. (1903–10, *b*)
1913 Sec. Lt., 9 Durh. L.I. Sept. Lt. France. Adjt. 151 Bde.,
50 Div. Wounded (gas) June 2, 1915. June 1916 Capt. 1919
Army of Occupn., Germany.

GATHERAL, T. M. (1899–1902)
1915 Sec. Lt., R.F.A., T.F., 3 W. Riding Bde. June 1916 Lt.
Nov. 1916 Actg. Capt. Wounded and prisoner (in Germany),
May 27, 1918.

†GAUNT, E. T. (1896–1901)
1910 Lt., R.A.M.C. July 1913 Capt., R.A.M.C. Malta. Jan. 1915 France. M.O. to H.A.C. Killed, Oct. 9, 1917, while dressing and evacuating wounded in the open.

GAUNT, J. K. (1895–1900)
Jan. 1914, Capt., R.A.M.C. Autumn 1914 Statry. Hosp. in France. Mentd. in Disp. 1915. 1918 Actg. Maj. Médaille d'Argent de l'Assistance Publique (1) July 1918, (2) June 1919.

GELLING, J. R. (1906–11, g)
Sept. 1914 Tpr., War. Yeo. Nov., Sgt. Jan. 1915 Sec. Lt., 11 R. War. R. France, Dec. 15. Transfd. 112 T.M.B., July 1916. Aug. 1916 Actg. Lt. July 1917 Lt. May Actg. Capt. Jan. 1918 Invalided home. Nov. 1918 France (2). Feb. 1919 attd. 15 Lan. Fus. (Bonn, Germany).

GELLING, P. R. (1909–14, g)
1914 Tpr., Worc. Yeo. Spr., Warwick Sectn., 16 M.G. Sqn., Egypt. Cdt., Cairo. Mar. 1918 Sec. Lt., E. York. R. (S. Bn.). Attd. 4 R. Suss. R. France : Germany (Rhine).

†GETHING, W. G. (1909–16, g)
Oct. 1916 Sec. Lt., 3 S. Staff. R. Feb. 1917 France. Killed at Ypres, Sept. 23, 1917.

GIBBS, H. V. (1909–12, b)
R.G.A. June 1918 Sec. Lt., Devon. R. (S. Bn.). Empd. under Air Ministry.

GIBSON, C. F. L., M.C. (1904–8, g)
Jan. 1915 Sec. Lt., 2/5 R. War. R., T.F. France. June 1916 Capt. Wounded 1916. Asst. Instr. 5th Army Inf. Sch., Aug. 1917. M.C. July 26, 1918.* Mentd. Dec. 1918.

GIBSON, H. D., M.C. (1908–9, b)
1914 Tpr., Staff. Yeo. 1915 Sec. Lt., 5 N. Staff. R., T.F. Attd. 137 T.M.B. Mentd. Ap. 1917. M.C. June 1917.* June 1916 Lt. Aug. 1917 to June 1919 Actg. Capt. Wounded and gassed Apr. 1918.

GIBSON, I. F. (1904–9, *b* ; Asst. Master, 1913–19)
Dec. 1915 Sec. Lt., K.E.S. B'ham O.T.C.

GIBSON, Rev. R. M. (1903–8, *b*)
Apr. 1917–Apr. 1918 C.F., 4th Cl. France. 32 Statry. Hosp., Boulogne. Attd. 2 Essex R., 4th Div. Monchy : Defence of Arras : La Bassée Canal.

GILL, C. L. (1909–17, *r*)
1917 Cdt., R.M.C., Sandhurst. Dec. 1918 Sec. Lt., R. War. R.

GILL, K. H. (1901–10, *r*)
1915 Lt., R.A.M.C., T.F., 1 Sn. Gen. Hosp. Mar. 1916 Capt. Egypt.

GILLMOR, Rev. F. J. C. (1882–6)
June 1907. June 1917 C.F., 4th Cl. 1917 C.F., 3rd Cl., Senior Chaplain for Berkshire, attd. 4 R. Berks. R.

†GILSON, R. Q. (1906–12, *r*)
1914 Camb. Univ. O.T C. Sec. Lt., 11 Suff. R. Lt. France. Killed near La Boisselle, July 1, 1916, leading his men into action.

GITTINGS, C. J. (1907–9, *b*)
1915 Sec. Lt., 4 R. War. R. Attd. R.F.C. Wounded (1) 1916. July 1917 Lt., S. Bn. Aug. 1918, attd. Reg. Bn. Wounded (2).

GITTINS, R. J., M.C. (1904–14, *g*)
1914 Pte., 16 R. War. R. Dec. 1914 Sec. Lt., 8 S. Staff. R. France. M.G. Coy. July 1916 Lt., attd. M.G.C. Actg. Capt., 95 Coy. M.C. Dec. 1916. Actg. Capt. Aug. 1917. 1917–Jan. 1919 Asst. Instr., Grantham.

GLANVILL, H. (1912–13, *r*)
Electrical Artificer, R.N. Devonport.

GLOSTER, L. J. (1907–8, *y*)
1914 Pte., 14 R. War. R. Sgt. 1915 Sec. Lt. France. 32 Divl. Cycl. Coy. Severely wounded July 19, 1916. Lt. Rel. Commn. June 1918.

1

GLANVILLE, H. (1906–08, *y*)
Jan. 1914 Pay. Asst. Clk, H.M.S. Crescent ; Jan. 1915 Clk. July 1917 P. Sub-Lt., H.M.S. Alsatian, 4 Cr. Sqn ; Nov. 1918 H.M.S. Carlisle.

GLOSTER, O. F. (1899–1906, *b*)
1915 Sec. Lt., 10 S. Staff. R. France. Severely wounded Jan. 1915. 1917 temp. Lt., recruiting. Rel. Commn. July 1917.

GLOVER, C. M. (1906–8, *g*)
1915 Pte., R.A.M.C., T.F., 1st Lond. San. Coy.

GODFREY, C. B. (1908–11, *r*)
1914 Pte., 14 R. War. R. Dec. 1914 Sec. Lt., 7 Leic. R., attd. 2 Bn., France: wounded 1915. India. July 1917 Lt., Lan. Fus. Attd. R.F.C. Sec. Lt., R.A.F. (Ad.). Aug. 1918 Actg. Capt. Staff Off., 3rd Cl., S.W. Area, Salisbury.

GODFREY, J. H. (1899–1902)
Oct. 1908 Lt., R.N. Aug. 1914 H.M.S. Charybdis, H.M.S. Euryalus. Lt.-Cdr. Order of the Nile. Aug. 1917 H.M.S. Egmont. Asst. to Chief of Staff, Malta, on Staff of Admiral C.i.C. Legion of Honour (Chevalier) Dec. 1919.

GOMPERTZ, H. (1914–16, *g*) Cdt., R.F.C., Hastings.

GOODE, T. F., T.D. (1880–3)
July 1914 Capt., A.S.C., T.F., S. Mid. Bde. No. 2 Warwick Bde. Coy. Mar. 1915 Actg. Maj. France, 48 Div. Capt., R.A.S.C. Territorial Decn., July 1919.

†GOODISON, G. H. (1913–16, *b*)
Pte., Queen's (R.W. Surrey R.). Killed Oct. 1, 1918.

GOODMAN, A. G. SUMNER (1897–9)
Sept. 1914 Pte., 19 R. Fus. (P. Sch. Bde). Nov. 1915 France. Wounded, at Givenchy, Feb. 1916. Dec. 1916 Sec. Lt. Jan. 1917 France (2), 23 Bn. Nov. 1917 attd. 2 Div., H.Q. Dec. 1918 Germany. 1919 Lt., H.Q., The Light Div., Army of the Rhine, 205 Equipment Coy.

GOODMAN, F. (1900–7, *r*)
1914 Sgt., R.E., D.R. France. 1915 Sec. Lt., R.E., S.R., Mot.-Cycl. Sectn. May 1915 Actg. Capt., 6 Divl. Sig. Coy. Mar. 1917 Actg. Capt. July 1917 Lt. Twice mentd. in Disp. ((2) Dec. 1918).

GOODMAN, H. J. (1901–3)
Lt., A.O.D.

GOODMAN, M. G. (1899–1900)
Jan. 1915 Sec. Lt., 12 R. War. R.   Lt. May 1916 Capt.   Empd.
under Min. of Munitions. Rel. Commn. May 1918.

GOODMAN, M. N. (1895–7)
German E. Africa.

GOODWAY, L. R. (1914–15, g)
1917 Inns of Court O.T.C. Cdt., R.F.C. 1918 Restd. Inns of
Court O.T.C. Artists Rif. O.T.C.

GOODWIN, ERNEST, O.B.E. (1889–96)
July 1915 to Jan. 1919 Staff Lt., Trench Warfare and Gun-Ammn.
Filling Depts., Min. of Munitions. Mentd. for Distg. War Services,
Feb. 1917, Mar. 1918.   June 1918 Staff Capt., Tech. Adviser,
O.B.E. Jan. 1918.

GOODWIN, E. B. (1907–10, b)
1915 Gnr., R.F.A., S.R., 13 By.   1916 L.-Cpl., Signals, Tank Corps.
France.

GOODWIN, O. H. (1908–9, b)
1915 Gnr., R.F.A., S.R., 13 By. Sec. Lt., R.F.A., S.R., 2 T.M.B.
Egypt.   Oct. 1917 Actg. Lt.   Jan. 1918 Lt. Wounded Nov.
1918.

GOOLD, C. A. (1906–10, y)
1916 Motor-Boatman, R.N.V.R., H.M.S. Satellite.

GOOLD, L. L., M.C. (1901–8, y)
1914 Pte., 14 R. War. R. Feb. 1915 Sec. Lt., 6 Res. Bn. Worc. R., S.R.
4th Bn., M.G. Coy. M.C. June 1917.*   July 1917 Lt., secd.
M.G.C., 157 Coy.   June 1918 Lt., M.G.C. (Motor).

GORDON, C. J. (1905–11, *)
Dec. 1914 Sec. Lt., 9 S. Staff. R. France.   Wounded (gas) 1916.
July 1916 Lt., attd. M.G.C. Rel. Commn. June 1918.

GORMAN, V. N. (1908–13, *y*)
Dec. 1914 Sec. Lt., 10 R. War. R. 1915–19 Staff-Sgt., Central Requisition Office, Rouen.

GOSLING, C. A. (1912–18, *y*)
B.U.O.T.C.

†GOSLING, D. E. (1907–10, *y*)
Aug. 1913 Lt., R.E., T.F., 1 N. Mid. Fd. Coy. France. Killed May 20, 1915, while digging out a buried officer.

GOUGH, J. (1904–6, *g*)
Apr. 1911 Lt., 1/7 Worc. R., T.F. 1916 Capt.

GOULD, F. E. (1912–18, *r*)
Sept. 1918 Cdt., 5 O.C.B., St. John's Coll., Cambridge.

GOULD, Rev. T. C. P. (1904–10, *r*)
Jan. 1918 C.F., 4th Cl. France.

GRAFF, C. J. A. V. (1891–6)
1914 Sgt., 14 R. War. R.

†GRAHAM, K. F. (1900–6, *y*)
1914 Pte., 16 Lond. R., T.F. (Q. West. Rif.). France. Killed at Gommecourt, July 1, 1916.

GRAHAM, T. J., V.D. (1871–4)
Oct. 1914 Maj. and Hon. Lt.-Col., ret., T.F., O.C. 2/6 R. War. R., T.F. 6 R. War. R., T.F. Res.

GRANT, K. W. (1907–12, *y*)
Nov. 1914 Sec. Lt., R.F.A. 1915 D/98 Bde., 22 Div., France. B/101 Bde., Salonica. Dec. 1915 Lt. Nov. 1917 Actg. Capt., 4 Res. Bde. July 1918 transfd. R.G.A. Oct. 1918 left for Salonica. Dec. Constantinople. G.S.I., G.H.Q., Constantinople. 2nd Class Agent, Intell. Corps, Aidin, Asia Minor.

GREATOREX, J. A. (1909–17, *r*)
1917 Cdt., 13 O.C.B., Newmarket. Nov. 1917 Sec. Lt., 4 S. Staff. R., 25 Div., France. Apr. 1918 Mt. Kemmel. Severely wounded at Pevy, nr. Fismes, before Reims, May 28, 1918.

GREATOREX, R. B. (1909–14, *r*)
Pte., A. Cycl. C. 1917 Signaller, 17 North'd Fus. Nov. 1916–
Apr. 1918 France, 6 Bn., 50 Div. Wounded Apr. 10, 1918
(Armentières).

GREAVES, A. W. (1912–14, *y*)
1914 Cpl., 18 K.R.Rif.C. France. Sgt. Severely wounded
July 1916. Sec. Lt., 5 Bn.; 1 Bn., France. Lt., Sept. 1918.
Army of Occupation in Germany.

GREAVES, H. (1909–11, *y*)
1914 Pte., 14 R. War. R. Nov. 1915 France. 1916 Sgt. Severely
wounded in attack on High Wood, July 1916. June 1917 Cdt.,
22 O.C.B., Jesus Coll., Camb. Aug. 1917 Sec. Lt., 1 Garr. Bn.,
Worc. R. Feb. 1919 Lt.

GREENBERG, M. S. (1898–9)
1914 Pte., 14 R. War. R. France. 1916 Cpl.

GREENHOUGH, R. (1910–12, *g*)
Aug. 1914 to July 1915 Tpr., 10 and 18 Hussars, 11 Res. Cav. Regt.
Invalided out. Artists Rif. O.T.C., Romford. Pte., 1 Artists Rif.,
France.

†GRIFFIN, H. S. (1900–5, *g*)
Feb. 1916 Artists Rif. O.T.C. Jan. 1917 Sec. Lt., King's (Shrops.
L.I.). France. Killed in action Apr. 3, 1917.

GRIFFITHS, H. L. (1907–9, *b*)
Jan. 1918 Sec. Lt., Gen. List, Intelligence Corps. Jan. 1918
France : Calais, Boulogne 1919 Security Sectn., Montjoie, Army
of the Rhine, Lt.

GRIME, A. G. (1910–12, *g*)
1917 Pte., A.S.C., 1st A.M.T. Dépôt. France.

GROOM, T. R. (1912–14, *g*)
1914 Pte., 14 R. War. R. Mar. 1915 Sec. Lt., 25 North'd Fus.
Mar. 1916 Lt., York. R. Oct. Trg. Res. Actg. Capt. Dec. 1917

62   OLD EDWARDIANS

Lt., Reg. Bn. Wounded May 1917. Mentd., Valuable War Services, Aug. 1918.

GROVER, J. D. (1910–12, *b*)
1914 Tpr., 2 County of Lond. Yeo. Oct. 1917 Sec. Lt., 2 Oxf. and Bucks. L.I. H.Q., 99 Bde. France. Aug. 1918, Army Sign. Service. May 1919 Gen. Res.

†GROVES, P. F. (1910–16, *b*)
1916 Spr., R.O.D., R.E. Died in hospital in France, Jan. 21, 1917.

GRUBE, GEORGE (1915–18, *y*)
Aug. 1918 Belgian Army, Camp d'Anvours, Sarthe, France, for artillery. Oct. Soldatan, 4e Cie. de renfort. Jan. 1919 Sgt. Interpreter, Belgian Mission, British G.H.Q. May Pte., Troupes Étapes, Belgian Army of Occupn., Gladbach, Germany.

GUEST, C. E. N. (1911–16, *g*)
1918 Cdt., R.A.F., Hastings, Shorncliffe.

GUEST, H. R., M.C. (1909–14, *g*)
Oct. 1915 Sec. Lt., 3 Oxf. and Bucks. L.I. 83 Prov. Bn. July 1917 Lt., 2/4 Bn., T.F. France. Severely wounded Sept. 3, 1917. M.C. Oct. 1917.*

GUEST, T. (1899–1906, *g*)
1914 Gnr., R.F.A., T.F., 3 S. Mid. Bde.

GUNNINGHAM, A. P. (1910–18, *r*)
Nov. 1918 Cdt., 2 Cav. O.C.S., Kildare. Apr. 1919 Sec. Lt., 2 Res. Regt. Cav.

HADDELSEY, H. H. (1908–10, *y*)
1914 Sgt., King's Own (York. L.I.). France. Sec. Lt., 7 Bn. Wounded (1) Oct. 1916. Lt., Mar. 1917. July 1917 Actg. Capt. Wounded (2) 1917. Sept. 1918 attd. Reg. Bn.

HADDOW, E. C. R., M.C. (1905–7, *g*)
Aug. 1914 Sec. Lt., R.F.A., T.F., 3 S. Mid. Bde. Aug. 1914–May 1916, training in England with 48 and 61 Divs. Dec. 1914 Lt. France May–Oct. 1916 61 S. Mid. Div. Amm. Col. June 1916

ROLL OF SERVICE 63

Capt., cdg. V/61 H.T.M.B. for a short time D.T.M.O., 61 Div. Nov.
1916–July 1917 D.T.M.O., Lahore Artillery, attd. Can. Div. :
Capture of Vimy Ridge, Apr. 9, 1917. Aug.–Sept. 1917 attd. H.Q.
xi Corps R.A. Oct. 1917–May 1918 D.T.M.O., 59 Div. Artillery;
retreat Mar. 21, 1918. May 1918–Feb. 1919 41 Div. Art. : in the
last fighting in Flanders Sept.–Oct. M.C. Feb. 1919.* Croix de
Guerre (Belge). Ment.

†HADLEY, C. V. (1907–12, *b*)
Sept. 1914 Spr., R.E., T F., 2 Wessex Fd. Coy. Dec. 1914 France :
Armentières, Ypres, Poperinghe. Sept. 1915 Sec. Lt., 10 Worc. R.
(in France). Wounded and missing, believed to have been killed,
at Albert, in 1st Battle of the Somme, July 1, 1916.

HADLEY, D. J. (1907–14, *g*)
1917 Pte., A.S.C., No. 5 Sectn., Drafts Coy. May 1918 Sec. Lt.,
Lab. Corps.

HADLEY, E. A. (1911–16, *b*)
July 1916 Gnr., R.G.A., T.F., Cornwall. July 1917 Italy, 390
Siege By. : the Carso. Oct. 1917 Egypt. Jan. 1918 Italy : Piave ;
Apr., Asiago Plateau. Oct. 1918 Cadet School, Brighton.

HADLEY, E. S. (1914–16, *b*)
June 1916 Cdt., H.M. Training Ship Worcester. June 1918 Mid.,
R.N.R. Sept. 1918 H.M.S. Blanche : with the Grand Fleet in the
North Sea till Feb. 1919 : took part in surrender of German fleet
Nov. 21, 1918.

HADLEY, G. H. (1906–10, *g*)
Aug. 1914 Tpr., 4 Hussars. Nov. 1914 Sec. Lt., 3 R. War. R. :
12 Bn. Jan. 1916 France, 16 Bn. : Feb.–July 1916 Somme;
July 1916 Lt. Sept. 1916 Neuve Chapelle, La Bassée. Mar. 1917
Vimy Ridge. Apr. 1917 Captured at Vimy Ridge. Prisoner in
Germany till Nov. 1918.

HADLEY, L. L., M.C. (1895–9)
Aug. 1914 Lt., R.A.M.C., attd. 8 Leic. R. Aug. 1915 Capt. M.C.
Jan. 1918.

HALL, J. FIELD (1880–3)

Nov. 1914–1919 Capt., R.A.M.C., T.F., M.O. attd. 2/22 Lond. R. June 1916 France.

HALLAM, A. (1895–7)

1917 Gnr., R.G.A.

HALLAM, G. (1901–7, g)

1914 Pte., 18 R. Fus. (P. Sch.). 1916 Sec. Lt., 3 R. War. R., S.R. France, 15 Bn. Twice wounded ((2) May 1917). Lt. 1918 Retd. List.

†HALLAM, H. (1898–1902)

1914 Tpr., War. Yeo. Egypt. 1915 severely wounded, Suvla Bay. Invalided, Mudros : home Dec. 1915. O.C.B., Oxford. 1916 Sec. Lt., R. War. R., T.F. France, 1/6 Bn. Killed Oct. 4, 1917.

HALL-EDWARDS, J. (1871–5)

Aug. 1914 to Oct. 1915 Senior Recruiting Surgeon, B'ham. Dec. 1914 Maj., R.A.M.C. Oct. 1915 S.M.O., Command Dépôt, Sutton Coldfield. Mar. 1917 to May 1919 Surgeon-radiographer to 1 S. Gen. Hosp., and Rubery, Hollymoor, Monyhull. Twice mentd. for Valuable War Services.

HAM, E. N. (1900–5, y)

Sept. 1914 Pte., Manch. R. (City Bn.) Sgt. Nov. 1915 C. Q.-M.-S., France. July 1916 C. S.-M., Wounded (1) Somme ; rejoined Bn., Oct. 1916. Somme, Arras. R. Q.-M.-S. Nov. 1917 Wounded (2) severely. Mar. 1918 R. Q.-M.-S., on permanent staff, W. Command Dépôt, Prescot, nr. Liverpool.

HAMMOND, N. W. (Asst. Master, 1919)

July 1919 Sec. Lt., temp. Lt., Unattd. List, T.F., K.E.S., B'ham Cont., O.T.C., from St. Edward's School Cont.

HANCOCKS, M. N. (1912–15, r)

1917 P.F.O., R.N.A.S. Apr. 1918 Lt. (A.), R.A.F., 213 Sqn., 61 Wing, Dunkirk.

HANDS, C. W. (1908–10, *g*)
1914 Tpr., War. Yeo. 1915 Sgt., Mot. Cycl. Sectn., R.E.

HARDWICK, W. H. (1897–1902)
1916 Bmbr., R.F.A., A/181 Bde., France.

†HARDWIDGE, W. J. (1915–17, *y*)
1917 Pte., 4 Res. Bn., D. of Corn. L.I., T.F. Apr. 1918 France, 1/5 Bn. Wounded and missing Apr. 23, 1918, since reported killed on or about that date.

HARLEY, C. B. (1910–14, *r*)
1914 Pte., 14 R. War. R. Wounded Aug. 1916. 1918 Discharged unfit.

HARLEY, W. R. (1899–1900)
Aut. and wint. 1916 Pte., D Coy., 1 R. War. R. 1917 Sec. Lt., 1 R. War. R. 10 Bn. Three times wounded ((3) severely at Marcoing, Dec. 1917). Sept. 1918 Home Service, 3 R. War. R. Lt., 10 Bn. Dec. 1918.

HARPER, J. H. (1900–4, *b*)
1915 Dr., A.S.C., T.F., 1/3 N. Mid. Fd. Amb.

HARRIS, C. L. (1914–15, *y*)
July 1917 Gnr., R.F.A., T.F., 3 Res. Bde., A By.

HARRIS, E. H. (1894–6)
1915 Sec. Lt., A.S.C., T.F., 1/3 N. Mid. Fd. Amb. July 1918 Capt., R.A.S.C.

†HARRIS, J. C. (1894–9)
Oct. 1912 Lt., R.A.M.C., T.F., 1/3 N. Mid. Fd. Amb. Apr. 1915 Capt. Died of wounds Aug. 1917.

†HARRIS, P. D. (1903–4, *g*)
1911 Sec. Lt., 3 N. Staff. R., S.R. 1914 Lt. Sept. 1914 France. Capt., 1 Bn. 1915 twice wounded. Invalided home. 1916 G.S.O.$_3$, 12 mths. Jan. 1917 Adjt., 1 N. Staff. R., France (2). Killed in action, nr. St. Quentin (repd. wounded and missing) Mar. 21, 1918.

K

HARRIS, R. (1894–9)
1915 Lt., A.S.C., Mersey Defences. Capt., May 1918.

HARRIS, W. H. (1901–4, g)
1917 2nd Cl. Air Mech., R.F.C.

HARRISON, C. H. (1912–13, y)
Tpr., War. Yeo., attd. Leic. R. France. Prisoner (repd. missing) July–Dec. 1918, in Sugar factory and road-making : interpreter. Feb. 1919 rejd. colours.

†HARRISON, E. R. (1899–1901)
1914 Lt., A.S.C., T.F., S. Mid. Bde. Coy. Sept. 1914 France. Jan. 1915 Capt., A.S.C., T.F., No. 4 S. Mid. Bde. Coy., 61 Div., in cd. of a Coy. with which he served nearly three years in France and Flanders. Mentd. in Disp., Dec. 1917. Died of double pneumonia, following influenza, at Abbeville, Dec. 25, 1918.

HARRISON, H. C., D.S.O. (1899–1907, y)
1914 Lt., R.M.A. (Sen. July 1908). May 1914 Asst. Adjt., Eastney Barracks. Sept. 1915 temp. Capt. Aug. 1915 till May 1919 temp. Maj., Secd. for service with R.G.A. S. Afr. Cont., 71 Transvaal Siege By. German S.W. Africa, Windhoek. 1916 trained S.A. batteries, Bexhill. France. Beaumont Hamel, July 1, 1916. Pozières. Twice mentd. in Disp. D.S.O. Aug. 1916.* Wounded (gas) Aug. 1916. France (2). Early 1917 invalided home. July 1917– July 1918 Instr., Sch. of Instn., Siege and Heavy Arty., Salisbury. Mentd. (3) Valuable War Services, and (4) German S.W. Africa (1915) Aug. 1918. July 1918 Bde.-Maj., 11th Corps, France (3). Wounded (2) Oct. 1918. Bt.-Maj., for distd. service in prosecution of the war, Jan. 1919. May 1919 Eastney Barracks.

HARRISS, W. (1892–3)
1916 Pte., 3/5 S. Staff. R., T.F. Dec. 1917 Sec. Lt., M.G.C. (Sen. Mar. 1917). France. Severely wounded Oct. 1917. Mentd. July 1919.

HARROWER, A. B. (1901–10, *y*)
1914 Pte., 5 Sea. Highrs. Sec. Lt., A.S.C., H.Q. Coy., 24 Divl. train. Lt. Capt. 1917 attd. 10 S.W. Bord. France. 1918 Home Service.

†HARROWER, A. P. (1907–11, *y*)
1914 Pte., 5 Sea. Highrs. Jan. 1915 Sec. Lt., 12 North'd Fus. Dec. 1915 21 Div., France. Fricourt. Wounded May 1916. 3 Bn. *Jan. 1917 France (2)* 1917 Lt., 11–12 Bn. Dec. France (3). Prisoner (repd. missing) *wounded (2)* Mar. 21, 1918. Died of wounds in German hands in hospital, Roisel, France, Mar. 26, 1918. ' On Mar. 21 he was awaiting a Medical Board. Though very ill, he volunteered to take up reinforcements and received mortal wounds in doing so.'

†HARTLEY, W. E. (1891–6)
Dec. 1915 R.N.C., Greenwich. May 1916 Naval Instr., H.M.S. Africa. Dec. 1916 H.M.S. Vanguard. Killed by explosion on H.M.S. Vanguard July 9, 1917.

HARTSHORNE, N. H., M.C. (1907–13, *r*)
Sept. 1914 Pte., 16 R. War. R. Jan. 1915 Sec. Lt., 11 S. Staff. R. Sept. 1915 sailed for Gallipoli, 7 S. Staff. R. Dec. 1915 Evacuation of Suvla Bay, Gallipoli : Imbros I. Feb. 1916 Alexandria. Mar. 1916 Suez Defences. June 1916 France. Aug. 1916 Actg. Lt., Gas Officer, 63 R.N.D. May 1917 Lt., transfd. to R.E. Nov. 1917 Actg. Capt., Commandant, xiii Corps Gas School. M.C. Jan. 1918. Feb. 1918 to Feb. 1919 Chemical Adviser, xiii Corps.

†HARVEY, W. H. (1909–14, *b*)
1915 Pte., 17 R. War. R., A Coy. 1916 Cpl., M.G.C. On active service in France for 2½ yrs. Sgt. Killed Aug. 11, 1918.

HARWOOD, F. L. (1910–18, *b*)
1918 P.F.O., R.N.A.S. Discharged through ill health.

HASELER, C. A. (1903–5, *y*)
1914 Pte., 14 R. War. R. France, Italy.

HASELER, M. R. (1907–10, *y*)
> 1914 Pte., Motor M.G. service. France. 1916 Invalided. Flt.-Cdt., R.A.F. Sec. Lt. (A.) Oct. 1918.

HAUGHTON, E. P. O. (1914–17, *b*)
> 1917 P.F.O., R.N.A.S. Injured in flying accident. 1918 Flt. Sub-Lt., Mudros (62 and 63 Wings, Thermi-Mitylene). Apr. 1918 Lt. (A.). Prisoner (Turkey), brought down in air-raid on Constantinople, Oct. 1918.

HAWKES, H., M.C. (1910–11, *b*)
> 1914 Sec. Lt., 5 S. Staff. R., T.F. 1915 Lt., France. Sept. 1915 Hohenzollern Redoubt, battle of Loos. Mentd. in Disp. M.C. Bde. Bombing Off. June 1916 Capt. 5 Res. Bn. Sept. 1918 Secd., Lt., Ind. Army R. of O., 2/48 Pioneers.

HAWKES, P. (1895–9)
> Feb. 1915 Dr. R.F.A. France, 122 By., till Apr. 1919. In many engagements.

HAWKES, P. J. (1900–3)
> July 1917 Pte., Artists Rif. May 1918 Sec. Lt., The King's (Shrops. L.I.). Sept. 1918 10 Bn., France.

†HAWKES, W. (1892–9)
> Oct. 1914 Rfn., 5 Rif. Brig. France. Three times wounded. Missing Mar. 21, 1918, at Flavy-le-Martel ; believed to have been killed, and buried at that place.

HAWKINS, D. J. R. (1901–7, *g*)
> Aug. 1914 to Oct. 1915 King's Afr. Rif. Sept. 1916 Sub-Lt., R.N.V.R., Lake Nyasa : Marine Trans. Dept., Fort Johnston. Mentd. in Disp. Jan. 1919. Mar. 1919 Lt.

HAWLEY, G. (1897–1903)
> Sec. Lt., A.S.C., M.T., attd. 175 Siege By., France. Apr. 1918 Lt. A.S.C. 1916 Ancre, Arras, Vimy. 1917 Ypres, Noyon. 1918 Somme to Le Cateau.

HAWLEY, H. (1901–6, *r*)
> Lt., A.O.D. June 1917 Capt.

HAYES, L. C. (1897–9)
(Jan. 1913) Capt., R.A.M.C. W. Indies. 1914 M.O., attd. 1 King's Own (R. Lanc. R.). France. Cambrai, Meteren. Wounded and gassed, Ypres, May 2, 1915. Mentd. for Distd. War Services Aug. 1919.

HAYES, R. A. (1899–1905, r)
1914 Supervisor, Mechl. and Expl. Sectn., Woolwich Arsenal. 1917 Asst. Manager.

HAYWOOD, B. (1899–1903)
1915 Nyasaland Vol. Force. Dec. 1916 Sub-Lt., R.N.V.R., Lake Nyasa.

HAYWOOD, C. F. (1902–5, y)
A.S.C., M.T. Was driving an ambulance in the French Army. 1917–18 Seven weeks in hospl. 1918 R.N.A.S.

HAYWOOD, N. A., M.B.E. (1896–1901)
1914 Tpr., 2 Co. of Lond. Yeo., T.F. 1917 Sec. Lt., Gen. List, Adjt., Egyptian Lab. Corps, Base Dépôt, France. May 1918 Actg. Lt., cdg. a Coy. Sept. 1918 Lt. Mentd. (Egypt) June 1919.

HAZELTON, E. (1911–14, g)
June 1915 Sec. Lt., R.F.A., T.F., 4 Welsh (Monmouthshire) Bde. Nov. 1915–Jan. 1916 France, R. Somme. Jan. 1916–Feb. 1919 Egypt and Palestine. June 1916 Lt., 268 Bde. Spring 1917 1st and 2nd battles of Gaza : summer, invalided : autumn, 75 D.A.C.: spring 1918, 37 Bde., R.F.A., summer, invalided : Nov. 1918 final offensive in Palestine.

†HEADLEY, A. N. (1897–1900)
Nov. 1914 Sub-Lt., R.N.V.R., H.M. Cruiser Maidstone. Lt. Lost in submarine between Nov. 30 and Dec. 3, 1916.

HEALD, P. B. (1899–1902)
B.U.O.T.C. Apr. 1915 Sec. Lt., 9 King's Own (R. Lanc. R.). Nov. 1915 France. Wounded 1916. Lt. May 1917 Capt.

HEATON, W. (1896–7)
1917 Sec. Lt., Gen. List, Interpreter. July 1918 Lt.

HEGGS, F. R. M. (1888–91)
Sept. 1912, May 1915 Capt., R.A.M.C., T.F., O.C. 3/1 Notts.
and Derby Mtd. Bde. Fd. Amb. Wounded (severely gassed) June
1918.

HEGGS, T. B. (1894–7)
June 1910 Capt., 4 The Buffs (E. Kent R.), T.F. June 1916–Mar.
1919 Maj., R.A.M.C.

HEINRICH, S. G. S. (1902–9, *b*)
1914 Pte., 6 R. War. R., T.F. 1915 Cpl. July 1916 Sgt. France.

HEMMING, F. J. (1902–11, *r*)
Apr. 1913 Sec. Lt., 5 S. Staff. R., T.F. Oct. 1914 Lt. June 1916
Capt. 46 N. Mid. Div. Cycl. Coy. Feb. 1915 France: Armen-
tières, Kemmel, Ypres, Vermelles, Richebourg. Oct. 1915 temp.
Capt. Jan.–Feb. 1916 Egypt. Mar. 1916 France (2), Souchez. 17
Corps Cyclist Bn. 1916–May 1918 Neuville St. Vaast, Arras,
Monchy. (Apr. 1917 for a short time No. 4 Coy., 3rd Army Traffic
Control). Mentd. May 1918. May 1918 T.F. Res. Empd. under
Min. of Munitions.

HEMUS, W. L. (1910–13, *r*)
Oct. 1914 Sec. Lt., 15 R. War. R. Nov. 1915 France. Twice
wounded ((1) 1915, (2) Sept. 1916). Actg. Capt., Trans. Workers
Bn., Worc. R. Jan. 1917 Lt. 1918 Sec. Lt., Hon. Capt. (A.),
R.A.F., Flying-boats, Felixstowe.

HENDERSON, R. B. (formerly Asst. Master, 1901)
Nov. 1915 Sec. Lt., R.G.A. 369 Bde. July 1916 Lt. Jan.–Feb.
1919, temp. Lt.-Col., while Commandant of the Gen. and Com-
mercial Coll. Feb.–Mar. 1916 temp. Maj., while Chief Instr.

†HERBERT, E. G., M.C. (1906–10, *b*)
Aug. 1914 Tpr., War. Yeo., T.F. (6 mths.). 1915 Sec. Lt., 13 R.
War. R. Lt. Nov. 1916 attd. M.G.C. France. Wounded Jan.
1917. Capt. 121 M.G. Coy. France. Jan. 1916 Sec. Lt. (Reg.
Army), R. War. R. Feb. 1918 Actg. Capt., 2nd in cd. of Coy.

Thanked in Divl. Order for 'most gallant behaviour through the whole battle', he 'displayed marked gallantry and leadership'. M.C. Sept. 1918.* Killed in action Apr. 1918.

HESELTINE, C. R. G. (1904–9, *b*)
1914 Pte., 14 R. War. R. 1915 17 Bn. 1916 Cpl. C. Q.-M.-S. Cdt., 18 O.C.B., Bath.

HICKS, R. J. E. (1907–16, *g*)
1918 Pte., Glouc. R., Home Service.

HIGGINS, H. L., M.C. (1908–12, *g*)
1914 Pte., 14 R. War. R. L.-Cpl. Apr. 1915 Sec. Lt. France. Severely wounded July 1916. M.C. Nov. 1916.* July 1917 Lt., Gen. List for duty with Min. of Natl. Service, Dec. 1917–Dec. 1918.

HILDICK, A. (1904–6, *y*)
1917 L.-Cpl., A.O.C.

†HILL, B. G. (1908–13, *g*)
Oct. 1914 Pte., 14 R. War. R. L.-Cpl. 1915 Sec. Lt., 3 R. War. R., S.R. July 1915 France, attd. 2 Bn., M.G. Coy. Wounded and missing, presumed killed, Loos, Sept. 1915.

HILL, E. L. (1906–13, *g*)
1913 Cdt., R.N. H.M.S. Highflyer. Aug. 1914 Mid. Sept. 1914 H.M.S. Endymion. Feb. 1915 H.M.S. Ajax. t.b.d. Moy, t.b.d. Patrician. Sub-Lt., 1916. t.b.d. Hydra. t.b.d. Liberty, 3rd flotilla. H.M.S. Bellerophon Apr. 1917. Temp. Lt. t.b.d. Moon. Lt. Mar. 1918. H.M.S. Laurel. H.M.S. Marlborough for Mediterranean. Jan. 1919. Malta. Constantinople. Black Sea. Brought off members of Russian Royal Family from Yalta. May–June 1919 Theodosia Bay, Krimea, defending peninsula of Kertch.

HILL, G. S. (1909–10, *g*)
1914 Sgnls. Dec. 1915 Sec. Lt., R.E. July 1916 Lt. 1918 Empd. Min. of Munitions.

HILL, R. M. (1909–10, g)
1916 Pte., A.S.C. Cdt., R.M.C., Sandhurst. Apr. 1917 Sec. Lt., Welsh R. July 1917 Q.-M., Capt.

†HIPKINS, N. (1909–11, b)
July 1917 LC., Sept. 1917 Actg. Capt. Capt. 1914 Pte., Lond. Scott. France. ~~14 Lan. R.~~ Sept. 1915 Sec. Lt., 2/6 S. Staff. R., T.F. Actg. Capt., 1/6 N. Staff. R., T.F. Killed at St. Quentin ~~Oct. 1917.~~ *Sept. 28, 1918.* Mentd. in Disp. Dec. 1918.

HOBBISS, D. H. (1901–6, y)
1914 L.-Cpl., 4 S. Staff. R. 1915 Cpl., 1 Bn. 2 Bn. Sgt. 1916 Sec. Lt., 5 Worc. R. May 1917 The King's (Shrops. L.I.), S. Bn. Feb. 1919 Lt. Actg. Capt. and Adjt., 12 Ches. R. France : Salonica : Greece : Bulgaria.

HOBBISS, H. W. (1891–6)
Jan. 1915 Sec. Lt., R.G.A., T.F., 2/1 S. Mid. (Warwickshire) Heavy By. France. June 1916 Lt. Sept. 1917 to Feb. 1918 Acting Capt., 2nd in cd. of By.

†HOBSON, M. W. (1901–5, r)
1914 Sgt., Worc. Yeo., T.F. 1915 Sqn. Q.-M.-S. Killed (repd. wounded and missing), Ograntine, Palestine, Apr. 23, 1916.

HODGES, H. J. (1903–5, r)
P.O., R.N.A.S.

HOLDEN, H. F. (1911–14, r)
Nov. 1914 Sec. Lt., 9 S. Staff. R. 191*5* Lt. ~~Temp.~~ *Actg.* Capt., 9 Bn., Pioneers. Severely wounded ~~Sept.~~ *July 19,* 1917. Rel. Commn. Dec. 1917.

HOLDER, T. G. (1895–1901)
1914 Pte., 14 R. War. R. Sept. 1915 Sec. Lt., 2/6 N. Staff. R., T.F. July 1917 Lt. Attd. Lab. Corps, Aug. 1918.

HOLDING, B. C. C. (1914–15, r)
1916 Gnr., No. 2 Sqn., R.H.A. Dépôt, Woolwich. *Oct. 1918 France.* 1919 U By., Army of Occupn., Cologne.

HOLDSWORTH, G. L. (1905–6, *g* ; 1910–12, *y*)
1914 Pte., R. Fus. (P. Sch.).   1915 Sec. Lt., R. Ir. R.   Rel. Commn.
on acct. of ill health.   1917 Pte., N.Z. Rif. Brig.   France, Nov.
1917 to Feb. 1918.   Passchendaele, &c.   Wounded (gas) Feb. 1918.
L.-Cpl., Details Coy.

HOLDSWORTH, M. E. (1905–15, *b*)
July 1915 Sec. Lt., 3 R. War. R., S.R.   Feb. 1916 attd. R.E., Sign.
Service Training Coy.   Sept. 1916 France, 1 Div. Sign. Coy. :
Somme.   1917 Nieuport, Le Cliton, Ypres Salient.   July 1917 Lt.,
Wireless Officer, 1 Div.   Apr.–Aug. 1918 Givenchy, Cuinchy,
Hohenzollern ; Aug., Arras ; Sept.–Oct., Somme, Hindenburg
Line ; Nov., Sambre–Oise Canal.   Dec. 1918–June 1919 Germany
(Rheinbach).   Mentd. July 1919.

HOLLAND, A. F. (1911–17, *y*)
1917 Cdt., R.M.C., Sandhurst.   Aug. 1918 Sec. Lt., 6 Res. D. Gds.

HOLLAND, H. (1904–10, *y*)
1914 Gnr., R.F.A.   1917 Bmdr.

HOLLAND, W. A. L. (1895–1901)
Sept. 1914–1919 Maj., R.A.M.C., T.F., 1/2 and 2/2 S. Mid. Fd. Ambs.

HOLLOWAY, G. (1897–8)
L.-Cpl., Essex R.   Bmdr., R.G.A.

HOLLOWAY, H. H. (1898–1900)
Nov. 1916 Sec. Lt., R.G.A., S.R.   May 1918 Lt.

HOLMES, D. F., M.C. (1900–6, *y*)
Oct. 1914 Lt., A.S.C., T.F., 1/3 S. Staff. Bde. Coy., N. Mid. Div.
Train.   1915 France.   Feb. 1919 secd. for service with N. Staff. R.
June 1916 Lt., A.S.C., T.F.   Oct.–Dec. 1918 Actg. Capt.,
cdg. a Coy., 46 Div. Train, attd. 4 N. Staff. R.   M.C. Mar. 1919.*
July 1919 Lt., T.F. Res.

HOLMES, J. L., (1901–6, *b*)
Aug. 1914 Pte., A.S.C., M.T. Aldershot.   Sept. Cpl. Oct. Sgt., drill instr.
Feb. 1915 W.O.   Dec. 1915 took a coy. to Whitchurch Salop. instr.
till Jan. 1918.   Jan. 1918 France; Doullens to Namur.

HOLMES, J. T. (1901–5, *y*)

1914 Cpl., A.S.C. 1916 Sec. Lt., R.F.A., T.F., 3 N. Mid. Bde. June 1916 Lt. Aug. 1918 Capt., Lab. Corps. 1919 Rel. Commn. on acc. of ill health.

HOLMES, N. C. (1900–2)

1914 to end of war, Pte., 2 Rhodesian Cont.; E. Africa.

HOLMES, W. J. K. (1894–8)

1914 Tpr., B.S.A. Police, S. Rhodesia. Pte., 2 Rhodesian Cont.; E. Africa.

†HOLROYD. J. O. (1899–1900)

1914 Sgt., 7 Norf. R. France. Died of wounds Oct. 11, 1915.

HOMES, W. P. (1907–12, *g*)

1915 Gnr., R.G.A., T.F., Smethwick Heavy By. Early 1916 France (1) on Vimy Ridge, near Bully Grenay; (2) battle of the Somme, ending near High Wood; (3) South end of British line on the Somme, advancing Mar. 1917 through Péronne to near St. Quentin. Nov. 1917 retd. home for Commission. Cadet School, Exeter. Sept. 1918 Sec. Lt., R.G.A.

HOOPER, R. B. (1910–12, *r*)

1917 Inns of Court O.T.C. Sec. Lt., R.F.C. (Flying Off.). France. Wounded, Cambrai, Nov. 20, 1917. 1918 R.A.F. July 1918 Aerial Gunnery Instr., New Romney. Apr. 1918 Lt.

HOPE, C. B. (1911–14, *y*)

1916 Pte., 5 S. Staff. R., T.F. Cpl. France. Wounded, Cambrai, Nov. 1917. Feb. 1919 Sec. Lt., S. Staff. R., S. Bn.

HOPKINS, E. L., M.C. and bar (1907–11, *r*)

1914 Cpl., 16 R. War. R. Feb. 1915 Sec. Lt., 6 Worc. R., S.R. 1916 attd. 2 Bn., France. Wounded (1) Oct. 1916. July 1917 Lt. (Reg. Cn.). June 1917 Actg. Capt. M.C. Apr. 1917 (Feb. 27–8, 1917).* Wounded (2) June 1917. Returned to England Oct. 1917 to June 1918. Attd. 1/6 Cycl. Bn., Norf. R., Longford. June 1918 France (2). Wounded (3) Aug. 1918. Bar to M.C. Mar. 1919 (Oct. 22–3, 1918).*

HOPKINS, F. A. R. (1909–12, *r*)
1916 Cpl., R.E., Spec. Bde. Feb. 1916 Sec. Lt., ' C ' Spec. Coy.
Nov. 1917 Lt.

HOPKINS, S. B. (1898–9)
1914 Pte., 14 R. War. R.

HOPPER, D. H. (1910–17, *g*)
1917 Cdt., R.G.A. July 1917 Sec. Lt., R.G.A., S.R. France:
Aug.–Oct. 1917, 253 Siege By., Ypres Salient ; Oct. 1917–Apr.
1918, 270 Siege By., Cambrai Sector. Wounded Apr. 5, 1918.
Empd. Min. of Labour. Jan. 1919 Lt.

HORNBY, A. J. W. (1907–11, *r*)
Jan. 1915 Sec. Lt., R.F.A. France, 9 Div. Oct. 1916 Lt.
Actg. Capt.

†HORNER, F. J., M.C. (1909–13, *g*)
1915 Sec. Lt., 10 R. War. R. 13 Bn. Lt., Feb. 1915. 1916
Salonica, attd. 2 Ches. R. Actg. Capt., Addl., Dec. 1917. Wounded
(1) Dec. 1917. Malta. Wounded (2) Apr. 1918. Died of wounds
Apr. 15, 1918. He was in command of his platoon, stemming
an overwhelming enemy advance ; he had already been wounded
in the right arm. M.C. June 1918.

HORSLEY, N. A. (1910–17, *r*)
1917 Cdt., R.G.A. Nov. 1917 Sec. Lt., R.G.A., S.R. 260 Siege
By., France.

HORTON, C. (1895–9)
1914 Eng.-Lt., R.N.V.R., H.M.S. Leviathan.

HORTON, C. E. (1911–15, *b*)
Sept. 1917 Sub-Lt., R.N.V.R., R.N. Barracks, Portsmouth.

HORTON, W. Claude (1897–9)
Sept. 1914 Lt., R.A.M.C., T.F. Sept. 1915–1919 Capt. Actg. Maj.
to Dec. 1918.

HOSKINS, A. (1901–5, *b*)
1915 Sec. Lt., Worc. R. Wounded 1915. July 1916 Lt.

HOWLETT, E.N. *(1904–08, y)*
Aug. 1914 Lt., S. Nig. Vol., Cameroon E.7., W. Afr. Wd. Nov 1914. Ret'. Gn. July
1915. — Germ. E. Afr. (Dar es Salaam) on Civil Service.

HOSKINS, W. J. (1880–1)
1914 Pte., 14 R. War. R.

HOSSELL, G. L. (1907–10, r)
1914 Pte., 15 R. War. R. France. Wounded 1916. Sec. Lt., 2 Dorset. R. France (2).

HOWARD, A. C., D.S.O., M.C. (1895–9)
Dec. 1914 Sec. Lt., R.E., T.F., 2/2 W. Riding Field Coy. July 1915 Actg. Maj. Oct. 1915–1918 France. June 1916 Lt. M.C. 1916. Feb. 1918 Actg. Lt.-Col., attd. R.E. C.R.E., 41 Div. 1918–1919 Cologne. D.S.O. June 1919. French Croix de Guerre. Three times mentd.

†HUDSON, J. W. W. (1907–13, g)
Nov. 1914 Sec. Lt., 5 R. War. R., T.F. May 1915 France. June 1915 Lt. Killed, opposite Gommecourt Wood, Nov. 30, 1915, by a sniper, while locating a German trench mortar.

HUGHES, F. C. (1895)
Oct. 1906 Capt., 5 S. Staff. R., T.F. Aug. 1915–1919 Maj., 1/5 Bn. France.

HUGHES, G. (1907–10, r)
July 1918 R.A.F.

HUGHES, H. W. (1913–15, y)
B.U.O.T.C. 1917 Cdt., R.E., Sig. Mar. 1918 Sec. Lt., R.E.

HUGHES, J. C. (1902–7, r)
Feb. 1915 Sec. Lt., R.G.A., T.F., S. Mid. (Warwickshire) Heavy By. June 1916 Lt.

HUGHES, W. (1904–8, b)
1914 Pte., 1/6 R. War. R., T.F. Lt., 3/6 R. War. R., T.F. July 1917. Attd. M.G.C. Salonica. Mentd. in Disp. Nov. 1918.

†HUGHES, W. B. (1912–16, y)
P.f.o. 1917 ████████, R.N.A.S. Apr. 1918 Sec. Lt. (A. and S.), R.A.F. Died as result of aeroplane accident, May 17, 1918.

HULL, R. R. (1909–10, *r*)
Pte., Worc. Yeo., T.F. Dischd. unfit through accident.

†HUMBY, F. H. (1903–5, *r*)
1914 Pte., 14 R. War. R. 1915 Sec. Lt., 3/6 R. War. R., T.F.
Actg. Lt. 1916 Actg. Capt. 2/6 Bn. France. Died of wounds
at Le Tréport Hosp., Nov. 9, 1918.

HUMPHERSON, W. R. (1910–16, *r*)
1916 Cdt., R.M.C., Sandhurst. Sec. Lt., 11 R. War. R. 1916
France. Apr. 1918 Lt., 1st Bn. 1918 Wireless Off., H.Q., 9th
Bde.

HUMPHREYS, H. H., O.B.E., M.C. (1895–6)
1915 Sec. Lt., A.S.C., M.T., Caterpillar Sectn., Aldershot. Dec.
1917 Maj., A.S.C., attd. Tank Corps. France. Mentd. in Disp.
M.C. 1919.

†HUMPHRIES, L. G. (1910–14, *r*)
Sept. 1916 Artists Ri⁂ June 1917 Sec. Lt., Gen. List, R.F.C.
Pilot. France. Killed in action Sept. 16, 1917, while photograph-
ing over the German lines.

HUNT, A. E. T., M.C. (1911–12, *r*)
Bmdr., R.F.A., T.F., 3 S. Mid. Bde., 48 Div. France. 1917
Sec. Lt., R.F.A., S.R. M.C. Jan. 1918.* Lt., Sept. 1918.

HUNT, J. C. B. (1904–5, *r*)
Oct. 1915 Sec. Lt., R.F.A., T.F., 2/3 S. Mid. Bde. Lt., June
1916.

HURST, J. H. D. (1909–14, *r*)
Jan. 1915 Sec. Lt., 2/6 Arg. and Suth'd Highrs., T.F. France,
1/6 Bn. Invalided home. 1916 France (2): 'The Labyrinth'.
Lt., June 1916. Invalided home. 5 Res. Bn. 1917 193 Bde.
Forestry Detachment. Apr. 1918 France (3) 10 Bn. Severely
wounded Aug. 1918. Rel. Commn. on acc. of ill health caused by
wounds, Aug. 1919.

HUTCHINSON, A. R. W. (1915–16, g)
1916 Cdt., R.G.A. 1917 Sec. Lt., R.G.A., S.R., 391 Siege By., Italy, The Carso. Aug. 1918 Lt.

†HUTCHINSON, H. J. (1904–10, y)
1914 Pte., 14 R. War. R. France. Killed July 30, 1916.

HUTTON, C. W. C. (1904–8, r)
1914 Tpr., War. Yeo., T.F. Dec. 1914 Sec. Lt., 8 S. Lan. R. 25 North'd Fus. 1916 Capt., York. R. 1917 Capt. and Adjt. Apr. 1918 Staff Capt., R.A.F., Salonica F.

HUTTON, T. W. (1904–7, r)
1915 Sec. Lt., 13 R. War. R. 1916 Actg. Lt. Tr. Res. July 1917 Lt. (Reg. Bn.).

HUXLEY, J. E. (1893–5)
July 1913 Lt., A.S.C., T.F., S. Mid. Bde. June 1916 Capt., empd. Min. of Munitions.

HYDE, C. W. (1907–11, y)
Nov. 1914 Sec. Lt., R.G.A. 1916 Lt., R.F.C. 1917 Capt., Flt. Cdr. Sept. 1918 Actg. Maj., R.F.A. (A.).

HYDE, G. L. (1913–15, b)
1914 Sec. Lt., 3 R. War. R., S.R. 1915 temp. Capt., Bde. Sig. Off., I. of W. 1916 France, attd. 7 D. of Corn. L.I. Sept. 1916 Sec. Lt., Ind. Army. Apr. 1917 Lt., 56 Punjabis, Chaman, Baluchistan. Actg. Capt., 2/153 Punjabis. Mentd. Mar. 1919. Mesopotamia. 1918 Capt. and Adjt., 2/153 Punjabis, 53 Div., Egypt. ?9, May 1918 Capt.

IBBOTSON, A. W., M.B.E., M.C. (1900–5, b)
1915 Sec. Lt., Indian Army R. of O., attd. 17th Cav. Feb. 1916 E. Africa. Lt. Feb. 1917, M.C. April 1917 attd. 18th Lancers. Sialkot. Aug. 1917 Staff School, Kashmir. Dec. 1917 G.S.O.₃, Mhow Div. Sept. 1918 Staff Capt., 13th Mounted Bde., Gulistan ; Nov. 1918 Staff Capt., Troops beyond Meshed, N.E. Persia and Turkestan. May 1919 England. June 1919 M.B.E. (Mil. Div.).

ICKE, J. H. T. (1901–5)
Sept. 1913 Lt., 2 S. Lan. R. Oct. 1915 Capt. Prisoner of War
in Germany, 1914. Returned, to Holland, Jan. 1918.

ILES, C. E. (1896–1900)
Sept. 1917 Capt., R.A M.C., attd. R.N.V.R.

ILLING, F. (1908–11, s)
1915 Pte., The King's Own (R. Lanc. R.). Transfd. 8 E. Lan. R.
France : Arras : Monchy ; Rocquelincourt. Wounded, outside
Monchy, Dec. 1917.

INGALL, D. H. (1900–?, y)
Jan. 1915 Sec. Lt., R.E., T.F., 59 Divl. Signal Coy. June 1915
Lt. Mar.–Dec. 1916 Ireland (Irish Rebellion). Mar. 1917 Asst.
Adjt,, Sig. Dépôt. Feb. 1918–Feb. 1919 Instr. in Wireless Signals.

IRVINE, A. G. C. (1876–83)
1915 Lt., R.A.M.C. 1916 Capt. Rel. Commn. July 1917.

IRWIN, H. J., M.M. (1907–8, g)
Pte., 14 R. War. R. France. M.M. 1916. Sec. Lt., R.M.L.I. Lt.,
Apr. 1918. Wounded and prisoner, Mar. 24, 1918.

ISAACS, E. (1881–9)
1914 Pte., R. Fus. (P. Sch.). Interpreter, afterwards in A.P.C.

JACKSON, J. P. (1910–15, y)
Aug. 1915 Pte., 29 R. Fus. (P. Sch.). 1917 Cdt., 2 O.C.B., R.F.A.,
Exeter. June 1918 Sec. Lt., R.G.A., T.F.

JACKSON, L. W. (1908–10, y)
1914 Pte., 14 R. War. R. Nov. 1915 France. Wounded July 1916.

JACKSON, W. A. L. (1887–91)
Sept. 1914 Lt., R.A.M.C., T.F., 3 N. Mid. Bde. Apr. 1915 Capt.,
attd. 5 S. Staff. R., T F. 1919 attd. 2/6 S. Staff. R., T.F. T.F.
Res.

JACKSON, W. E. (1908–10, y)
1914 Pte., 14 R. War. R. 1916 Sgt. Wounded June 1916.

JACKSON, W. H. (1902–4, y)
1914 Pte., 14 R. War. R.

JACOBS, A. J. (1913–15, g)
1917 Inns of Court O.T.C. Oct. 1918 Sec. Lt., Tank Corps.

JACOBS, E. S. (1905–9, g)
1914 Pte., 14 R. War. R. 1915 Sec. Lt., R. Monmouthshire R.E.,
S.R. June 1917 Secd. R.F.C. (Obs.). Apr. 1918 Lt., R.A.F.
(A.). Flying Instr., Yatesbury.

†JACOT, C. W. (1915–17, r)
1917 Sec. Lt., R.F.C., Castle Bromwich. Flying Officer. Killed
in flying accident at Curdworth, June 23, 1917.

JACOT, E. W. (1912–14, r)
Aug. 1914 Sec. Lt., 14 R. War. R. Aug. 1915 Lt. Nov. 1915
France. Wounded, Somme, July 1916. 52 Tr. Res. Bn. Apr.
1917 Actg. Capt., Tr. Res. May 1918 Grad. Bn. Dec. 1918 attd.
16th Bn., France (2).

JAMES, E. A. (1913–17, b)
1917 Cdt., R.E., Sign., Haynes Pk., Bedford. May 1918 Sec. Lt.,
R.E. 2nd Corps Sign. Coy., France. Wounded (gas) Sept. 1918.
Attd. 29th Div. Cable Sectn., Army of Occupn., Altenberg, Germany : Leverkusen.

JEAVONS, E. V. (1896–9)
Aug. 1914 Capt., 5 R. War. R., T.F. 1915 France. Dec. 1915
Q.-M. Oct. 1917 Home Service. Q.-M., 7th Bn.

JENKINS, Digby (1892–6)
Dec. 1915 Enlisted. Apr. 1916 Gnr., R.G.A., 41 Coy., 143 Siege By.
1916–17 Belgium, 207 Siege By. ; 1918–19 France, 120 Siege By.

JENKINS, Douglas L. (1901–7, g)
1912–14 Tpr., Calcutta L.H. Dec. 1914 Sec. Lt., I.A., R. of O.,
38 Dogras, Malakand, N.W. Frontier, India. Feb.–Sept. 1915
Spec. Serv. Offr., Patiala State Inf., 32 Impl. Serv. Bde., I.E.F.,
' E '. Sept. 1915–Feb. 1916 Offr. i/c Supplies, No. 2 Sectn., Suez
Canal Defences. Dec. 1915 Lt. Feb.–Sept. 1916 Offr. i/c Supplies
and Transport, Indian troops, E.E.F. Oct. 1916–Jan. 1917 Comman-

dant 24 Mule Corps and D.A.D.T., Mohmand Field Force, N.W. Frontier, India. Feb.–June 1917 Pilot, R.F.C., E.E.F. Aug. 1917–Feb. 1918 Instr., No. 1 Wing Cadet Bde., R.F.C. Feb. 1918– May 1919 Chief Instr. in Signalling, No. 5 Wing Cadet Bde., R.A.F., Dec. 1918 Capt.

†JENKINS, G. C. (1906–11, *r*)

Sept. 1914 Pte., 21 R. Fus. (P. Sch.). 1915 Sgt. France till Spring of 1916. July 1916 Sec. Lt., York. and Lanc. R. Tr. Res. Bn. Apr. 1917 France (2). 2/5 York. and Lanc. R. May 3, 1917 Missing, believed killed, while leading his men in a bombing attack at Bullecourt.

JENKINS, HARRY LAWRENCE (1899–1901)

Dec. 1913 Actg. Sub-Lt., R.N.R. Apr. 1915 Sub-Lt., Actg. Lt. Ap. 1917 Lt. H.M.S. Ithuriel.

JENKINS, HERBERT LESLIE (1903–8, *y*)

1914 Pte., 14 R. War. R. France. Twice wounded ((2) 1916). 1917 Home Service, Ireland, H.Q., Provl. Bn., Midd'x. R., T.F.

†JENKINS, J. R. (1912–14, *r*)

1914 Pte., 14 R. War. R. Nov. 1915 France. Severely wounded Jan. 6, 1916. Died of wounds.

JENSEN, A. G. (1914–15, *b*)

Sept. 1917 Signalman, R.N.V.R. Apr. 1918 Mediterranean, in a hydrophone trawler.

†JERVIS, A. CYRIL (1900–6, *b*)

1914 Pte., 14 R. War. R. Mar. 1915 Sec. Lt., 3 King's (L'pool R.), S.R. Dec. 1915 Actg. Capt., 4 Bn., France. Lt. attd. K. Afr. Rif. July 1917 Actg. Capt. Aug. 1917 Capt. E. Africa. Killed July 3, 1918.

JERVIS, B. A. (1900) M.C.

1915 Sec. Lt., 1 Worc. Yeo. Gallipoli. 1915–Dec. 1918 Prisoner in Turkey (Yozgat). June 1916 Lt. M.C. May 1919.

†JERVIS, J. CEDRIC (1903–9, *b*)

1914 Pte., R. Fus. (P. Sch.). 1915 Sec. Lt., 21 Bn. 1916 transfd.

Gen. List, R.F.C. Observer, 5 Sqn., France. Killed in action Oct. 26, 1916.

JERVIS, N. E., M.C. (1903–9, *b*)

1914 Pte., 14 R. War. R. July 1915 Sec. Lt., 16 Bn. Oct. 1915 17 Bn. Actg. Lt., Tr. Res. Sec. Lt., attd. Reg. Bn. Feb. 1917 France. Wounded June 1917. M.C. Aug. 1917.* Apr. 1918 attd. M.G.C., Rugeley.

JESSOP, J. W. (1898–1904, *b*)

1915 Inns of Court O.T.C. Mar. 1917 Sec. Lt., 2/8 R. War. R., T.F. France. Wounded Dec. 4, 1917. May 1918 attd. M.G.C. Sept. 1918 Lt.

†JOHNSON, A. E. (1900–3)

Sept. 1914 Pte., 14 R. War. R. Nov. 1915 France: Vaux, Arras, Somme. Killed July 30, 1916, in the first wave of an attack on Delville Wood.

JOHNSON, A. V. (1907–9, *b*)

1914 Pte., War. Yeo. Jan. 1915 Sec. Lt., 11 Worc. R. 12 Bn.

JOHNSON, A. W. (1914–16, *b*)

Aug.–Dec. 1918 Cadet R.A.F. No. 2 Sch. of Aeronautics, Oxford.

JOHNSON, E. B. (1910–17, *b*)

1918 Wireless Opr., Marconi Service, H.M.T. Boveric. Mediterranean.

†JOHNSON, F. C. (1902–9, *b*)

1914 Pte., 15 R. War. R. Twenty months in France. Sgt. Killed, at Oppy Wood, July 1, 1917.

JOHNSON, F. H. (1899–1901)

Feb. 1915 Sec. Lt., R.G.A., T.F., 1/1 Warwickshire Heavy By. Mar. 1915 France. Armentières. Temp. Lt. June 1916 Lt. Somme battle to Martinpuich. Oct. 1916 invalided home. Empd. Min. of Mun., Sheffield.

JOHNSON, R. P. (1900–4, *b*) 1915 Sgt., R.E., Sign. Sectn. France.

JOHNSON, T. L. (1906–8, *b*)   1914 Spr., R.E., Wireless.

JOHNSON, T. W. M. (1911–16, *b*)
1917 Cdt., R.M.A., Woolwich.   June 1918 Sec. Lt., R.G.A.   Sept. 1918 France.

JOHNSON, W. H. (1902–8, *b*)
1916 Sec. Lt., R.F.A.   France.   Invalided out.

†JONAS, F. I. (1905–8, *y*)
Pte., 26 R. Fus.   Killed in France July 21, 1916.

JONES, B. W. (1888–95)   1917 Capt., R.A.M.C.   France.

JONES, C. C. (1905–6, *y*)
July 1912 Lt., R.A.M.C.   France.   Mar. 1915 Capt.   O.C. No. 7 Statry. Hosp., St. Omer.   Missing June 1918.   Prisoner in Germany : Rastatt, Langenzelys.   1919 Egypt.

JONES, E. E. (1908–12, *b*)   1914 Pte., 16 R. War. R.

JONES, E. W. (1910–13, *b*)
Sept. 1914 Sec. Lt., 6 R. War. R., T.F.   1915 Lt., 2/6 Bn.   June 1916 Capt.   Twice wounded (July 1, 1916, Aug. 31, 1918).   1918 attd. N. Lan. R., Egyptian E.F.   Mar. 1915 to July 1916 France ; Feb. 1917 to May 1918 E.E.F. ; May 1918 to Feb. 1919 France (2). Belgian Croix de Guerre.

†JONES, F. W. (1903–8, *g*)
Sept. 1914 Pte., 6 R. War. R., T.F.   Mar. 1915 France, Signaller. Nov. 1915 Sec. Lt., 3/8 Bn.   Oct. 1916 Lt.   Nov. 1915 France (2). Wounded Nov. 25, 1916, while helping a soldier who had lost his unit ; died of wounds at Westminster Dec. 21, 1916.

JONES, J. M. (1913–14, *b*)
1916 Sec. Lt., Welsh Horse.   Lt.   Secd. Ind. Army.   Oct. 1917 attd. 39 Cent. India Horse.

JONES, M. (1912–15, *b*)   Aug. 1918 Sec. Lt., R. Fus., S. Bn.

†JONES, N. E. (1905–8, *b*)
1914 Pte., 14 R. War. R.   1915 Cpl.   France.   Missing, presumed killed, July 22, 1916.

JONES, R. (1891–6)
1916 Tpr., King Edward's Horse.

JONES, W. R. Lloyd (1909–10, *b*)
Apr. 1917 Lt., Ind. Army, 108 Pioneer R. 1918 Actg. Capt., Adjt. Mesopotamia.

JORDAN, L. G. (1897–1902)
1915 Pte., 34 Can. Inf., D Coy.

JORDAN, V. F. (1911–15, *b*)
1916 Inns of Court O.T.C. 1917 Sec. Lt., 3 North'd Fus., S. Bn. France. Severely injured by bomb, Apr. 1917. Rel. Commn. Apr. 1919.

JOSEPH, E. V. (1901–7, *g*)
Oct. 1914 Sec. Lt., R.F.A. 79 Bde., Amm. Col. France. Oct. 1916 Lt. Wounded. 1919 Capt.

JOSEPH, G. L. (1887–90) Sept. 1918 Sec. Lt., R.A.S.C.

JOSEPH, H. (1892–5)
1916 Sec. Lt., R.E., T.F., Tyne Elect. Eng. Mar. 1918 Lt. Anti-aircraft Searchlight Statn.

JOSEPH, L. H. (1893–6)
1918 Cpl., R.A.S.C., M.T., attd. 122 Siege By., R.G.A., France. Home Service, M.T. Dépôt.

JOSEPH, M. W. (1900–5, *g*)
Fought in South African Rebellion 1915.

JUDGE, T. (1909–12, *r*)
1914 Pte., 14 R. War. R. 1917 L.-Cpl., A.S.C., M.T., 27 Coy.

†KEATES, R. J., M.C. (1891–5)
1914 A.B. Seaman, R.N.V.R., A.-A. Div. (night duty). 1915 Chief P.O., Anti-aircraft defences of London. Apr. 1917 Sec. Lt., R.G.A., S.R. France. M.C. Oct. 1917,* for saving a man's life at Boesinghe, in September, when he was gassed himself. Jan.

1918 Actg. Capt. and Adjt., 23 Bde.   Was at Péronne, Mar. 1917.
Killed Aug. 20, 1918, near Albert.

KEEBLE, C. H. (1910–13, r)
Apr. 1915 Tpr., 3 Co. of Lond. Yeo., T.F.   1 year Suez Canal, with
8 Mtd. Bde.   6 mths. Salonica.   Palestine, to capture of Jerusalem.
Invalided.   Apr. 1918 France, M.G.C.   Wounded (gas), Douai.

KEEP, A. S., M.C. (1904–8, g)
1914 Pte., 14 R. War. R.   1915 Sec. Lt., 14 R. War. R.   Oct. 1916
Sec. Lt., R.F.C.   July 1917 Lt.   R.A.F. (A.) France.   M.C. Sept.
1918.*   Wounded Aug. 1918.   Dec. 1918 Actg. Capt.

KEEP, C. E. (1915–17, g)
1917 Cdt., 5 O.C.B., St. John's Coll., Camb.   Mar. 1918 Sec. Lt.,
The King's (L'pool R.), S. Bn., Cork.

†KEKEWICH, R. G., C.B. (1865–7)
Maj.-Gen.   Col., The Buffs (E. Kent R.), Retd.   Divl. Commander,
Salisbury.   Died Nov. 5, 1914.

KEMP, T. C. (1906–9, r)   1914 Pte., 14 R. War. R.

KENTISH, W. (1900–2)
1914 Pte., 14 R. War. R.   June 1915 Sec. Lt., 3/8 R. War. R.,
T.F.   Nov. 1915 Actg. Lt.   July 1916 Lt.   Apr. 1918–Feb. 1919
Actg. Capt., 10 Bn.   Wounded Oct. 1918.

KERBY, Rev. E. T., M.C. (1886–96)
Mar. 1914–1919 C.F., 4 Cl., attd. 7 Manch. R., T.F.   Wounded,
1915.   Egypt.   Mentd. 1916.   M.C. 1916.

KEY, K. T. (1899–1902)
1914 Sec. Lt., 5 R. War. R., T.F.   June 1915 Lt.   France.   June
1916 Capt.

†KEYS, M. (1911–12, b)
Returned from Australia on the outbreak of war.   Oct. 1914 Sec.
Lt., 10 Bord. R.   July 1915 France.   Wounded Aug. 30, 1916.
Died of wounds Aug. 31, 1916.

KIMPTON, H. K. (1892–9)

1916 Driver-Mech., M.T., B.S.A. Police, N.W. Rhodesia.

KIMPTON, W. H., T.D. (1892–5)

Aug. 1912 Capt., R.A.M.C., T.F., Q.-M., 1 S. Mid. Fd. Amb.
1916 Lt., A.S.C. June 1916 Capt. 1917 Capt., R.A.S.C., T.F.,
S. Mid. Divl. Train. 1917–1919 France. Territorial Decn. Mar.
1919.

KING, ARTHUR (1902–3)

1914 Pte., 4 Res. Bn., Wilts. R. 1917 Bmdr., R.G.A., Avington
Park, Winchester.

KING, G. G. (1906–11, y)

1914 Tpr., War. Yeo., T.F. 1918 9 Impl. Camel Corps, Egyptian
E.F.

KING, L. (1909–14, y)

1917 Min. of Munitions. May 1918 Cpl., 13 Som. L.I., Genl.
Foreman Labourer. Sgt., attd. 51 Grad. Bn., R. War. R., for
Educational Work.

†KING, N. T. (1911, y)

1916 Sec. Lt., 3 D. Gds. 1918 Lt. France. Killed Mar. 23,
1918.at Noreuil.

KINGS, W. R. (1898–1900)

1914 Pte., 14 R. War. R. 1915 L.-Cpl. Nov. 1915 France. 1916
Cpl. Sgt.

KINO, J. J., M.C. (1896–1900)

1916 Sec. Lt., R.F.A. Oct. 1916 Lt. Wounded July 1917. Apr.
1918–Mar. 1919, Actg. Capt., attd. 282 Siege By., R.F.A., T.F.
Mentd. in Disp. Dec. 1918. M.C. June 1919.

KIRK, H. G. (1901–3)

1914 Pte., 14 R. War. R. 1916 Sec. Lt., R.F.C., 10 Kite Balloon
Sectn. 1917 27 Sectn., Salonica. 1918 Lt., R.A.F. (A). In
England.

KIRKBY, W. H. (Asst. Master, 1899–)
May 1909–May 1919 Capt., Unattd. List, T.F., O.C., K.E.S.
Birmingham Cont., Jun. Div., O.T.C.

KNYVETT, J. S. (1900–4, *y*)
Aug. 1913 Lt., 2 R. War. R. France. Feb. 1915 Capt. Wounded
(1) Oct. 1914, (2) Sept. 1915. 1916 Secd., G.S.O.$_3$, Humber
Command. 1917 2 R. War. R., France. To July 1918 Actg. Maj.
2nd in cd., 7 Lan. Fus., attd. 15 R. War. R. Jan. 1919 Actg. Adjt.,
16th Bn. Sen. Offrs' Course. May 1919 Recruiting Off., Leam-
ington.

LAING, R. R. J. (1906–11, *b*)
1915 Sec. Lt. 3/8 R. War. R., T.F. 1/8 Bn., France. Feb.
1917 Lt.

LAMB, F. B. (1901–7, *b*)
Oct. 1914 Sec. Lt., A.S.C. Oct. 1914–Aug. 1915, France, 6 Divl.
Supply Col. Mar. 1915 Lt. July 1915 Capt. Sept. 1915 France (2)
in charge of A.S.C. attd. 30 (6 in.) Siege By., R.G.A. Apr. 1916 in
charge of A.S.C. attd. 65 (12 in. How.) Siege By., R.G.A. Dec.
1916 transfd. Tank C., Engineer Off., 2 Bn. : 1917 Messines ;
July–Sept. 1917 Ypres ; Equancourt, Marcoing, Gouzeaucourt,
Nov. 1917. Feb. 1918 Actg. Maj., 1 Advanced Workshops.
Mar. 1918 Dainville (Arras). From June 1918 with H.Q., Tank C.
Aug. 1918 Tank Inspectorate, attd. to M.W.D. Design Dept.
Oct. 1918 temp. Maj. 1919 Tank Design and Experimental Dept.,
War Office.

LAMB, F. W. M. (1906–13, *r*)
Apr. 1918 Lt., R.A.M.C. Apr. 1918 France ; attd. 7 Stationary
Hosp., Boulogne : attd. 26 Fd. Amb., and 25 Fd. Amb., near
Amiens : at Boves, in charge of a Dressing Station : in Soisson-
Reims sector : Divl. Rest. Station, Dravegny (close to Fère-en-
Tardenois) : Bouvancourt (close to Fismes) : 26 Fd. Amb.,
8 Div. (latterly in part of French Army). Taken prisoner, May 27,
while temporarily attd. 25 Fd. Amb., the whole of which was

captured. In Germany, 3 wks. at Rastatt, Baden ; 3 months in Stralsund, Pomerania, on Baltic Coast, in Officers' camp : Sept. sent down through Berlin with a guard to a men's camp in Silesia, close to Austrian border, in charge of all British sick in the camp till repatriated Jan. 1919. Apr. 1919 Capt. 2/1 S. Gen. Hosp.: 1 B'ham War Hosp., Northfield.

LAMB, J. H. (1898–1901)

Aug. 1914 temp. Surg., R.N.V.R. (permanent). Sept. 1914–Aug. 1916 H.M.S. Calgarian, 9 Cruiser Sqd., N. America and W. Indies. Off Tagus, N.W. African Coast, Azores, Gibraltar, Bermuda, Halifax, N.S., St. John's, Newfoundland, U.S. Coast ; North Atlantic patrols. Torpedoed. Aug. 1916–July 1918 H.M.S. Arrogant, Dover. July 1918–Mar. 1919 H.M.S. Sir Thomas Picton, British Adriatic Forces, under Italian Admiral protecting left flank of Allied lines on Balkan front : Valona, Durazzo, Fiume, Ancona, Brindisi, Malta ; Bougies, Oran (Algeria). Surgeon Lt., unattd. list.

LAMBOURNE, A. W., M.C. (1892–5)

1915 Sec. Lt., R.E., T.F., N. Mid. Fd. Coy. June 1916 Lt. Mar. 1918 Actg. Capt., R.E. Three years in France, the first two with the 46 Div. Commanding Camouflage Factory, Rouen. M.C. (Amiens front in German advance, 1918) Jan. 1919.

LAMBOURNE, R. G. H. (1901–4, b)

A.S.C., M.T.

LAMPLUGH, A. G. (1906–11, g)

Aug. 1914 Cpl., 4 Hussars. Jan. 1915 Lt., 8 N. Staff. R., 19th Div. Bombing Off. Severely wounded, while on patrol duty, Feb. 27, 1915. 1917 Gen. List, R.F.C., Flying Off. Mesopotamia. Apr. 1918 Lt., R.A.F. (A). Aug. 1918, May–June 1919 Capt. (A). Castle Bromwich. Oct. 1919 Short service commn., Fl. Off. (A.).

†LAMPLUGH, S. C. (1909–10, g)

Oct. 1914 Pte., 16 R. War. R. Jan. 1915 France, 2nd Cl. Air Mech., R.F.C. Dec. 1916 Observer. Killed in action Mar. 6, 1917.

†LANCASTER, J. N. (1903–5, g)

Three years in B.U.O.T.C. Aug. 1914 Sec. Lt., 9 Worc. R. Killed in Gallipoli Aug. 10, 1915.

LANDON, J. W., M.B.E. (1891–4)

May 1909 Sec. Lt. (temp. Capt. in the Army), Unattd. List, T.F. Camb. Univ. O.T.C., Fortress Coy. Eng. Dec. 1914 Sec. Lt., Gen. Spec. List, Asst. Instr. in Fortification, Sch. of Mil. Engineering, Chatham. Mar. 1917 Capt., Spec. List, while Asst. Instr. of Mil. Eng. 1919 M.B.E., Mil. Div.

†LANE, S. H. (1909–11, r)

1914 Pte., 14 R. War. R. L.-Cpl. 1915 Sec. Lt., R.G.A., 58 Siege By., France. 1916 Actg. Capt., 38 Heavy By. July 1917 Actg. Maj., in cd. of 290 S. By. Five times mentd. in Disp. (4) May 1918, (5) Dec. 1918. Killed Apr. 5, 1918.

LANGLEY, A. S., C.M.G. (Asst. Master, 1905–, House Master, 1910–, b)

Feb. 1913 Capt., K.E.S. O.T.C. May 1916 Lt., R.N.V.R., Executive Offr., R.N.A.S. Dépôt, Stratford, E. Stratford then had a strength of 4 offrs. and 60 men, and was chiefly engaged in the small-scale production of anhydrous prussic acid and research on poison gases. The dépôt steadily increased in strength and became the centre of chemical research and production for Naval purposes. Large quantities of poison gas liquids were supplied to the Army, and various kinds of smoke-producing gear to the three services, including all the smoke-producing devices and skilled personnel to work them in the Zeebrugge operations. On the formation of the R.A.F., the R.N.A.S. Dépôt was retained by the Admiralty as the R.N. Experimental Station, Stratford. June 1917 Lt.-Cdr. Nov. 1917 ' First Lieutenant ' at Stratford under Wing-Cdr. F. A. Brock, R.N. Mentd. May 1918. May–Aug. 1918 Offr. in charge at Stratford. Sept.–Oct. 1918 Offr. in charge, R.N. Anti-Gas Section. Nov. 1918 O.C. R.N. Expl. Statn., Stratford : Actg. Cdr. By Nov. 1918 the Stratford Command included the Expl. Statn. ; the R.N. Expl. Base, Dover ; the R.N. Anti-Gas

Sectn. with dépôts at Tottenham and Stamford Hill, togr. with Maintenance Dépôts for inspection and repair of anti-gas gear at Kirkwall, Rosyth, Harwich, Dover, and Portsmouth (these were worked by W.R.N.S. personnel) ; and Instructional Gas Schools for Naval Offrs. at Rosyth and Dover. Nov. 1918 Member of Admiralty Anti-Gas Committee. Apr. 1919 C.M.G. June 1919 Admiralty Representative on Chemical Warfare Organization Committee.

LANGRIDGE, B. (1909–13, b)
1915 Sec. Lt., Cycl. Res. Bn., Hunts. R., T.F.

LANGRIDGE, F. F. (1908–11, b)
Dec. 1915 Sec. Lt., 6 Essex R.

LARKIN, S. S. (1900-2)
Sec. Lt., S. Staff. R.

LARKINS, D. F. (1908–11, g)
Dec. 1914 Sec. Lt., 11 N. Staff. R.

†LARKINS, J. C. (1907–11, g)
Oct. 1914, Sec. Lt., 2 R. War. R. France. Killed June 4, 1916.

LAST, C. A. (1896–9, 1902–3)
1914 Pte., H.A.C. Dec. 1914 Sec. Lt., R.F.A., T.F., 4 Lond. How. Bde., Amm. Col. 7 Bde. 11 Bde. 1915 France, 36 Div. Nov. 1915 Salonica. June 1916 Lt. End of 1916 invalided home. Nov. 1917 Secd. Railway Traffic Off. France. Ytres. Apr. 1918 Vignacourt. Apr. 1919 Spec. Appt., H.Q., Admin. Services and Depts.

LAST, F. B. (1902–5, g)
1914 Pte., R.A.M.C. 1915–Dec. 1917 France, 2 Div. Mar. 1918 Cdt., R.E. Sch., Newark.

†LAST, L. S. (1905–6, y)
1914 Driver, H.A.C., B By. 1915 Egypt. Summer 1916 returned to England. Oct. 1916 Sec. Lt., R.F.A. Salonica. Aug. 1917

tranfd. R.F.C. Flying Officer (Pilot) Feb. 1918. Instructor. Killed in flying accident, Egypt, Feb. 21, 1918.

LATOUR, A. F. (1911–14, *r*)
1916 Artists Rif. O.T.C. 1917 Sec. Lt., Pioneer Bn., Worc. R. Wounded, Cambrai, Mar. 1918. Empd. Min. of Labour. Nov. 1918 Lt. Rel. Commn. Jan. 1919.

LATOUR, R. L. T. (1909–12, *r*)
Dec. 1917 Sec. Lt., Gen. List, R.F.C. Sec. Lt. (Obs.), R.A.F. Nov. 1918 Sec. Lt. (T.). Mar. 1919 Unempd. List.

LAW, C. D. (1909–17, *y*)
1917 Cdt., O.C.U., R.E., Sig. Aug. 1918 Sec. Lt., R.E., Sig. Nov. 1918 Salonica F , Signal Dépôt ; G.H.Q., Salonica. Dec. 1918 O.C. No. 5 Wagon Wireless Section. Jan.–Mar. 1919 Osmania Wireless Station, Turkey.

LAWLEDGE, E. C. (1910–13, *b*)
1916 Sec. Lt., 4 R. War. R., S.R. 2 Bn., France. Wounded 1917. July 1917 Lt. Oct. 1918 France (2) 25 Div., 1/8 Bn., T.F. Le Cateau, Landrecies, Sambre Canal, Cambrai.

†LAWLEDGE, F. M. (1893)
1915 Pte., 17 R. Fus. Feb. 1916 Sec. Lt., R.E. Attd. R.F.C. Killed Oct. 1916.

LAWLEY, T. H. (1898–1901)
Oct. 1914 Sec. Lt., 3/5 R. War. R., T.F. Jan. 1915 Actg. Capt. Lt. 1916 Capt. Wounded, 1916.

LAWLEY, W. W. (1906–8, *r*)
1914 Pte., 14 R. War. R. France. 1916 L.-Cpl.

†LAWRENCE, R. R. (1909–11, *y*)
1914 Pte., 14 R. War. R. Jan. 1915 Sec. Lt., 8 The King's (Shrops. L.I.). Missing (presumed killed on or about) Aug. 24, 1916.

LAWSON, W. W. J. (1894–6)
Oct. 1914 Lt., R.A.M.C., T.F., 3 W. Rid. Fd. Amb. Apr. 1915 Capt.

LEA, F. M. (1911–18, *b*)
Mar. 1918 Cdt., R.M.A., Woolwich. Army of the Rhine.

LEACROFT, J. F. (1904–8, *y*)
Oct. 1914 Lt., 11 Worc. R. Dec. 1915 Capt., R.G.A. Jan. 1919, Bt.-Maj.

†LEACROFT, R. F. (1904–9, *y*)
Sept. 1914 Can. Cont., A.S.C. Jan. 1915 Sec. Lt., 12 Worc. R. (Permanent Commn. antedated Jan. 7, 1915). Attd. 2 Worc. R., France, June 1915. Killed by machine guns, while occupying a crater after the explosion of a German mine, 1915.

LEE, A. (Asst. Master, 1918–   )
Apr. 1918 Sec. Lt., K.E.S., Birmingham O.T.C.

LEE, A. F. (1899–1903)
Mar. 1918 Sec. Lt., Tank Corps. Actg. Capt.

LEE, F. H. (1899–1903)
1914 M.T. Service, Botha's Force, S. Afr. Mech. Staff-Sgt., A.S.C. 1917 Sec. Lt., M.G.C. Sept. 1918 Lt., Actg. Capt. Feb. 1918 Tank Eng. Mentd. in Disp.

LEE, G. R. (1892–8)
1914 R.F.A., T.F., 1 City of Lond. Bde. Oct. 1917 Sec. Lt., R.F.A., S.R.

LEE, H. G. (1907–10, *b*)
Inns of Court O.T.C. 1918 Sec. Lt., Tank Corps.

LEE, T. L. (1901–7, *g*)
July 1918 L.-Cpl., Res. Bn., Q. West. Rif.

LEES, A. A., M.C. (1900–8, *b*)
1914 Lt., R.A.M.C. 1916 36 Gen. Hosp., Salonica. June 1917–June 1919 Capt. M.C. Jan. 1918.

LEES, W. G. (1909–11, *b*)
1915 Sec. Lt., 3/5 R. War. R., T.F. June 1916 Lt., France. 1917 Actg. Capt., 1/5 Bn. Invalided England, Sept. 1917.

LENCH, H, (1908–10, *y*)
Nov. 1915 Signaller, 2/6 S. Staff. R., T.F. Irish Rebellion.
France, Sept. 1917 Ypres, Nov. 1917 Cambrai. Captured at
Bullecourt, Mar. 1918 : prisoner in Germany till Nov. 1918.

LEVERS, G. J. (1904–10, *g*)   Pte., A.S.C.

LEVINE, A. E. (1906–9, *g*)   R.E.

†LEWIS, I. F. (1896–1901)
1915 Pte., 17 R. War. R. Wounded and missing, presumed killed,
at Ypres, Oct. 9, 1917.

LEWIS, J. (1903–6, *b*)   1915 Pte., 11 Aust. Inf.

†LINE, B. C. (1911–14, *y*)
1916 Gnr., R.F.A., T.F., 3 S. Mid. Bde. Signaller, France. Killed
Apr. 28, 1917.

LINE, F. F. (1912–13, *y*)
1914–1919 Pte., 14 R. War. R.

LINE, J., A.F.C. (1905–11, *y*)
Dec. 1914 Sec. Lt., A.S.C., 11 Divl. Train. 1916 Salonica. July
1915 Lt.   848 H.Q. Coy., Pack Echelon, 26 Divl. Train.   1917
attd. Sec. Lt., R.F.C., Aboukir, Egypt. Home. Oct. 1918
Instr., Grantham. A.F.C., Nov. 1918.

LINE, L. A. N. (1909–17, *y*)
1918 Cdt., 8 O.C.B., Lichfield. Sept. 1918, Sec. Lt., 7 Res. R. War.
R., T.F. Nov. 1918 France, attd. 6 Leic. R.

LINE, W. R. A. (1910–11, *y*)
1914 Pte., 14 R. War. R. Nov. 1915 to 1919 France. Cpl., Dressing
Station.

LISBONA, V. M. (1909–16, *b*)
1917 Cdt., 9 O.C.B., Gailes, Ayrshire. Aug. 1917 Sec. Lt., 3 N.
Staff. R., S.R. Oct. 1917–Jan. 1918 8 Bn., France : Ypres,
Cambrai. Invalided home. Feb. 1919 Lt., 3 Bn.

LISLE, C. F. J. (1912–17, *r*)

Sept. 1917 P.F.O., R.N.A.S. Apr. 1918 Sec. Lt., R.A.F. (A), Isle of Thanet. Armament Offr., Mullion.

LISTER, CECIL, D.S.O. and bar, M.C. (1895–1902)

Feb. 1913 Capt., 5 S. Staff. R., T.F. Aug. 4, 1914 mobilized. Feb. 1915–July 1919 France, 137 Bde., 46 Div. : served at different times with all 4 Bns. of 137 Bde. Oct. 1915 Battle of Loos, Hohenzollern Redoubt. M.C. 1915. Dec. 1915–Feb. 1916 Egypt, Suez Canal. Mar. 1916 France (2). In the line at Neuville St. Vaast. July 1, 1916 1st Battle of the Somme, Gommecourt—very severe casualties—slightly wounded. Aug. 1916 Capt., North'n R. (Reg. Cn.). Mar. 1917 2nd in cd., 5 N. Staff. R., in hurried and unsuccessful attack on Bucquoy by 2 Bns., with some of 7 Div. June 1917 2nd in cd., 6 N. Staff. R., Lens (gained much ground) : to end of 1917, in front of Hulluch, raiding and being raided. Dec. 1917 Actg. Lt.-Col., cdg. 6 S. Staff. R., till July 1919. Apr.–Aug. 1918, in line N. of Béthune, after Portuguese break : heavy gas casualties ; gassed May 1. Good work by the whole Div., snaffling German posts in daylight. Sept., moved S. : Sept. 29, crossed St. Quentin Canal and broke Hindenburg Line : the Div. took 4,000 pris. and 80 guns. D.S.O. (gazetted Mar. 1919)*. Oct.–Nov. pursuit of the Germans, finishing nr. Landrecies. For a month in 1916, Instr., 46 Divl. Offrs'. School ; 2 mths. in 1917, Commandant, 46 Divl. Dépôt Bn. Five times mentd., 1915 ; Apr. 1917 ; May 1918 ; Dec. 1918 ; July 1919. Bar to D.S.O., Jan. 1919. Temp. Lt.-Col., May 10, 1918.

†LISTER, F. W., M.C. (1904–7, *g*)

Aug. 1914 W. Afr. Rif. 1915 Sec. Lt., 3/1 Worc. Yeo., T.F. June 1916 Lt. Actg. Capt. Capt., S. Staff. R., S. Bn. France. Capt., Apr. 1917. Attd. Tank Corps, 3 Coy., 1 Bn. M.C. (for Sept. 1918) Dec. 1918.* Sept. 1918 Actg. Maj., wh. cdg. a Coy. Sec. in cd., 21 Bn., Wareham. Died at Wareham from pneumonia Feb. 24, 1919.

†LISTER, M. W. (1893–8)

July 1915 Sec. Lt., 3/5 S. Staff. R., T.F. Jan. 1917 France ;

Capt. (Coy. Commander), 9 (Pioneer) Bn. : engaged in prepara-
tions for our attacks of spring and summer 1917, including the
storming of Messines Ridge. Killed in billets by a long-range
H.V. shell, July 19, 1917, near Dickebusch : buried in the cemetery
next the church.

LLOYD, B. A. (1897–1902)
Apr. 1915–1919 Capt., R.A.M.C., 1 Sn. Gen. Hosp.

LLOYD, J. H. (1908–14, *r*)
Nov. 1915 Pte., 14 Lond. R. (Lond. Scottish). Aug. 1916 France :
a year at base. Severely wounded during advance into Bullecourt, Aug. 31, 1918. Sept. 1918–Mar. 1919 in England.

LLOYD, N. C. (1908–15, *r*)
1st Cl. Air Mech., R.F.C., B Flt., 21 Sqn. France. Ypres.

LLOYD-JONES, W. R. : see Jones, W. R. Lloyd.

LOFTHOUSE, R. H. (1907–14, *b*)
Gnr., R.H.A. 1917 1128 By., R.F.A.

LONG, A. J. (1900–9, *r*)
1915 Sec. Lt., 3 N. Staff. R., S.R. France, attd. 8 Leic. R. Dec.
1915 Lt. Wounded, Somme, Sept. 1916. 1917 France (2), attd.
Portuguese cont., Liaison Off.

LONG, F. H. (1908–12, *r*)
Mar. 1916 Pte., R. Fus. (Bankers' Bn.). Dec. 1916 N. Lan. R., France.
Invalided, 'permanent base', G.H.Q., Rouen, June 1917. Sgt.

LONG, F. W. C. (1911–14, *r*)
Early 1917 Spr., R.E., Sign. Dépôt. France. Wounded (gas)
Sept. 29, 1917.

LONG, WILSON C. (1906–12, *r*)
Rfn., K.R. Rif. C. Jan. 1916 France. Wounded 1918.

LONGLEY, C. W., M.C. M.M. (1897–1900)
1915 Gnr., R.F.A., T.F., 1 S. Mid. Bde. B/240 Bde., France.
M.M. Nov. 1916. Sec. Lt., R.F.A. Lt., July 1917. M.C. (Sept.
1917) Jan. 1918.* Feb. 1919 2 S. Mid. Bde.

†LORY, V. A. M. (1911–16, *r*)
1917 Pte., R. War. R. Died May 23, 1917.

†LOVEKIN, E. (1909–11, *r*)
Aug. 1917 Pte., A.S.C., H.Q., 67 Divl. Train. L.-Cpl. Nov. 1918,
R.A.S.C. Base Supply Dépôt, Constantinople. Died at Constantinople, Feb. 27, 1919.

LUCAS, O. (1903–7, *y*)
1914 Lt., R.N. Aerial Div., Armoured Motor Car Sectn. 1916
Sec. Lt., A.S.C. Supervisor (Inventions), provision of Aeroplane
parts. July 1917 Lt.

LUNTS, L. (1902–8, *r*)
1916 Pte., 35 Can. Inf., A Coy. 1917 Driver, Can. F.A.

LYAL, D. H. (1901–8, *b*)
1916 Artists Rif. O.T.C. Sec. Lt., 12 Lond. R., T.F. Jan. 1918
Lt. Actg. Capt., Adjt., 1918.

LYCETT, C. V. L. (1903–12, *y*)
Sept. 1914 Sec. Lt., R.E., S.R., Res. Sigs. Mar.–Apr. 1915 France.
Wounded, nr. Ypres, Apr. 25, 1915. July 1915 Lt. Dec. 1915–
May 1916, France (2) : 3 Divl. Sgnls. : G.H.Q., Wireless Off.
Instr., Wireless Signal Dépôt, Worcester. Dec. 1916 2 Wireless
Sigs., Mesopotamia E.F. Magil. Persia. Nov. 1917 Capt. 1918
Capt., Wireless Press Sectn., Baghdad. June 1918 No. 4 Wireless Observation Group, Mes. E.F. Mentd. in Disp., Nov.
1918. Jan. 1919 No. 3 Wireless Obsn. Group, Constantinople, for
S. Russia.

LYTHGOE, F. S. G. (1899–1902)
1915 Q.-M.-S., 3/5 R. War. R., T.F. Sec. Lt., Mon. R., T.F.
Secd. The King's (L'pool R.). 1918 Lt., Lab. Corps.

†LYTHGOE, J. W. (1900–5, *y*)
1914 Pte., 14 R. War. R. Feb. 1915 Sec. Lt. Nov. 1915 France.
Lt. Killed July 22, 1916.

McARDLE, R. (1912–13, *y*)
  1917 Cdt., 2 Cav. O.C.U., The Curragh. Apr. 1918 Sec. Lt.,
  1 Res. Regt., Cav.

†McBEAN, D. (1903–6, *g*)
  Sept. 1914 Sec. Lt., 8 R. Welsh Fus. Feb. 1915 Lt., attd. 10 Bn.
  Gallipoli. Killed Mar. 15, 1916.

McCALL, W. B. (1910–16, *g*)
  1918 L.-Cpl., B.U.O.T.C.

McCARDIE, W. J. (1880–3)
  Sept. 1908–1919 Capt., R.A.M.C., T.F., 1 Sn. Gen. Hosp.

McCORMACK, B. H. (1911–14, *g*)
  1917 Inns of Court O.T.C. Sec. Lt., R.F.C. (Fl. Off.), N. Carley,
  nr. Lincoln. Wounded 1918. June 1918 Lt., R.A.F. (Admin.)
  Offr. in charge of running engines. Lt. (A).

MACDONALD, A. J. W. (1907–10, *r*)
  1915 Drummer, 3 Wilts R., A Coy. Pte., 3/5 Bn. H.Q., Alexandria District.

MacFARLANE, W. M. (1909–13, *y*)
  June 1915 Sec. Lt., 3 Cam'n Highrs., S.R. Severely wounded,
  Somme, Sept. 1916. Rel. Commn. Sept. 1918.

McGAVIN, D. J., D.S.O. (1892–5)
  June 1917 Col., N.Z. Mil. Forces, A.D.M.S., N.Z. Med. Corps.

McKENZIE, A. B. (1900–5, *g*)
  Cdt., O.C.B. Apr. 1917 Sec. Lt., 16 Manch. R. Oct. 1918 Lt. :
  attd. Notts. and Derby R., E.E.F. Turkish Pris. of War Camp,
  Quesna, Egypt. Also served in France.

McKENZIE, J. F. R. (1899–1904, *g*)
  1914 Pte., S. Wales Bord., Brecknockshire Bn., T.F. 1917 L.-Cpl.
  Cpl. At Aden, and at Mhow, Central India.

McKENZIE, S. N. (1911–13, *y*)
  1915 Pte., 10 Reinforcements, 16 Aust. Inf. 1916 Sec. Lt.,
  France. 48 Bn. June 1917 Lt. Mentd. (Bullecourt) Dec. 1917.

McMICHAEL, D. (1912–16, *y*)
B.U.O.T.C. Feb. 1918 Cdt., R.E., Newark. June 1918, Sec. Lt.,
R.E., T.F. Sept. 1918 No. 4 Siege Coy., R. Anglesey R.E. France.
Marched through Belgium with 4 Army, aftds. joining 2 Army.
Entered Germany, Dec. Army of the Rhine.

McNAIR, C. B. (1910–15, *b*)
B.U.O.T.C. Motor-Mech., R.N.A.S., Motor-boat service. 1918 Air
Mech., 1st Eng. Great Yarmouth, in attendance on seaplanes.

MACNIVEN, D. (1908–9, *r*)
Aug. 1914 Sec. Lt., 8 R. War. R., T.F. Lt. June 1916 Capt.
Mar. 1917 Spec. List, cdg. a T.M.B.

MACSWINEY, D. G. (1901–11, *g*)
1918 Cdt., R.A.F. June 1918 Sec. Lt. (A. & S.) Felixstowe.

†MACSWINEY, F. D. (1903–11, *y*)
Pte., 49 Can. Inf. France. Died of wounds July 1916.

†MADDERS, H. F. (1891–7)
Nov. 1915 Sec. Lt., R.F.A., S.R. 1 B. Res. Bde. Killed July 1, 1916.

MADELEY, J. T. (1896–7)
1915 Pte., H.A.C. Nov. 1915 Lt., 17 Ches. R. May 1917 Capt.,
S. Bn. 1918 empd. under Colonial Office.

MAGRANE, J. V. V. (1901–3)
June 1909 Lt., R.N., Navigating Off., H.M.S. Blanche (lt.
cruiser). 1916 Legion of Honour (Croix de Chevalier). Mentd.
in Disp. Jan. 1917–1919 H.M.S. Comus. June 1917 Lt.-Cdr.

MAITLAND, V. G. (1893–4) 1917 Capt., R.A.M.C.

MAJOR, A. B. (1907–10, *g*) O.S., R.N.R. 1917 Signaller.

†MALINS, E. F. (1913–17, *b*)
B.U.O.T.C. May 1917 Cdt., O.C.B., Yealmpton. Aug. 1917
Sec. Lt., 2 S. Wales Bord. Oct. 1917 France, 29 Div. Wounded
at Neuf Berquin Apr. 11, died of wounds Apr. 14, 1918.

MALINS, W. H. (1888–93)

Aug. 1916 Lt., T.F. Res. Empd. Min. of Nat. Service.

MANLY, G. B. (1893–4)

Oct. 1916 to Nov. 1918 Pte., A.S.C., M.T., 11 Pontoon Park. 1916–1917 Arras ; 1918 Somme ; attd. to Aust. Corps in great advance, finishing at Roisel.

†MANN, Horace (1894–8)

s.ᴀ.   Sec. Lt., 3 Dorset R., July 1917 Lt. Served for some time in the East, chiefly Egypt. 1918 attd. K. Afr. Rif., E. Africa. Capt. Died of enteric fever at Zomba, Nyasaland, Dec. 25, 1918. Mentd. in Lt.-Gen. Van Deventer's Dispatch of Jan. 1919 (Gaz. June 1919) for gallant and distinguished service in the field.

MANNOX, F. C. (1911–16, g)

Nov. 1916 Pte., North'd Fus. Feb. 1917 L.-Cpl. 85 Tr. Res. Bn. Nov. 1917 Cdt., 7 O.C.B., Fermoy, Ireland. Apr. 1918 Sec. Lt., 5 R. Mun. Fus. France July 1918. Wounded, Cambrai, Oct. 7, 1918.

†MANSELL, C. P. (1905–8, g)

1914 Pte., 14 R. War. R. 1915 Sec. Lt., A.S.C. Transfd. 16 R. War. R. Nov. 1915 17 Bn. 1916 France. Killed at Guillemont. Sept. 3, 1916.

†MANSELL, W. R. (1904–8, r)

1914 Pte., 15 R. War. R. Cpl. July 1915 Sec. Lt., 3/5 S. Staff. R., T.F. : Musketry Offr. July 1916 France, 1/5 Bn. Lt. Bn. Bombing Offr. Sept., invalided home. 3/5 Bn. Oct. 1917 2 Bn., France (2). Dec. 1917 Actg. Capt. Severely wounded, St. Quentin, Mar. 24, 1918 ; died of wounds at 3 Can. Hosp., Étaples, Apr. 16, 1918.

MANTON, G. C. (1908–9, b)

1914 Cpl., D.R., R.E. France. Jan. 1917 Sec. Lt., Hamps. R. (Reg. Bn.) Wounded. Rel. Commn. Feb. 1919.

MARGRETT, H. C. (1909–17, *b*)
1917 P.F.O., R.N.A.S. Aug. 1917 Invalided, R. N. Hosp., Chatham. Sub-Lt. Westgate-on-Sea. Seaplanes. May 1918 Sec. Lt. (A. and S.), R.A.F. Lt.

MARKS, C. S. I. (1911–16, *r*)
1917 Gnr., R.M.A.

†MARKS, I. D. (1910–13, *r*)
1915 Sec. Lt., 11 W. Riding R. France. Killed July 10, 1916.

MARRIS, R. G. (1915–16, *g*)
1918 Cdt., R.A.F., Hastings, Folkestone.

MARSH, G. W. (1911–16, *g*)
Sec. Lt., R.F.C.

MARSH, S. E. (1906–11, *g*)
1917 Gnr., R.F.A.

†MARSHALL, P. S. (1907–15, *g*)
Feb. 1915 Sec. Lt., R.F.A., T.F., 3 S. Mid. Bde. May 1916 France, B/307 Bde. June 1917 Lt. Did some excellent work at the extreme South of the British line. Killed near Ypres Aug. 15, 1917, while his section was engaged in wire-cutting from a very forward position.

MARTYN, R. O. F. (1906–7, *b*)
Sept. 1915 Sec. Lt., 11 S. Staff. R. Actg. Lt., Tr. Res. Bn. Attd. Reg. Bn. July 1917 Lt. Actg. Capt., 6 L.N. Lan. R. Oct. 1918 Lt., Ind. Army.

†MASON, JOHN (1888–90)
1914 Col.-Sgt., R.M.L.I. Killed in action Sept. 1914.

†MASON, P. G., D.S.O. (1885–90)
1914 Maj., 3 D. Gds. France. D.S.O. 1915. May 30–June 2, in command of Hooge Fort. Legion of Honour 1915. Mentd. Killed in action Sept. 26, 1915.

MATTHEWS, G. C. (1913–15, *y*)
 1918 Cdt., R.A.F., Rendcomb.

†MATTHEWS, H. J. (1901–4, *b*)
 '14 O.T.C. · Pte., R.A.M.C., 3/1 S. Mid. Bde., Fd. Amb. Died of ~~pneumonia~~ *wounds*,
 '15 left front. in Palestine, ~~1918.~~ *Nov. 7, 1917*

MAY, E. W. N., M.C. (1909–13, *r*)
 Mar. 1915 Sec. Lt., R.F.A., T.F., 2/3 S. Mid. Bde. June 1916 Lt.
 Feb. 1918 Actg. Capt. Attd. T.M.B. Div. T.M. Offr., to Jan.
 1919. M.C. June 1919.

MENCE, H. G. V. (1910–12, *g*)
 B.U.O.T.C. May 1917 Lt., R.A.M.C., S.R. Sept. 1917 Meso-
 potamia E.F. 1917–1919 Military Hospital at Kut. Aug. 1918
 Capt.

MERRY, Thomas (1892–4)
 Aug. 1915 Lt., R.E. Capt., Asst. Dir. of Docks. July 1918 Actg.
 Maj., D.A.D. Docks.

MILLER, D. C. (1903–11, *g*)
 Apr. 1915 Sec. Lt., Camb. Univ. O.T.C. : O.C. Coy. : 2nd in cd.
 of Bn. 1915 Sec. Lt., R.F.C. 1916 Fl. Off. (Pilot), No. 8 Sqn.,
 France. 1917 Capt., Flt.-Cdr., No. 21 Sqn., France. 1917 Capt.,
 Flt. Cdr. 1918 Actg. Maj., R.A.F. (A.), Sqn.-Cdr. On Board of
 Examiners for Schools of Aeronautics : commanded No. 20 and
 No. 15 Sqns. in England, and was 2nd in command of No. 39
 Training Dépôt.

> †MILLIGAN, H. W. (1896–1900)
 1914 Ceylon Planters Rif. Corps. July 1915 Sec. Lt., 1 Lan. Fus.
 Gallipoli landing Apr. 14, 1915. Wounded (1) Gallipoli. 1916 Lt.
 France. Wounded 3 times in France. Killed at Noyelle Nov. 21,
 1917.

MILLINGTON, F. (1906–7, *g*)
 Salonica.

MILLER, NEVILLE (1892–4)
 Sept. 1914 Pte., 14 R. War. R. Nov. 1915 France. Wounded,
 Somme, July 22, 1916. Jan. 1917 Sec-Lt., 1/5 S. Staff. R., T.F.
 Apr. 1917 France (2) Killed, nr. R. Scarpe, June 28, 1917.

†MILLNER, W. (1889–1902)

Oct. 1914 Capt., 1/5 S. Staff. R., T.F. France. Killed at Hohenzollern Redoubt, Oct. 13, 1915.

MILLS, AUSTEN (1913–14, *b*)

1917 Pte., Notts. and Derby R. Wounded Dec. 1917.

MILLS, S. J. O. (1898–1904, *b*)

July 1917 Driver, H.A.C.

†MILLWARD, B. J. (1909–13, *y*)

Aug. 1915 Sec. Lt., 12 E. York. R. June 1916 Resigned Commn.
Pte., Manch. R. Transfd. The King's (L'pool R.). Nov. 1916
France. Wounded Mar. 1917. Jan. 1918 France (2). Killed bet.
Apr. 19 and 22, 1918.

MILNER, C. E., M.C. (1904–7, *r*)

1915 Sec. Lt., A.S.C., Transport and Supply Column. Capt.,
R.A.S.C. M.C. June 1918.

MINDELSOHN, H. G. (1897–1902)

1917 Flt.-Sgt., R.F.C., M.T., Rep. Park, Leeds. 1918 R.A.F.

MINDELSOHN, M. L. (1914–17, *y*)

B.U.O.T.C. 1918 Cdt., R.A.F.

MITFORD, B. R., C.B., D.S.O. (1887–91)

Sept. 1914 Col., R. of O., Hon. Brig.-Gen. (late Staff) (Gent. at
Arms). Bde. Cdr., 72 Inf. Bde. 1917 Maj.-Gen.

MITTON, E. J. (1901–5, *y*)

July 1912 Lt., R.E., T.F., Southern Cable Sig. Coy. Nov. 1914
France. Army Signals, 1 Echelon, G.H.Q. Oct. 1915 Capt.
Mar. 1917–Nov. 1918 Lt., Actg. Maj., R.E. Three times mentd.
Capt. Nov. 1918 Spa.

†MITTON, T. E. (1911–16, *b*)

Feb. 1916 Sec. Lt., R.E., Sig. Mar. 1917 France, 1 Echelon,
G.H.Q. Sig. Coy. Accidentally killed on the railway, nr. Ypres,
Dec. 24, 1917.

MOLE, K. L. (1910–15, *y*)

June 1915 Sec. Lt., 4 R. War. R., S.R. France, attd. 2 Bn.
Wounded, Somme, 1916. 1917 France (2), attd. 1 Bn. Wounded
(2), Fampoux, Apr. 1917. France (3) Lt., attd. 2 Bn. 4 Bn. :
Apr. 1918 severely injured by bomb explosion. Secy., Officers'
course, B'ham. Jan. 1919 Retd. List.

MOORE, A. G. (1908–13, *g*)

1916 O.S., R.N.V.R. 1917 Wireless Telegraphist.

MOORE, B. HERBERT (1913, *g*)

W.T., R.N.V.R., attd. R.G.A. 1917 Wounded. Oct. 1918 Cdt.,
R.G.A., Maresfield.

†MOORE, C. F. (1907–14, *g*)

May 1914 Sec. Lt., 3 Worc. R., S.R. France (1) Wounded
Nov. 3, 1914. France (2). Killed Mar. 13, 1915, in an assault on
the German trenches to prevent them from reinforcing Neuve
Chapelle. Buried at Kemmel.

MOORE, E. D. (1906–9, *r*)

Aug. 1914 Sgt., 6 R. War. R., T.F. Mar. 1915 Sec. Lt., 1/6 Bn.
France. Mar. 1916 Actg. Lt. June 1916 Lt. July 1916 to Jan.
1919 Actg. Capt. Apr. 1917 Secd., Asst. Instr., 3 Corps Sch.
Nov. 1918–Jan. 1919 2/6 R. War. R.

MOORE, F. (1889–93)

1914 Tpr., Worc. Yeo., T.F.

†MOORE, G. W. B. (1912–15, *g*)

1915 Cdt., R.M.C., Sandhurst. Sec. Lt., 2 Lein. R., Ireland.
1918 Lt. France. Invalided home, London Hosp. France (2).
Killed at Ledeghem, Belgium, Oct. 14, 1918 ; buried in the Com-
munal Cemetery.

MOORE, H. C. (1914–17, *g*)

B.U.O.T.C.

MOORE, H. E. (1891–4)

1914 Pte., 16 Midd'x. R. (P. Sch.).

MOORE, R. D., M.C. (1881–2)
Sept. 1915, Capt., R.A.M.C., T.F., 2 S. Mid. Fd. Amb. 1917–1918 France. M.C. Feb. 1918.* 1918 Maj.

MORGAN, J. L. S. (1913–16, g)
1918 Pte., 4 Res. Bn., Devon. R., Co. Donegal.

MORGAN, J. S. R. (1908–10, g)
1916 Inns of Court O.T.C. Sec. Lt., R.F.C. Severely wounded in daylight air-raid over London, June 1917. Rel. Commn. June 1918.

MORLEY, A. P. (1912–17, y)
Oct. 1917 P.F.O., R.N.A.S., Kite Balloon Sectn., Sheerness. Sub-Lt. 1918 Brindisi. Lt., R.A.F. Mudros. Nov. 1918 Home for Aeroplane training. Lt. (A.).

MORLEY, E. G. (1901–5, g)
1915 Cpl., A.S.C., M.T. Sgt. C.-S.-M. Jan. 1917 Sec. Lt. July 1918 Lt. Dec. 1918 Actg. Capt., R.A.S.C. 2½ yrs. in Paris, in charge of 1 Heavy Repair Shops.

MORLEY, F. H. (1899–1903)
Lt., Baltic Wheat Exchange Corps. 1917 Inns of Court O.T.C. ; Sgt. Instr., Poison gas, till Apr. 1919.

†MORRISON, E. S. (1903–7, y)
Jan. 1917 Pte., Can. Inf. Sgt. France. Wounded and gassed, Ypres. Sec. Lt., R.F.C. Flt.-Lt. (Pilot), R.A.F. Killed in France July 1, 1918.

†MORRISON, J. W. (1904–6, y)
Sept. 1915 Sec. Lt., 17 R. War. R. France. Died of wounds 1916.

MORTON, H. C. V. (1906–8, g)
1917 Cdt., 1 Cav. Cdt. Sqn. Sec. Lt., 2 War. Yeo., T.F. May 1918 Lt.

MOTTERAM, H. P. (1876–84)
June 1916–1917 Lt., R.A.M.C. Salonica.

†MOULD, C. W. (1907–9, g)
Sept. 1914 Sec. Lt., 5 The King's (Shrops. L.I.). France. Killed in Flanders Sept. 25–6, 1915.

MOULD, Rev. D. H. S. (1905–9, y)
1916 C.F., 4th Cl., attd. North'n R. France. Wounded Aug. 1917. 3 Lond. Gen. Hosp., Wandsworth. 1918 Mesopotamia, 15 C.C.S., Egyptian E.F., Palestine. Dec. 1918 at Damascus.

MOULD, H. A. H. (1910–12, y)
1914 Pte., R.A.M.C., 52 Fd. Amb. Apr. 1915 Sec. Lt., 19 North'd Fus. France. 1916 Lt. Invalided home. 1918 attd. R.A.F. Aug. 1918 Sec. Lt. (O.), Hon. Lt. France (2). Wounded Aug. 1918. Sept. 1918 Lt., North'd Fus. and R.A.F.

MOULE, E. S. (1902–6, y)
1916 Sec. Lt., S. Afr. Sigs., H.Q. Mar. 1918 Sec. Lt., R.G.A., S.R.

MOUNTFORD, L. W. (1912–17, y)
1918 Pte., Inns of Court O.T.C. Nov. 1918 Pte., 12 Res. Bn., M.G.C.

MOUSLEY, N. K. (1910–14, b)
Nov. 1918 Paymaster Sub-Lt. R.N.V.R. Mar. 1919 H.M.S. Venus.

MUNCASTER, J. W., D.C.M. (1896–8)
1916 Sgt., 31 Can. Inf. France. D.C.M. 1917 Sec. Lt., Can. Forestry Corps. Retd. to Canada 1918.

†MURRAY-BROWNE, G. (1898–9)   Le-Cdr.
Dec. 1907 Lt., R.N. June 1913 H.M.S. Indefatigable. Killed in Battle of Jutland May 31, 1916.

MURSELL, H. T. (1881–2)
1915 Lt.-Col., A.D.M.S., Johannesburg.

NATHAN, L., M.M. (1899)
1915 Pte., 9 Lond. R. (Q. Victoria's Rif.). 1917 Sgt. France. M.M. 1917. Wounded and prisoner 1917.

NATHAN, R. (1898–9)
1917 Bmbr., R.G.A., 36 Coy., Renney By., nr. Plymouth.

P

NATTRASS, F. J. (1906, *r*)

Feb. 1915 Lt., R.A.M.C., T.F. Aug. 1915 Capt. Two years in France. (1) 1st N. Gen. Hosp. ; (2) 62 C.C.S. ; (3) attd. 2 S. Wales Bord., 29 Div. Wounded and prisoner, Apr. 11, 1918. Jan. 1919 repatriated. 1919 Orthopaedic Centre, Newcastle-on-Tyne.

NAYLOR, Rev. A. T. A., O.B.E. (1903–5, *y*)

Dec. 1914 C.F., 4th Cl. France. 1916 England. 1917 France (2), Guards' Base Dépôt, Havre. Mentd. in Disp. Dec. 1917. Dec. 1917–Jan. 1918 S.C.F. at Guards' Base, Havre, temp. 1st Cl. Mentd. (2) Dec. 1918. O.B.E. (Mil.) Jan. 1919.

NEAL, E. J. (1907–11, *y*)

1914 Pte., 14 R. War. R. 1915 2nd Cl. Air Mech., R.F.C. India. 1916 Sgt., R.F.C., 31 Sqn., Lahore.

NEEDHAM, F. W. (1913–16, *y*)

1918 O.S., R.N.V.R. Empd. in sound-ranging, nr. Lowestoft.

NEVILLE, R. W. D. (1903–8, *g*)

1916 Sec. Lt., 10 Leic. R. 1917 Lt. Sept. 1917 attd. Reg. Bn., France. Severely wounded, Somme, 1916. 1918 Rel. Commn.

NEWEY, F., O.B.E. (1903–11, *r*)

Nov. 1914–Apr. 1915 Dresser, Lady Paget's combined Serbian Relief Fund and St. John's Amb. Unit, Serbia. Cross of Serbian Red Cross, 1915. 1915 in England. 1916 21 Stationary Hosp., Salonica F. Aug. 1917 Capt., 84 Fd. Amb. Mentd. in Disp. Nov. 1918, Mar. 1919. O.B.E. (Mil.), Balkans, June 1919.

NEWTON, H. H. H. (1904–7, *r*)

Mar. 1915 R.F.C., Transport Sectn. 1916 France. 1917 home, for promotion, transport, 59 Sqn. Mar. 1918 transfd., Rif. Brig. Aug. 1918 7 O.C.B., Fermoy, Ireland. Mar. 1919 Sec. Lt., Worc. R. and demobd.

NICHOLL, F. M. (1894–5)

Joined the Forces in India: empd. in superintending manufacture of munitions at Oorgaum.

†NICHOLL, O. J. (1894–9)

July 1916 Pte., 7 Aust. Fd. Amb. 1917 France. April–June 1918 Arras, Messines. Seriously Injured. *Died Nov. 25, 192?, the result of war wounds, in Tasmania.*

†NICHOLS, T. L. (1905–11, *r*)

1914 Pte., 16 R. War. R. Aug. 1915 Sec. Lt., 17 Bn. France, 15 Bn. Wounded. France (2). Killed May 1917.

NICHOLS, W. H. (1894–9)

July 1917–Oct. 1918 France. C. Q.-M.-S., 76 Aux. M.T. (Steam and Petrol) Coy., R.A.S.C.

NICOLSON, J. H. M. (1909–12, *y*)

1917 Pte., A.S.C., Drafts B.S.P.D., Bath.

NOCK, H. C. (1914–15, *b*)

1917 O.S., W.R.B., R.N.V.R., Portsmouth. 1918 Cdt., 8 O.C.B., Lichfield.

NORMAN, C. R., M.C. (1899–1901)

Sept. 1914 Sec. Lt., Cornwall Fortress R.E., T.F., No. 2 Works Coy. Feb. 1715 Lt. Sept. 1916 transfd. 1/3 Wessex Field Coy., Wessex Div. Feb. 1917 France, 57 Div. June 1917, May 1918 Actg. Capt. Severely gassed, Armentières, July 29, 1917. June 1918 to N. Russia, Archangel, with 1 Exped. Force. Nov. 1918 Actg. Maj. M.C. Feb. 1919.* Croix de Guerre Oct. 1919.

NORTHWOOD, J. D. D'A. (1911–13, *b*)

Sept. 1914 Pte., 14 R. War. R. Nov. L.-Cpl., France. July 21, 1916 wounded (High Wood). Feb. 1917 Cdt., R.F.C., Oxford. Apr. 1917 Sec. Lt., Gen. List, R.F.C. Aug. 1917–Mar. 1918 France (2) (Pilot). Apr. 1918 Lt., R.A.F. (A.). Sept. 1918 Actg. Capt. (A.), London defences. Mentd. in Disp. Jan. 1919.

ODELL, F. B. (1897–8)

Pte., M.G.C. Prisoner at Cambrai, Nov. 30, 1917.

OLD, R. E. (1910–13, *r*)

Aug. 1914 joined up. Oct. 1915 Sec. Lt., 11 Devon. R. July 1916 France. Severely wounded Sept. 6, 1916. Ireland. 1918 Lt.

Unattd. List, Ind. Army; 52 Sikhs. May 1918 (ranking from July 1917) Lt. Apr. 1918, proceeded to India. 2/8 Pioneers. Apr. 1919 Persia. June 1919 Afghanistan. Capt.

OLDLAND, O. W. (1914, *b*)
Sept. 1917 P.F.O., R.N.A.S. Resigned Feb. 1918. Oct. 1918 'C', M.G.C., T.B., Rugeley.

OLLEY, J. B. (1911–13, *r*) 1914 Pte., 15 R. War. R.

ONIONS, G. G. (1896–1900)
1915 M.T., French Army. Mar. 1918 Lt., Gen. List, Equipt. Off., R.F.C., Sec. Lt., Actg. Lt., R.A.F.

†ONIONS, W. L. (1904–10, *g*)
1914 Pte., 14 R. War. R. France. Killed in Battle of Somme, July 22–3, 1916.

ORFORD, R. J. (1904, *g*) 1915 Pte., 14 R. War. R.

ORME, T. J., M.C. (1906–8, *g*)
Nov. 1914 Pte., 14 R. War. R. 1915 Cpl., 17 Bn. Sept. 1915 transfd. M.G.C. C.-S.-M., Grantham. Feb. 1917 Sec. Lt. July 1917 France. M.C. (Ypres, Sept. 1917),* Apr. 1918.

ORR, E. P. (1901–9, *r*)
Aug. 1914 Lt., 5 E. Surr. R., T.F. July 1915 Actg. Capt., 2/5 Bn. June 1916 Lt., 1/5 Bn. Mesopotamia. Invalided home. May 1918 Actg. Capt. July 1919 Capt., T.F. Res.

ORR, Rev. G. E. (1893–1902)
Two years in Aust. M.G.C. Apr. 1919 Sec. Lt., Unattd. List, T.F., Louth School O.T.C.

ORR, Rev. H. C. (1897–1907, *g*) Dec. 1915 C.F., 4th Cl., Malta.

†ORTON-SMITH, G. E. (1904–5, *y*)
1914 Cpl., 6 R. War. R., T.F. Oct. 1915 Sec. Lt. France. Repd. Missing, Mar. 31, 1917. Died of wounds in Germany.

ORWIN, J. M. (1899–1901)
1915 Sec. Lt., Hymers Coll. O.T.C.

Gnr., R.H.A., W.By. Meerut. July '917 Mesopt.

†OTTEY, R. G. (1902–5, *y*)

> 1915 Artists Rif. O.T.C. 1916 Sec. Lt., Leic. R., S.R. Attd. R.F.C. Missing 1917, presumed killed.

PAGE, H. A. (1902)

> 1917 Cdt., R.F.C., No. 1 Cdt. Wing, Hastings. Capt., R.A.F. (K.B.).

PAGETT, E. A. (1904–6, *b*)

> 1914–19 Cpl., City of Lond. Yeo. (Rough Riders), T.F. Salonica. Egyptian E.F.

PALMER, A. B. (1911–16, *r*)

> June 1917 B.U.O.T.C. May 1918 Cpl. Sept. 1918 Cdt., 5 O.C.B., Cambridge, attd. 5 Worc. R. Mar. 1919 Sec. Lt., R. War. R., S. Bn.

PALMER, W. A. (1906–7, *b*)

> 1914 Cpl., 14 R. War. R. Apr. 1915 Sec. Lt., 17 Bn. 16 Bn., France. Wounded July 1916. July 1917 Lt. Sept. 1917 transfd. 2/9 Glouc. R.

PARDOE, R. H. (1882–5)

> Mar. 1916 Sec. Lt., Unattd. List, T.F., Handsworth G.S. O.T.C. Jan. 1918 Lt.

†PARKER, C. W. H. (1905–14, *y*)

> Oct. 1914 Sec. Lt., 5 Res. Worc. R., S.R., attd. 1 Norf. R. France, 3 Bn., Worc. R. 1 battle of Ypres. Invalided home Dec. 1914. Feb. 1915 attd. W. Afr. Force for Cameroons. Torpedoed in the Falaba Mar. 17, 1915. Nine mths.' home service, 6 Bn. May 1915 Lt. Mar. 1916 France (2) No. 2, I.B.D. 2 Bn. Actg. Capt. Bazentin-le-Petit ; High Wood, July 1916. Secd. R.F.C., 5th Sqn., Obsr. Killed in flying accident Dec. 27, 1916.

PARKER, S. W. (1910–14, *y*)

> 1914 Pte., 14 R. War. R. France. 10 Corps Cycl. Bn. Mar. 1919 Sec. Lt., R. War. R., S. Bn. and demobd.

PARKES, L. F. (1900–2)

> Jan. 1916 Sec. Lt., Unattd. List, T.F., B.U.O.T.C. Dec. 1917 Lt.

PARR, N. (1904–9, *g*)

B.U.O.T.C.   Dec. 1914 Sec. Lt., 6 The King's (Shrops. L.I.). France 1916.   At Ypres and most of the Somme fighting.   Wintered on the Somme.   1917 followed up German retirement from the Somme.   Hindenburg Line.   Bullecourt.   Feb. 1917 Lt.   July 1917 Actg. Capt., Addl., attd. M.G.C.   Pilkem Ridge.   Early part of Passchendaele.   Severely wounded (twice in one day), N. of Langemarck, Sept. 23, 1917.   Sept. 1918 Discharged through ill health caused by wounds with rank of Capt.

PARRY, D. H. (1909–12, *y*)

July 1915 Sec. Lt., R.E., T.F., 3/1 East Anglian Div. Fd. Coy.   June 1916 Lt.   Mentd. (Egypt), June 1919.   Actg. Capt., till July 1919.

PARSEY, E. M. (1914–18, *y*)

1918 Gnr., R.M.A.

†PARSONS, B. F. (1905–8, *r*)

1914 Pte., 6 R. War. R., T.F.   1916 Sec. Lt., R.F.C.   Killed in flying accident, Charlton Park, Malmesbury, Jan. 22, 1917.

PARSONS, F. R. (1907–12, *r*)

1916 Sec. Lt., 10 Suff. R.   Sept. 1916 Lt., M.G.C.

PARSONS, T. H. (1899–1904, *r*)

1915 Lt., R.A.M.C., T.F., 2 S. Mid. Fd. Amb., Transport Off. 1917 Lt., A.S.C.   France.   Rel. Commn.

PARTON, W. H. (1910–14, *b*)

Tpr., Yeo., T.F.   Pte., M.G.C.   France.

†PARTRIDGE, A. J. (1905–6, *r*)

July 1915 Sec. Lt., 9 R. Berks. R.   Apr. 1916 France ; attd. 5 Bn. Missing, at Ovillers, in Battle of the Somme, July 3, 1916 (officially repd. killed, Mar. 1917).

PARTRIDGE, G. W. (1899–1902)

1917 2 Artists Rif.   Feb. 1918 Sec. Lt., 5 S. Staff. R., T.F. Serving under Air Ministry.

PARTRIDGE, Rev. J. W. (1901–9, *y*)

Nov. 1918 C.F., 4th Cl.   Egypt.

PARTRIDGE, T. H. (1900–3)
Dec. 1918 Lt., A.P.M., Black Watch (R. Highrs.). Egypt.

PARTRIDGE, Rev. W. W. (1894–1901)
1917 C.F., R.F.C. Oct. 1918 temp. C.F., 4th Cl.

PASCAL, E. (1913–17, *y*)
1917 Cdt., R.E., Newark. Mar. 1918 Sec. Lt. N. Wales. 1918
Cdt., R.A.F., Reading.

PATRICK, A. S. (1910–12, *b*)
Volunteer, 2 Prov. Br., B.C. 1914 R. Ir. Fus., Can. Cont. Pte.,
G. Gds. Cpl., 4th Bn.

†**PATTERSON, G.** (1901–7, *r*)
1912 Sec. Lt., R.E., T.F., 1 N. Mid. Fd. Coy. Nov. 1914 Lt.,
France. Killed Oct. 13, 1915, at Hohenzollern Redoubt, while
taking part in ' a gallant rush '.

PATTERSON, H. (1902–10, *g*)
Jan. 1915 Sec. Lt., R.E., T.F., 1 N. Mid. Fd. Coy. 1915 France.
Severely wounded 1915. June 1916 Lt. May 1918 Capt., Lab.
Corps.

PATTMAN, H. A. (1902–9, *y*)
Oct. 1914 Sec. Lt., 15 R. War. R. Nov. 1915 Lt., 17 Bn. May
1916 Lt., A.S.C., M.T. Ireland. 1918 R.A.S.C., Workshop Off.,
France.

†**PAYTON, R. S.** (1906–13, *r*)
1914 Sgt., 14 R. War. R. Dec. 1914 Sec. Lt., M.G. Off. Nov. 1915
Lt. France. Killed, while leading his machine guns into action,
Somme, July 22, 1916

PAYTON, W. H. (1904–11, *r*)
1916 Sec. Lt., Ind. Army R. of O., attd. 1 Gurkha Rif. 1917 Capt.
1918 attd. Khyber Rif. Jamrud. On Afghan frontier, Landi
Kotal fort.

PAYTON, W. N. (1902–8, *r*)
1914 Pte., Malay Fed. States Vol. Rif. 1918 Sgt.

†PEARSON, F. S. (1878–83)

Oct. 1914 Lt.-Col., A.S.C., T.F. Res. Transport and Supply Col., S. Mid. Div., H.Q. Died from riding accident, near Wareham, Dorset, Sept. 5, 1916.

†PEARSON, H. (1911–15, g)

1916 B.U.O.T.C. Sept. 1917 Sec. Lt., R.F.A. Nov. 1917 France. Died of wounds Oct. 1, 1918.

PEARSON, WILLIAM (1888–94)

Lt., R.E. Oct. 1916 to Mar. 1919 France. 181 Tunnelling Coy. 184 Tunnelling Coy. May 1918 empd. under Directorate of Requisitions and Hirings.

PEART, G. C., M.M. (1880–6)

Sept. 1914 Pte., 14 R. War. R. Nov. 1915 France. Aug. 1916 Lt., 2 K.O. Sco. Bord., Transport Offr. M.M., Nov. 1916. July 1917 invalided home. Apr. 1918 France (2), 6 K.O. Sco. Bord., 9 Div. Kemmel Hill, Meteren, Hoogenacker. Advance from Ypres, Ledeghem, Harlebeke, Lys to Germany; Wald on the Rhine till Apr. 1919. Mentd. July 1919.

PEATTIE, J. B. (1910–15, g)

1915 Pte., Gordon Highrs. 1916–17 7 Bn., France, 51 Div. Wounded (slightly). Cpl. Nov. 1916 at capture of Beaumont-Hamel. 1917 invalided home. Attd. Argyle and Suth'd Highrs., Cam'n Highrs., Sea. Highrs. 1918 Cdt., 24 O.C.B., Winchester, Tank Corps.

PECK, C. W. (1911–16, y)

1918 Wireless operator, Marconi Co. June–Aug. 1919 2 W.O., S.S. Llangorse, Mercht. Service.

PEMBERTON, R. T., D.S.O. (1881–5)

Feb. 1911, Sept. 1914 Capt., Adjt., A.S.C., T.F., H.Q., 1 N. Mid. Div. Train. Mentd. in Disp., D.S.O., 1916. June 1916 Maj.

†PEPPER, S. W. (1904–8, r)

1914 Pte., 14 R. War. R. June 1915 Sec. Lt., 8 Bn., T.F., M.G. Sectn. Dec. 1915 France, attd. a Gar. Bn. 2 mths. Lt.

Wounded, Serre, July 1, 1916. Apr. 1917 France (2). Actg. Capt., July 1917. Killed (repd. missing) Aug. 27, 1917. (Mortally wounded, died a few hours later.)

†PERKINS, C. H. (1911–13, *y*)

Nov. 1914 Cpl., 16 R. War. R. Sept. 1915 Sec. Lt., 13 York. R. May 1916 France, 15 York. R., Bombing Offr. Oct. 1916 Lt., 10 York. R., attd. 62 Inf. Bde., H.Q. : attd. 62 T.M.B. Feb. 1918 2 York. R., attd. 21 T.M.B. Mar.–May 1918 Actg. Capt., cdg. T.M.B. Died at Calais of wounds caused by aerial bomb, July 23, 1918. He was all through the Mametz Wood battle.

PERKINS, H. A. (1904–9, *y*)

1914 Pte., 14 R. War. R. Sgt. Secd. Min. of Mun.

PERKINS, W. H. (1908–15, *y*)

1917 Cdt., Wellington Coll., India. Torpedoed on the way to India. June 1917 Sec. Lt., Unattd. List, Ind. Army. Mesopot. E.F. June 1918 Lt.

PERRY-KEENE, A. L. A. (1912–14, *r*)

June 1917 Sec. Lt., R.F.C. (A.) R.A.F.

PETIT, Rev. O. S. (1884–90)

Aug. 1915–Dec. 1918 C.F., 4th Cl., 1 S. Gen. Hosp. Hon. C.F.

PHELPS, E. J. (1902–5, *b*)

1914 Pte., 14 R. War. R. 1916 L.-Cpl. 1917 Inns of Court O.T.C. Oct. 1917 Sec. Lt., R.F.C., Equipt. Off., 2nd Cl. Lt., R.A.F. July 1918 Actg. Capt. (T.).

PHILLIPS, A. A. (1906–9, *b*)

1914 Gnr., R.H.A., T.F., Warwickshire By. Bmbr.

PHILLIPS, E. B. (1903–5, *b*)

Tpr., Can. L.H.

PHILLIPS, J. S., M.C. (1908–12, *b*)

Sept. 1914 Sec. Lt., 9 S. Staff. R. (Pioneers). Lt. Mentd. 1917. Mar. 1917 Capt. France ; Italy. M.C. June 1918.

†PHILLIPS, R. H. (1911–14, *b*)

Dec. 1915 Sec. Lt., 13 R. War. R. 15 Bn., France. Killed Sept. 25, 1916.

PHILLIPS, W. J. (1912–16, *b*)

1917 Cdt., R.M.C., Sandhurst. Dec. 1917 Sec. Lt., 3 R. War. R. May 1918 secd. M.G.C. (Inf.). France. May 1919 Gen. Res., R. War. R.

PHILLP, A. B. (1887–90)

Dec. 1914 Farrier-Sgt., Aust. L.H. Up to autumn 1916 Egypt and Sinai Desert. Summer 1917 Capt., Eng. Sectn., Aust. Mtd. Div. (Railway, S. of Gaza). June 1918 Sec. Lt., R.E. June–Aug. 1918, mending bridges, making roads, &c., in Jordan Valley, and at Damascus and Aleppo. Sept. 1918 Staff-Capt., Aust. Eng., till June 1919. Twice Mentd., 1918, June 1919.

PHIPPS, F. N. (1907–11, *b*)

June 1915 Sec. Lt., 3/8 R. War. R., T.F. July 1916 Lt. 2/8 Bn. Dec. 1917 secd. M.G.C. M.G.C. (Motor) July 1918–Feb. 1919

PHIPPS, F. Reginald, O.B.E. (1889–92)

Jan.–May 1917 Capt., R.E., O.C. 311 Road Constn. Coy., France, on the Somme, near Bray. Oct. 1917 Actg. Maj. Till Feb. 1919 D. A. D. of Roads to 15 Army Corps. Nieuport, Hazebrouck, Armentières, Bailleul, Meteren, Lille.

PHIPSON, E. S., D.S.O. (1898–1902)

1911 Capt., Ind. Med. Service, Deputy Sanitary Commr., Burma. 1914, on mobilization, M.O., 1/6 Gurkha Rif., I.A. Nov. 1914 left India : 29 Ind. Inf. Bde., Suez Canal Def. Force. Jan.–Feb. 1915 operations near Kantara. May 1, 1915 Gallipoli, landed at Cape Helles : operations near Pink Farm, Gurkha Bluff, Bruce's Ravine, Fusilier Bluff, Chanak Bair, Hill 60, and Susak Kuyu. Mentd. (Dec. 1915) for Chanak Bair, and awarded D.S.O. Nov. 1915 Invalided to Egypt. Jan. 1916–Mar. 1917 Bacteriologist, No. 5 Ind. Gen. Hosp., Alexandria. Apr. 1917 Recalled to India : Asst. Health Offr., Bombay. Oct. 1918 Health Offr., Simla.

PICKERING, W. V. (1909–11, *y*)
1914 Pte., 14 R. War. R.

PICKMERE, J. R. (1895–9)
1914 Sgt., 14 R. War. R. Sept. 1915 Sec. Lt., R.E. July 1917 Lt.
Mentd. June 1918.

†PIPE, D. A. (1895–9)
1914 Pte., Lond. Scottish, T.F. 1915 Sec. Lt., 3 Arg. and Suth'd
Highrs. Nov. 1915 Lt., R.M.L.I. France : Vimy Ridge, Beau-
court, Somme. 1917 Capt. Killed Oct. 30, 1917.

PLATER, F. E. (1906–12, *b*)
1915 Tpr., 1/1 Worc. Yeo., T.F. Jan. 1916 D Sqn., E.E.F. Cpl.
In Palestine till June 1919.

POLLARD, B. (1912–15, *b*)
June 1918 Pte., R. War. R. Transfd. R. Berks. R.

POLLARD, S. (1908–12, *b*)
Aug.–Dec. 1916 Orderly, Red Cross Hosp. Jan. 1917 Gnr., R.F.A.
Aug. 1917 Cdt., No. 3 R.F.A. Cdt. Sch. Jan. 1918 Sec. Lt.,
R.F.A., 5a Res. Bde. June 1918 empd. under M.I.D. (location of
aircraft by sound). Aug.–Nov. 1918 France.

POLLITT, H. T. (1907–15, *r*)
1915 Cdt., R.M.A., Woolwich. June 1916 India. Cdt., I.A.,
Quetta. Feb. 1917 Sec. Lt., 2 Rajputs. 20 Deccan Horse. Mar.
1917 France. Nov. 30, 1917 Cambrai (Revelon Ridge). Mar. 1918
to May 1919 E.E.F. : Egypt, Syria, Palestine.

POLLOCK, N. C. (1893–5)
1915 Staff Driver, R.A.M.C., 1 S. Gen. Hosp. 1917 Sec. Lt.
R.A.S.C. Sept. 1918 Lt.

POLLOCK, WILLIAM (1903–8, *b*)
Aug. 1915 Sec. Lt., 14 S. Wales Bord. Aug. 1916 France, 12 Bn.
Loos district ; Somme ; German retreat. Wounded May 1917.
July 1917 Lt. France (2) Apr. 1918, 5 Bn., 19 Div. South, in

the Champagne. May 27, German attack in Reims district (21 days) ; Bethune district. Oct.-Nov. near Cambrai to between Mons and Maubeuge.

POOLER, W. R. H. (1909–17, *y*)

1917 Cdt., R.F.A., 3 O.C.S., Weedon. Jan. 1918 Sec. Lt., R.F.A. T.F., 1 S. Mid. Bde. Mar. 1918, France, S.A.A. Sectn., 4 D.A.C. Oct. 1918 Y/4 T.M.B. July 1919 Lt.

PORTER, B. A. (1896–7)

Dec. 1916 Sec. Lt., R.G.A., S.R. June 1918 Lt.

†POUNTNEY, P. (1906, *b*)

Oct. 1915 Sec. Lt., 11 Gordon Highrs. Secd. M.G.C. France. Wounded June 7, 1916. Lt. Killed June 7, 1917.

†POWELL, H. S., M.C. (1906–9, *y*)

1914 Pte., 14 R. War. R. L.-Cpl. July 1915 Sec. Lt., 3/6 R. War. R., T.F. Actg. Lt., Dec. 1915. 1916 Lt. 1/6 Bn., France. Bde. Bombing Off. Actg. Capt., cdg. C Coy., Sept. 1917. Wounded. Aug. 1917 returned to Bn. M.C. Mar. 1918.* Died of wounds (received prev. day), Oct. 5, 1917. (at Poelcapelle)

POWELL, H. W. (1895–8)

1916 R.N.A.S.

POWELL, T. D. (1904–8, *y*)

1914 Pte., 14 R. War. R. 1916 Cpl., 17 Bn. Aug. 1917 Sec. Lt., 6 Worc. R., S.R. Feb. 1919 Lt.

†POWER, B. C. (1909–12, *g*)

1914 Pte., R. War. R. France. Missing, presumed killed, on the Somme, July 21, 1916.

†POYNTING, A. (1895–8)

Aug. 1914 Sec. Lt., 1/6 R. War. R., T.F. France. Secd. Bde. M.G. Coy. Killed 1916.

PRATT, F. W. H. (1902–7, *r*)

1916 Pte., 2 S. Afr. Inf. Bde. With 5 S. Afr. Inf. in E. Africa. Invalided, Cape Town.

†PREEDY, L. J. (1912–13, *r*)

Pte., 28 Lond. R. (Artists Rif.). 1917 Sec. Lt., 1 R. War. R. Nov. 1917 France. Killed, nr. Feuchy, S. of R. Scarpe, Mar. 31, 1918, in attempting to bring in a wounded man.

†PRETIOUS, B. J. (1900)

Dec. 1915 enlisted in Australian E.F. Early summer 1916 France. Killed at Pozières, Aug. 26, 1916, while working a Lewis gun, in his first engagement.

PRICE, B. E. (1914, *b*)

1914 H.M. Training Ship Worcester. Jan. 1917 Mid., R.N.R. H.M.S. Amphitrite. Apr. 1917–1918 H.M.S. Southampton.

PRICE, G. H. (1912–15, *b*)

Sept. 1917 Air-Craftsman, 2 Cl., R.N.A.S. Mar. 1918 A.-C., 1 Cl. Home Service. Apr. 1918 R.A.F. Sept. 1918 on Meteorological duties.

PRICE, H. C. (1910–13, *b*)

1917 P.F.O., R.N.A.S. June 1918 Sec. Lt. (A.) R.A.F. France, 214 Sqn. (Handley Pages).

PRICE, T. SLATER, O.B.E. (1887–90)

Dec. 1917 Lt.-Cdr., R.N.V.R., R.N. Experimental Station, Stratford. From latter part of 1917 was in charge of the Research Laboratory and the Prussic Acid and Smoke Mixture Producing Plants. His work on chloro-sulphuric acid led to the production of the 'artificial fog' at Zeebrugge. During 1918 the Admiralty Chemical Representative on the Chemical Warfare Committee. O.B.E.

PRIEST, R. C. (1895–1901)

July 1912 Capt., R.A.M.C.

PRIEST, T. S. (19~~03–05~~, *g*)   1915 Sgt.

PRITCHETT, V. E. C. (1901–7, *r*)

Sept. 1914 Pte., 1/2 S. Mid. Fd. Amb., T.F., 48 Div. Mar. 1915 France. Invalided (France) Mar. 1916. Aug. 1916 2/2 S. Mid. Fd. Amb., T.F., 61 Div. Invalided Dec. 1918.

PROSSER, C. K. K. (1914–16, *y*)

Aug. 1916–Sept. 1917 Gnr., R.G.A., Spike Island. 1917 Cdt., 3 O.C.S. Oct. 1917–Apr. 1919 Sec. Lt., R.G.A., S.R. Nov. 1917–Jan. 1919 France, 99 Siege By. Lens, Arras, Neuve Chapelle. In the German attack of Apr. 9, 1918, the By. blew up or lost all its guns, suffering heavy casualties, one section being captured. Merville (Nieppe Forest). Aug. 1918 advanced through Calonne-sur-la-Lys and Lestrem over the Aubers Ridge to Lille, where they had a great reception : thence to Blandain, finishing up on R. Scheldt, just N. of Tournai. Wounded Apr. 9, 1918. Mentd. July 1919.

PROSSER, E. (1888–91)

July 1917 Gunner, R.G.A. : Coast Defence, Spike Island, Queens-town. June 1918–Dec. 1918 R.F.A., H.Q., 67 Div.

PROSSER, W. D. (1914–16, *y*)

1917 L.-Cpl., T.R. Bn. : 52 Devon. R. 1918 Cdt., 8 O.C.B., Lichfield. Sept. 1918 Sec. Lt., Dorset. R., S. Bn. France, attd. Wilts. R., 50 Div.

PRYCE, A. C. H. (1906–11, *y*)

1917 Leading Seaman, 63 R.N.D., Drake Bn. Aug. 1916 Sub-Lt., R.N.V.R. for 63 R.N.D.

PURSER, G. W. (1917–18, *b*)

Dec. 1918 Cdt., Ind. Army, R.M.C., Quetta.

RAMSDALE, A. E. (1874–5)   1916 Pte., R.A.M.C., Chelmsford.

RAVENHILL, E. L. B. (1894–1902)

Aug. 7, 1914–Feb. 1915, Lt., 5 W. Can. Cav., 1 Can. E.F. Mar.–Aug. 1915 Transport Off., 4 Cav. Bde., France. May 2–8 2 Battle of Ypres. Aug. 1, 1915 Capt. Aug. 15, 1915 Sec. Lt., 3 C. Gds., S.R. France (2). Sept. 27, 1915 Battle of Loos. Oct. 1915–May 1916 Transport Off. : Laventie, Loos, and Ypres sectors. May Invalided home. Nov. 1916–Jan. 1917 5 Res. Bn., C. Gds. Jan.–Nov. 1917 Transport Off., 1 Guards Bde. M.G. Coy.,

RASTON, BERTRAND (1913–14, *y*)
Sept. 1914 Pte., R.A.M.C. Nov. 1915 Sec. Lt., Midd'x R. France, Somme (July 1916), Ypres. Wd. Sept. 1916.

France (3) : St. Pierre Vaast, Sailly Saillisel, Le Transloy, Ypres sectors. July 31–Oct. 15 3 Battle of Ypres. Nov. 1, 1917– July 8, 1918 Home Service. July 8–Aug. 30 France (4) : 2 in cd. No. 8 Coy., 4 Guards M.G. Regt. Aug. 17 commencement of Great Advance ; storming of Moyenneville ; through the whole advance, particularly the crossing of Canal du Nord, capture of Flesquières Ridge, thence by way of Serenvillers, Wambaix, Boussières, St. Python, to Bavai : entered Maubeuge with Guards. Germany.

RAVENHILL, T. H., M.C. (1890–1900)

Sept. 1914 Lt., R.A.M.C., till Jan. 1915 M.O., 63 Bde. Feb.–June 1915 attd. Serbian Army, British Military Mission ; Nish, Kragugevatz, Belgrade. June 1915 Tigue Gen. Hosp., Malta. July– Aug. 1915 Gallipoli, attd. 11 C.C.S. Aug.–Sept. 1915 ' Clan MacGillivray ' Hosp. Ship, Suvla Bay. Sept., invalided. Oct. 1915–Mar. 1916, M.O., Mil. Hosp., Tidworth. Mar. 1916–Jan. 1918 France, 96 Fd. Amb., 30 Div. July 1916–Jan. 1918 O.C. Bearers. 1916 Battle of the Somme. Apr. 9–23, 1917 1 and 2 Battles of Arras. June 1917 Battle of Messines. July 31, 1917 3 Battle of Ypres. In sectors Maricourt (Somme) ; Givenchy ; Bailleulval ; Mercatel ; Heninel ; Zillebeke ; Wytschaete and Messines ; Passchendaele Ridge. Jan.–Nov. 1918 O.C. 22 Motor Amb. Convoy. Sept. 1915 Capt. Mentd. Order of St. Sava of Serbia, 5 Class, May 1916. M.C. June 1917 (Aug. 1917).*

RAWLINS, E. H. P., M S.M. (1904–8, r)

1914 Pte., R.A.M.C., 61 F.A. France, 20 Div., Sgt. Sept. 1918 transfd. H.Q., 3 Div. Q.-M.-S. M.S.M. June 1919. Army of Occupn., Cologne.

RAYNER, O. T. (1902–5, y) , M . B .E

Nov. 1915 Lt., Spec. List. May 1918 Capt. Gz.Lit.M . B .E. , Ci. Div.

RAYNER, W. E. (1900–2)   1914 Singapore Vol. Art.

READE, T. H. (1908–9, r)

Sept. 1914 Pte., 6 S. Staff. R., T.F. Feb. 1915 Sec. Lt., 11 R. War. R. July 1916 Lt. M.G.C.

REDFERN, C. F. (1889–91)

Aug. 1917 Sec. Lt., Tech. Off., Lab. Corps : France, 26 Lab
Ypres salient ; Passchendaele push (Aug.–Oct.), on roads, t
gun tracks, and defences.   Apr. 1918 empd. on engineerinɡ
on N. front : Godewaersveldte, Boeschepe, Berthen, Locre,
outre, Wytschaete, Kemmel, Messines, &c.

REDPATH, W. (1910, g)   1916 A.B., R.N.

RENNIE, Rev. W. H. M. (1902–4, r)

Sept. 1918 C.F., 4th Cl., attd. 13 Durh. L.I., 74 Bde.

RETALLACK, W. C., M.C. (1892–7)

Lt., 5 R. War. R., T.F.   Oct. 1914 Actg. Capt., 1/5 Bn.   Jaɪ
Capt. Mar. 1915, France.   May 1915 Adjt.   Mentd. Apr
June 1916 Actg. Maj.   Sept. 1916 Actg. Lt.-Col.   M.C. Jan
Wounded (1) July, (2) severely, Aug. 1917.   Chief Instr. De
Res. Commn. May 1919.

REVELY, L. P. (1907–13, g)   1915 Pte., 18 R. Fus.

REVELY, Rev. O. P. (1906–9, g)

Sept. 1918 Actg. Chaplain, R.N., H.M.S. Highflyer. Jaɪ
H.M.S. Vivid, for R.N. Barracks, Devonport.

RICHARDS, G. R. (1909–17, g)

1918 Cdt., R.M.A., Woolwich.   Jan. 1919 Sec. Lt., R.E., A
Occupn., Germany.

†RICHARDS, W. C. (1911–13, g)

1914 Pte., 6 S. Staff. R., T.F.   France.   Killed 1916.

†RICHARDSON, F. H. (1910–12, g)

7 Bn., 1st. Can. Cont. Mar. 1915 France. 1914 Pte., ~~in~~ Can. Inf.   Killed ~~1916~~ gas attack, Ypres, Apr

RICHARDSON, S. H. (1901–8, g)

1914 Sec. Lt., Cape Union Def. Force.   Dec. 1915 Sec. Lt.,]
Sept. 1918 Actg. Capt. S.R., 5a Res. Bde.   July 1917 Lt.   Ireland, Rebellion
and Adj., R.G.A. ~~Volunteered~~, Mountain By., India ; ~~transfd. R.G.A.~~   Rawal

RICHARDSON, S. O. B. (1900–6, y)

Feb. 1914 Sec. Lt., 1/8 R. War. R., T.F.   Dec. Actg. Lt.
Lt.   France.   Feb. 1916 Invalided.   June 1916 Capt.   191

2/5 K.O.S.B., The Curragh. Mar. 1919 Instructional Duties. Egypt. General Staff (Training), Zeitoun, E.E.F.

RICHARDSON, T. J. (1874)
Sept. 1907 Capt., Unattd. List, O.T.C. Oct. 1914. Empd., Dépôt, S. Staff. R. Mar. 1915 Maj., 2 in cd., 11 N. Staff. R. 1917 Rel. commn., empd. Min. of Pensions.

RICHARDSON, W. A. R. (1900–3)
1914 Pte., 14 R. War. R. June 1915 Sec. Lt., 7 Dorset. R. Nov. 1916 Lt., M.G.C.

RIDDELL, D. E., M.B.E. (1905–8, b)
Oct. 1914 Sec. Lt., 1/5 R. War. R., T.F. June 1915 Lt. France. June 1916 Capt. 1917 secd. Min. of Mun., 2 Asst. Supt., Research Lab., Ord. factory, Woolwich. M.B.E. (Mil.), June 1919.

RIDDELL, H. (1903–8, b)
1914 Cpl., R.E., D.R. Injured 1914. 1916 Sub-Lt., R.N.V.R.

RIDDELL, W. G. (1905–8, b)
June 1915 Sec. Lt., 3/5 R. War. R., T.F. Sept. 1915 Actg. Lt. June 1916 Lt. May–Dec. 1916 Actg. Capt. Feb. 1917 attd. 12 (Yeo.) Bn., Norf. R., Egyptian E.F. Nov. 1917–Oct. 1918 Adjt. Feb. 1917–Apr. 1918 Egypt and Palestine : 2 Battle of Gaza ; operations round Gaza previous to successful attack of Oct. 1917, resulting in capture of Gaza and Beersheba : the advance till after the capture of Jerusalem, Dec. 1917 ; end of Dec., N. of Jerusalem: occupation of line from the sea, 15 mls. N. of Jerusalem, Jiljilia–Sinjil–Turmus Aya, including fighting round Nebi Samwil, Beitunia, Ram Allah, Yebrud, Burt Bardawile, and astride the Nablus Road. May 1918–Jan. 1919 France and Flanders : re-capture of Bailleul, Ploegsteert Wood, the advance across the Lys to Courtrai : fighting round Ingoyghem and across the Scheldt just S. of Oudenarde. Dec. 1918 secd. Bde. Intell. Offr. Oct. 1919 Capt., T.F. Res.

RIGAL, G. (1903–5, r)
1915 Pte., 1 Kimberley R. Cpl. Wounded 1916. Nov. 1916 Sec. Lt., 1 S. Afr. Inf. May 1918 Lt.

R

RIGAL, I. (1903–5, *r*)
1915 Pte., 1 Kimberley R. Sgt.

ROBBINS, N. (1909–12, *y*)
1914 Pte., 14 R. War. R. May 1915 Sec. Lt., 2/5 Bn., T.F. France.
Sept. 1916 Res. Commn. Training volunteers, Fed. Malay States.

ROBERTS, A. B. P., M.C. (1904–10, *r*)
Aug. 1914 Sgt., 14 R. War. R. Oct., Sec. Lt., 16 Bn. France
Nov. 1915 to May 1916. Invalided home. May 1915 Lt. July
1916 France (2), attd. T.M.B. Wounded Oct. 1916. Attd.
Tank Corps. Nov. 1917 Capt., transfd. Gen. List, Staff Capt.
Cambrai. Oct. 1918 Staff Course, Cambridge. M.C. Jan. 1919.
Apr. 1919 H.Q., for Embarkation duties.

ROBERTS, A. C. (1908–15, *r*)
1915 Pte., 17 R. War. R. : 16 Bn. 18 mths. in France. Jan. 1918
invalided home.

ROBERTS, A. S., M.C. (1907–9, *r*)
Sept. 1914 Pte., 6 R. War. R., T.F. Jan. 1915 Cpl. Mar. France.
Aug. 1917 Sec. Lt. Nov. Italy. Apr. 1918 Lt. M.C. June 1918.
Actg. Capt. and Adjt. Mentd. June 1919.

ROBERTS, J. E. H., O.B.E. (1891–1900)
Aug. 1914 Lt., R.A.M.C., attd. 5 Gen. Hosp., France. Aug. 1915
Capt. Mentd. 1915. 1918 Actg. Maj. O.B.E. (Mil.) June 1919.

†ROBERTS, L. I. H. (1900–5, *b*)
1914 Lt., 56 Can. Inf. Sec. Lt., 12 R. War. R. France. Killed
Sept. 1916.

ROBERTS, S. Arthur (1893–1900)
1914 Sec. Lt., Calcutta Scott. R., India. Sept. 1917 Lt., R.A.,
1 King George's Own Sappers and Miners, Egyptian E.F. (Water-
engineer.) Mentd. Jan. 1919 (for Mar. to Sept. 1918). 1919
Taurus tunnel, Baghdad Railway.

ROBERTS, T. A. M. (1914–16, *r*)
1918 P.F.O., R.N.A.S. Cdt., R.A.F.

ROBERTSON, J. K. A., M.C. (1911–15, *b*)
1915 Cdt., R.M.C., Sandhurst (senior Sgt.). 1916 Sec. Lt., 8 R. Highrs. (Black Watch). Apr. 1917 France. Oct. 1917 Lt., Actg. Adjt. M.C. Dec. 1917.* Wounded (1) Oct. 1917, (2) Apr. 1918.

ROBINSON, G. E. (1897–1900)
June 1915 Sec. Lt., R.F.A., 179 Bde. Sept. 1916 Actg. Capt. July 1917 Lt.

ROBINSON, P. E. (1903–12, *g*)
Nov. 1912 Sec. Lt., 5 R. War. R., T.F. Oct. 1914 Lt., 1/5 Bn. France with 2/5 Bn. Invalided home. Res. Commn. 1916.

ROBINSON, S. H., M.C. (1905–8, *y*)
Sept. 1914 Lt., R.F.A., T.F., 1/3 S. Mid. Bde. France. Mentd. 1915. M.C. Jan. 1916. 1917 Capt. Res. Commn. Dec. 1917.

ROBOTHAM, C. (1909–13, *y*)
Air Mech., R.N.A.S.

RODD, J. H. (1907–8, *y*)
1914 Pte., R. Fus. (P. Sch.). Apr. 1915 Sec. Lt., 4 R. Dub. Fus.

ROE, J. F. (1888–97)
Dec. 1915 Sec. Lt., Camel Transport Corps, Egypt. Jan. 1916– Mar. 1919 with the Corps, up to Jaffa. Dec. 1916 Lt. Mentd. Jan. 1918.

ROGERS, F. H., M.C. (1901–3)
Nov. 1915 Sec. Lt., R.E. Sept. 1916 Lt. France. Dec. 1917 Actg. Capt., 255 Tunnelling Coy. M.C. Jan. 1919.

†ROGERS, P. A. (1901–3)
1914 Botha's Force, Armoured train, German S.W. Afr. S. Afr. M.G. Bde., France. Sept. 1917 Sec. Lt., R.E. Killed May 27, 1918.

ROGERS, S. E. (1901–4, *y*)

1914 Lt., Rand L.I., Botha's Force. Jan. 1916 German S.W. Afr. Nov. 1914 Lt., 3 S. Afr. Inf. July 1916 Capt., 2 Bn. France. Severely wounded (1) Gauche Wood. Nov. 1917 France (2). Wounded (2) and Prisoner, Mar. 22, 1918, after 28 hrs.' engagement. Returned home Sept. 1918.

†ROLASON, L. N. (1901–5, *y*)

Sept. 1914 Tpr., 1/3 Co. of Lond. Yeo., T.F. Yeomanry charge at Suvla Bay. Wounded (1) 1915. 1917 Cdt., Bristol. Mar. 1917 Sec. Lt., 2/9 Lond. R., T.F. (Queen Victoria's Rif.). France. Wounded (2) May 27, 1917. Killed Sept. 26, 1917.

ROOKER, T. G. (1908–13, *y*)

Oct. 1914 Pte., R.A.M.C. (2 years). End of 1916 transfd. A.S.C. 1 Cl. Mech., Tank Corps. Mar. 1917 Cpl., France. Ypres, Cambrai, Bourlon Wood, Flesquières, Gouzeaucourt. Wounded at Roisel, Mar. 21, 1918. Invalided home. Cdt., Winchester.

ROSE, N. F., M.B.E. (1908–10, *b*)

1914 Pte., 14 R. War. R. Cpl. 1916 Sec. Lt., 10 R. War. R. France. Wounded July 1916. Lt., Aug. 1916. Attd. M.G.C. Oct. 1918 Actg. Capt., empd. Min. of Mun. M.B.E. (Mil.) June 1919.

†ROSE, R. V. (1911–13, *y*)

1914 Pte., 1/6 R. War. R., T.F. L.-Cpl. France. 1916 Cdt., G.H.Q., France. Sec. Lt., 1/6 R. War. R., T.F. Killed July 2, 1916.

ROSENBERG, C. M. (1906–11, *b*)

Jan. 1916 Sec. Lt., 3/6 S. Staff. R., T.F. June 1916 Lt., 9 Bn. France.

ROSENBERG, H. W. (1906–12, *b*)

1916 D.R., R.F.C. 1917 2 Cl. Air Mech., R.F.C., 78 Sqn., Hornchurch, Essex.

ROUND, A. J., M.C. (1912–13, *y*)

B.U.O.T.C. July 1915 Sec. Lt., 9 S. Wales Bord. July 1917 Lt. Salonica F. (18 mths.) 10 mths. Bde. Bombing Off. Cdg. a Coy. Wounded Sept. 18, 1918 (left front attack, Lake Doiran front). M.C. Jan. 1919.* Croix de Guerre, with palm, May 1919.

ROWE, C. F. (1880–1)

1914–15 Chief Supply and Transport Off., Nigeria E.F., N. Cameroons, W. Afr. Capt. Mentd.

ROWNEY, L. C. (1910–14, *b*)

1915 Pte., A.S.C., 19 Divl. Train. Gallipoli. Sec. Lt., 3 Midd'x R. Salonica F. Invalided home. Oct. 1917 Lt. 1918 attd. Sec. Lt., Hon. Lt. (A.), R.A.F. France. Brought down 8 German machines, and was 3 times brought down himself.

ROWSE, R. Anthony (1877–9)

1914 Maj., R.F.A., T.F., 3 S. Mid. Bde. Mentd. 1916. 1917 Lt.-Col.

RUSBY, R. H., D.F.C. (1910–13, *g*)

Aug. 1914 Sec. Lt., 4 (City of Bristol) Bn., Glouc. R., T.F. Dec. 1914 Actg. Lt. Lt., 2/4 Bn. France. Wounded (1) 1916. Apr. 1917 Capt. Attd. R.F.C. Wounded (2) Jan. 1918. Flt.-Cdr., Mar. 1918. Capt., R.A.F. D.F.C. July 1918.

ST. JOHNSTON, J. H., M.C. (1910–17, *r*)

1917 Cdt., R.E., Newark. Feb. 1918 Sec. Lt., R.E., 98 Fd. Coy. July 1918 France. Harpies Brook. M.C. Mar. 1919.* Army of the Rhine. Aug. 1919 Lt.

†SALAMAN, L. H. (1893–1901)

1914 A.B., R.N.V.R. Hawke Bn., R.N.D. Died of wounds in Gallipoli, June 19, 1915.

SALT, W. E. S. (1913–18, *y*)

1918 Pte., 36 Tr. Res. Bn.

SAMBIDGE, G. C. (1898–1902)

Nov. 1914 Sec. Lt., 4 R. War. R., S.R. Jan. 1915 Lt. Mar. 1915 Capt., attd. 1 Nigeria Regt., W. Afr. Frontier F. Torpedoed in S.S. Falaba. Cameroons. Nigeria.

SAMPSON, H. H., O.B.E., M.C. (1900–3)
Mar. 1916 Capt., R.A.M.C. France. M.C. 1916. Jan. 1918
Actg. Maj. 19 C.C.S. O.B.E. (Mil.) June 1919.

SAMSON, G. W. (1885–93)
Dec. 1916 Sec. Lt., R.G.A., S.R. Hong-Kong. May 1918 Lt.

SANBY, L. O. (1903–6, g)
1914 Pte., 15 R. War. R.

†SANBY, W. W. (1909–11, g)
1914 Pte., 14 R. War. R. Apr. 1915 Sec. Lt., 20 North'd Fus.
Jan. 1916 France. Killed July 1, 1916.

†SANDERS, G. E. (1910–12, b)
Sept. 1915 Sec. Lt., 17 R. War. R. France. Lt., 15 Bn. Actg.
Capt. Missing, presumed killed, Oct. 9, 1917.

SANDERS, H. J., D.S.O., M.C. (1903–5, y)
1914 Pte., 14 R. War. R. Sept. 1915 Sec. Lt. (3/24) 1/24 Lond.
R., T.F. France. May 1916–Apr. 1917 Actg. Lt. M.C. Nov.
1916.* July 1917 Lt. Oct. 1917, Apr. 1918 Actg. Capt. Mentd.
D.S.O. Feb. 1919.* Actg. Maj. while 2 in cd., Jan–Feb. 1919.

†SANDERS, T. F. P. (1905–9, b)
1914 Pte., 14 R. War. R. France. Died of wounds Apr. 20, 1916.

SANDERS, V. G. (1909–12, b)
1914 Pte., 14 R. War. R. Sec. Lt., Tank Corps. France, 16 Coy.,
6 Bn., 3 Army troops. May 1918 Lt. Oct. 1918–Jan. 1919
Actg. Capt., cdg. Sectn.

SANDS, A. L. (1909–13, g)
1917 Cdt., No. 2 O.C.S., R.G.A., Uckfield. Feb. 1918 Sec. Lt.,
R.G.A., S.R., 509 Siege By. Sept. 1918 France, 514 Siege By.
(12 in.). Arras to Cambrai. Düren, W. of Cologne, Germany.

SANDS, H. H. A. (1907–15, g)
1915 Sec. Lt., 3 R. War. R., S.R. Attd. 2 Bn., France. Accidentally
injured, June 6, 1916. Jan. 1917 Lt. Nov. 1917 Actg. Capt.,
51 Grad. Bn. Bde. Bombing Off.

†SANDS, L. K. (1903–11, *g*)

Sept. 1914 Sec. Lt., 10 Lan. Fus.   Feb. 1915 Lt.   July 1915 France.   Actg. Capt., Bn. Bombing Officer.   Sanctuary Wood. Died of machine-gun wounds (recd. the previous day) Apr. 28, 1916.

SANGER, A. J. (1913–15, *y*)

1917 Air Mech., R.F.C., Retford.

SANGER, O. L. (1913–16, *y*)

1917 L.-Cpl., 252 Inf. Bn., Colchester.   Cpl.   1918 Cdt., 14 O.C.B., Catterick.   Sept. 1918 Sec. Lt., R. Suss. R.   Nov. 1918 attd. 8 R. Ir. R., 25 Div., France.

SANGER, W. (1907–10, *y*)

1915 Tpr., Cullman's Horse, S. Afr. 2 Rhodesian Horse. Garrison of S.W. Africa : E. Africa.   Asst. Inspr. of Area, E. Africa.

SANGSTER, C. B. (1912–14, *r*)

1915 L.-Cpl., 17 R. War. R.   Cpl.   Transfd. M.G.C.

SANKEY, W. V. (1890–3)

1915 Pte., 16 Queen's West. Rif. (Lond. R.), T.F.   1916 Sec. Lt., 3 Ches. R.

SANTO, V. G. (1897–9)

Nov. 1916 Sec. Lt., R.E.   May 1918 Lt.

SAPCOTE, T. M. (1912–18, *r*)

1918 O.T., R.N.V.R., Aberdeen.   Tel.

SARSONS, A. W. (1894–8)

1917 Eng.-Lt., R.N.V.R.   Attd. R.N.A.S.   Apr. 1918 Capt. (T.), R.A.F.

SARSONS, H. B. (1901–5, *r*)

1914 Tpr., War. Yeo., T.F.   Sec. Lt., 1 War Yeo.   July 1917 Lt. Apr. 1918 secd. M.G.C. (Inf.).

SATCHELL, E. P. (1874–6)

Apr. 1915 Lt., R.A.M.C.   Apr. 1916 Capt.

SAUNDBY, R. H. M. S., M.C., A.F.C. (1910–14, *y*)
June 1914 Sec. Lt., 5 R. War. R., T.F. Invalided. 1915 attd.
R.F.C. Lt. June 1916 Capt. Flying Officer, France, 24 Sqn.,
14 Wing, 4 Army. Slightly wounded 1916. England, Apr. 1917.
Feb. 1917 Flt.-Cdr.: Experimental Stations, Orfordness. Brought
down Zeppelin 48, near Saxmundham, July 2, 1917: M.C.*
41 Sqn., Scampton. July 1918 Sqn.-Cdr. A.F.C. Jan. 1919.
38 T.D.S., Tadcaster. ' Flying Colours ', published Dec. 1918.
Oct. 1919 Flt.-Lt. (permanent commn.) (A.).

†SAUNDBY, W. S. F. (1912–15, *y*)
1915 Cdt., R.M.C., Sandhurst. 1916 Sec. Lt., York R., attd.
R.F.C. France. Missing, now presumed to have been killed,
Nov. 17, 1917.

SAUNDERS, A. H. (1903–8, *b*)
Jan. 1916 Instr. Lt., R.N., H.M.S. Monarch. 1918 R.N. Coll.,
Dartmouth.

SAUNDERS, B. R., M.C. (1907–10, *b*)
Aug. 1914 Pte., 6 R. War. R., T.F. Oct. 1914 Sec. Lt., 2/6 R.
War. R., T.F. July 1915 Actg. Lt. May 1916 France. Dec. 1917
Lt. Actg. Capt., Sig. Sectn. Wounded Sept. 1917. M.C. Oct.
1917.* Actg. Capt., Dec. 1917–Feb. 1918.

SAUNDERS, F. B. (1902–8, *b*)
Aug. 1914 Sec. Lt., 9 R. Scots R., T.F. Jan. 1915 Lt., O.C.
Lothian Inf. Bde. Sig. Sectn. 1915 Instr., Scottish Command
Sig. Sch. 1916 attd. 65 Lowland Div., R.E., T.F. 1918 Off. in
charge of Sig., G.H.Q., N. Dist., Ireland. Jan. 1919 Army of the
Rhine.

SAWYER, A. W. (1914–16, *r*)
1917 Inns of Court O.T.C. 1918 Sec. Lt. (A.), R.A.F.

SAYER, A. H., M.C. and bar (1900–7, *b*)
1914 Pte., 14 R. War. R. Jan. 1915 Sec. Lt., 16 R. War. R.
Nov. 1915 France, 15 Bde., 5 Div. Dec. 1915 Lt. Nov. 1915–

Feb. 1916 Mametz. Feb. 1916 Arras : July, Longueval : Sept., capture of Falfemont Farm and Morval. July 1916 Capt. Oct. 1916–Mar. 1917 Sector round Neuve Chapelle and Festubert. Apr. 1917 Vimy Ridge : round La Coulotte : before Arleux. May 1917 Adjt. June, capture of Oppy Wood and trenches ; holding these trenches till Sept. : 3 Battle of Ypres ; attack on Polderhoek Chateau : to Nov., before Gheluvelt, N. of Menin Road. Nov. 1917 to Mar. 1918 Italy ; Piave, S. of Montello. Apr. 1918 back to France : Aire : Nieppe Forest. Aug. 21 The Great Advance : Bucquoy and Achiet-le-Petit : wounded Aug. 21, 1918. Oct. 1918 Senior Offrs'. Course, Aldershot. M.C. Jan. 1918 ; bar to M.C. June 1919.

†SAYER, L., M.C. and bar (1908–10, b)
1914 Pte., 14 R. War. R. Jan. 1915 Sec. Lt., 16 R. War. R. Lt. Nov. 1915 France. Was in all the actions with the Bn. (see A. H. Sayer above). Wounded in attack on Morval, Sept. 27, 1916. Rejoined in Italy 4 months later. Mar. 1917 Actg. Capt. M.C. (for work in attack on Morval), Jan. 1917. 1917 Capt. Killed Aug. 23, 1918, obtaining bar to M.C. (Dec. 1918) * for his work, Aug. 21–3 at Bucquoy and Achiet-le-Petit.

†SCORER, W. H. (1901–3)
1914 B.U.O.T.C. June 1915 Sec. Lt., 8 Wilts. R. Sept. 1915 Dardanelles. Suvla Bay. Dec. 1915 Invalided home. July 1917 7 Wilts. R., Salonica F., Patrol work. Actg. Capt. July 1918 Overland to France, 2 in cd. of Coy. Wounded, Le Catelet. *Peronne* Died of wounds, Oct. 1918. Mentd. July 1919.

SCOTT, E. S. (1912–14, b)
1915 Pte., 3/12 Lond. R. (The Rangers), T.F.

SCOTT, G. J. (1913–17, b)
1917 Cdt., R.N. Sept. 1917 Mid., H.M.S. King George V.

SCOTT, G. N. (1902–3)
1916 Sec. Lt., 5 N. Staff. R., T.F. Feb. 1917 Lt., R.E., T.F. 1918 Empd. Min. of Lab.

SCHWABEN , C.W. (1902)
Pte., 13 Lond. R . Died on active service in Alexandria Dec. 23,'917.

SEARLS, T. H., M.C. (1901–7, *g*)
1914–Apr. 1915 Pte., R.A.M.C. May 1915 Univ. of Lond. O.T.C.
May 1915 Sec. Lt., 11, attd. 2 S. Staff. R. France, 7 Div. Wounded
(1) Bully Grenay, Mar. 1916 ; (2) Vimy Ridge, May 29, 1916 ;
(3) Le Sars, Sept. 1916 ; (4) Oppy, Apr. 1917 ; (5) Italy, June
1918. Jan. 1916 Lt. M.C. June 1918.* Dec. 1918 Instr., Educ.
Scheme, Newcastle-on-Tyne.

SECCOMBE, L. H. (1892–3)
Lt. (T.), R.A.F. 1918 Capt., R.A.F., Air Ministry. Aug. 1918
Lt., Actg. Capt. (Admin.).

†SECKER, F. T. (1909–10, *y*)
1916 Pte., 26 R. Fus. (Bankers' Bn.). Killed June 7, 1917.

†SEERS, G. O. (1893–1902)
1914 Pte., 23 Lond. R., T.F. France. Killed, Givenchy, May 25,
1915.

SHAKESPEARE, C. (1910–11, *g*)
1914 Pte., 14 R. War. R.

SHARP, W. H. C. (1895–1902)
1918 Pte., Inns of Court O.T.C.

SHAW, E. L. (1906–10, *r*)
1915 2 Artists Rif. O.T.C. Sept. 1916 Sec. Lt., S. Staff. R.
Dec. 1916 France, 7 Bn. Apr. 1917 transfd. R.F.C. July 1917
Sec. Lt. (O.). Ap. 1918 Lt. (O.), R.A.F.

SHAW, G. S. (1909–16, *r*)
1916 B.U.O.T.C. 1917 P.F.O., R.N.A.S., Vendôme. Flt. Sub-Lt.
R.N.A.S. ; Submarine patrol, Plymouth. 1918 France. Lt. (A.
and S.), R.A.F.

†SHAW, H. LYNN (1884–6)
1914 Capt., T.R. of O., 5 R. War. R., T.F. Sept. 1914 Capt., 10
R. War. R. 1916 Maj. Killed July 3, 1916.

SHAW, J. A. (1910–13, *r*)

Oct. 1916 Pte., 9 R. War. R. Early 1917 India : Mesopot. Exp. Force. 1919 Sgt., H.Q., 36 Indian Bde., Kasvin, Persia.

†SHAW, RALPH, D.S.O. (1909–15, *r*)

July 1915 Sec. Lt., 3 R. War. R., S.R. 1916 11 Bn., France. Actg. Lt. Mentd. D.S.O. (for action at Greenland Hill, Apr. 23, 1917)* June 1917. Lt., gazetted June 1917. Wounded and missing, afterwards found to have been killed, Apr. 28, 1917.

†SHEFFIELD, H. W. (1909–15, *y*)

1915–Apr. 1916 Cdt., R.M.C., Sandhurst. Sec. Lt., 1 E. York. R. June 15, 1916 France (1) : near Albert, in action July 3 (third day). After refitting, in action at Mametz Wood (meeting 2 R. War. R. before the battle), wounded (1). Apr. 1917 France (2) : wounded (2), May, at Fontaine-le-Croisille. Invalided home. Dec. 1917 France (3). Mar. 1918 (Oct. 1917) Lt., 2 in cd. of his Coy. In the German attack of Mar. 21 he was in charge of 2 platoons : while kneeling on the parapet, encouraging his men, he was killed, Mar. 23, 1918, near Epéhy.

SHEPPARD, C. P. (1905–9, *g*)

1916 Sub-Lt., R.N.V.R. France. Attd. R.N.A.S. Flt. Sub-Lt., Dover, Seaplanes. 1918 Lt., R.A.F. (S.). Lt., R.N.V.R., Motor Boat Service, Southampton, M.L. 358. Feb. 1919 Motor Boats on Rhine.

SHEPPARD, M. L. (1911–15, *y*)

July 1918 Sub-Lt., R.N.V.R. Destroyer.

SHEPPARD, R. ST. J. (1917–18, *y*)

Apr. 1918 P.F.O., R.N.A.S. R.A.F. Vendôme. Injured in aeroplane accident.

SHIRLAW, COLIN (1905–9, *y*)

1914 Driv.-Mech., A.S.C. M.T. 1915 L.-Cpl. July 1917 Sec. Lt., A.S.C.

SHIRLAW, GILBERT R. (1902–6, *y*)

1914 Lt., A.S.C., M.T., Aust. Cont., 9 Aust. A.S.C., M.T. Jan. 1917 Maj., 1 Aust. Div. Suppl. Col. France.

SHIMWELL, A. G. (1912–14, *g*)

S.A.M.T. South Africa.

SHIRLAW, GODFREY (1904–7, *y*)
1917 Pte., A.S.C., M.T., 65 Motor Air Line Signals, Salonica F.

SHORTT, I. (1906–8, *r*)
1918 Pte., A.S.C., M.T., attd. 17 Siege By., R.G.A., France.

SIDDAWAY, K. G. (1909–16, *g*)
1917 attd. R.F.C. Nov. 1917 Sec. Lt. (Fl. Off.), R.F.C. Lt., R.A.F.

†SILK, E. G. (1895–1900)
Aug. 1914 Pte., 14 R. War. R. France. Killed, at Ytres, Sept. 20, 1918.

SILVERSTON, CLIVE J. (1895–1901)
1917 2 Cl. Air Mech., R.F.C. Sec. Lt., R.F.C., 21 Sqn., France. Apr. 1917 Lt., Equipt. Off., 3 Cl. 1918 Sec. Lt., Hon. Lt. (T.), R.A.F.

SILVERSTON, CYRIL J. (1890–6)
Dec. 1915 Rfn., 2/16 Co. of Lond. R. (Q. West. Rif.). Mar. 1916 Pioneer, R.E. Apr. 1916–May 1917 France. Aug. 1917 Cdt., R.G.A., 2 O.C.S. Feb. 1918 Sec. Lt., R.G.A., S.R.

SIMPKIN, C. (1915–16, *b*)
June 1918 R.N.V.R.

SIMPSON, C. (1891)
A.B., R.N.V.R. Nov. 9, 1915 to Feb. 12, 1919 H.M.Ships King Alfred (battleship), Orwell (Destroyer), Princess and Macedonia (armed liners). North Sea; patrol Plymouth–Holyhead; Convoys India, Africa, S. America; bombarding, German E. Africa, and capture of Dar-es-Salaam. Good Conduct Badge, 3 yrs.' service.

SKIRROW, G. H. (1905–7, *b*)
1914 Sgt., 5 R. War. R., T.F. Feb. 1915 Sec. Lt., 1/5 R. War. R., T.F., attd. R.F.C. Salonica F.

SLIM, W. J., M.C. (1909–10, *b*)
Aug. 1914 Sec. Lt., 9 R. War. R. Feb. 1915 Lt., 12 Res. Bn. Wounded (1) 1915. Oct. 1915 Lt., W.I.R. Temp. Capt., 9 Bn.

Gallipoli.

Sept. 1915

Mespot Wounded (2) Apr. 1917. G.S.O.₃, H.Q. Staff of the Army in India. M.C.

†SMART, E. D. (1903–9, *b*)
Oct. 1914 Pte., 14 R. War. R. L.-Cpl. Summer 1916 Sec. Lt., 10 Bn. Missing at the capture of Grandcourt, presumed killed, Nov. 18, 1916.

SMITH, ARTHUR (1906–8 *g*)
Pte., 2/2 S. Mid. F.A. 1917 France.

SMITH, A. E. (1897–1903)
1914 R.E. Jan. 1915 Sec. Lt., 9 S. Staff. R. (Pioneer Bn.). Aug. 1915 France. Wounded at Martinpuich (Somme) Sept. 25, 1916. Apr. 1917 Lt., R.E. Oct. 1917 till Armistice, Q Spec. Coy., R.E. Nov. 1918 lent to Impl. War Graves Commn., Doullens.

†SMITH, A. P. (1902–9, *r*)
Oct. 1914 Lt., R.A.M.C., 32 Fd. Amb., 10 Div. France. Apr. 1915 Capt. Missing, presumed killed, 1915, in Gallipoli.

SMITH, C. S. (1906–10, *g*)
Nov. 1914 Sec. Lt., R.E. T.F., 1 N. Mid. Div. Sig. Coy. France. June 1916 Lt. Jan. 1917 Actg. Capt.

SMITH, E. W. (1903–5, *r*)
5 R. War. R., T.F. Jan. 1918 Sec. Lt., 16 R. War. R. 1919 Army of Occupation, Germany.

†SMITH, GEOFFREY BACHE (1905–13, *g*)
Dec. 1914 Sec. Lt., 8 Oxf. and Bucks. L.I. Sec. Lt., 19 Lan. Fus. June 1915 Lt. France. Died of wounds (received 3 days earlier), at Warlencourt, Dec. 3, 1916.

†SMITH, G. BARKER (1893–8)
Pte., 26 R. Fus. Died of wounds at Étaples, Oct. 12, 1916.

†SMITH, G. M. (1910–14, *g*)
Pte., 13 Worc. R., Blandford. Aug. 1916 Sec. Lt. 10 Leic. R. France. Battle of the Somme. Slightly wounded (1). Intelli-

gence Officer. Died of wounds (recd. prev. day), Oct. 6, 1917.
Buried at Godewarsvelde, near Hazebrouck.

SMITH, IRVING W. (1896–1900)
1917 Pte., A.S.C. Sgt., Hy. Arty. M.T., H.Q., A.S.C., M.T.,
Bulford Camp.

SMITH, J. H. (1911–16, *g*)
Pte., 4 R. War. R. 1917 L.-Cpl., attd. 262 Inf. Bn., Lewis Gun
Sectn. Sec. Lt., 4 York. and Lanc. R. Lt., R.A.F., 61 Sqn., Roch-
ford, Essex (London Defences).

SMITH, L. ARTHUR (1893–7)
1917 Pte., A.S.C., M.T. Mar. 1918 729 M.T. Coy., Mesopot. E.F.
1918 Cdt., O.C.B., India. Mar. 1918 to Mar. 1919 Sec. Lt., 1 R.
Suss. R.

†SMITH, ROGER (1903–7, *r*)
1914 Pte., A.S.C. 1915 L.-Cpl. 10 days in France. Sept. 1915
Sec. Lt., 9 S. Wales Bord., attd. R. W. Fus. Mesopot. E.F.
Killed Jan. 25, 1917.

SMITH, STANLEY, O.B.E. (1898–1901)
June 1913 Capt., A.S.C., T.F., 1 N. Mid. Div. Mar. 1915
France, O.C. 4 Coy., 46 Div. Apr. 1919 O.C. 50 Divl. R.A.S.C.
O.B.E. (Mil.) June 1919.

SMITH, T. G. (1897–9)
1914 Tpr., War. Yeo.

SMITHIES, I. E. (1909–10, 1912–13, *y*)
1917 R.N.A.S.

SMOUT, A. J. G. (1902–4, *g*)
1915–16 C. S.-M., B.U.O.T.C.

SMOUT, C. F. V. (1908–11, *b*)
Sept. 1914 to Dec. 1918 L.-Cpl., R.A.M.C., T.F., 1 S. Gen. Hosp.
1916 1 Cl. Dresser, France. Mentd. ' for amputating a man's
leg while lying wounded on a shell-swept road '.

SNOW, F. T. B. (1910, *b*)
    1918 P.F.O., R.A.F.

†SOMERVILLE, H. R. (1897–1901)
    Aug. 1914 Pte., 10 R. Fus. (Midd'x R.). France. 1916 Cpl.
    Died of wounds, received nr. Beaumont-Hamel, Nov. 1916.

SOMERVILLE, W. A. (1899–1902)
    1914 Tpr., War. Yeo.

†SPELLER, C. E. W. (1906–11, *b*)
    1914 L.-Cpl., 11 Hussars. Died in hospital at Aldershot, Dec. 22,
    1914.

SPENCER, C. L. (1901–6)
    Cpl., R.A.S.C., G.H.Q., Res. M.T. Coy., Belgium.

†SPENCER, ELIOT (1902–9, *y*)
    1914 Pte., 16 R. War. R. 1915 L.-Cpl. Sept. 1915 Sec. Lt.,
    3/5 R. War. R., T.F. 1916 Lt. Jan. 1917 France, 1/6 Bn.
    Wounded Aug. 27, 1917 : died of wounds in London, Feb. 18,
    1918.

SPENCER, N. F., M.M. (1902–6, *y*)
    1914 Gnr., R.G.A. Bombr., 65 Siege By., France. 1917 Sgt.
    Mentd. 1917 (he recd. congratulations of Gen. in cd. of 15 Corps
    for July–Aug. 1917). M.M. for Mar. 28, 1918.

SPENCER, P. C. (1909–15, *y*)
    Nov. 1917–May 1919 Inns of Court O.T.C. May–Sept. 1919 Pte.,
    1 D. of Corn. L.I., Ireland.

SPRINGTHORPE, G. W. (1900–3)
    1917 Inns of Court O.T.C. Aug. 1917 Sec. Lt., R.G.A., S.R.
    Feb. 1919 Lt.

SPURWAY, E. E. R. (1903–10, *g*)
    1917 B.U.O.T.C. Nov. 1918 Lt., R.A.M.C., S.R.

SQUIERS, J. G. (1906–8, *y*)
    1914 Bowker's Horse, S. Africa. 1918 Sec. Lt., G.H.Q., Dar-es-
    Salaam.

STANBURY, A. G. (1899–1904, *b*)

Oct. 1915 Sec. Lt., 6 Res. Rif. Brig. July 1917 Lt., secd. M.G.C. Actg. Capt. (1) German S.W. Africa (a) with Southern Army through Port Nolloth in Namaqualand to the R. Orange at Raman's Drift. (2) Boer Rebellion. (3) German S.W. (b) with Eastern Army under Col. Berranjé from Kimberley via Kuruman through the Kalahari Desert to Keetmanshoef. (4) Sinn Fein Rebellion, Ireland, Apr. 1916. (5) France 1916. The Somme (including 6 wks. in Delville Wood) ; both battles of Arras, 1917– 18 ; 3 big attacks in the Ypres Salient (including Passchendaele, 1917) ; the advance of 1918. Mentd. Dec. 1917.

STANLEY, A. B. (1912–14, *b*)

Aug. 6, 1914 joined R.E. France, Feb. 1915. Aug. 1917 Sec. Lt., R.F.C. : Pilot. Jan. 1918 Lt., R.A.F., Wing Navigation Offr. till Mar. 1919.

STANNARD, H. M. (1899–1902)

Dec. 1915 Sec. Lt., 2/6 Hamps. R., T.F. Secd. W.O., Spec. Appt. (Staff Lt., 2 Cl.) till Feb. 1919. June 1917 Lt. Temp. Capt.

STANSBIE, E. H. (1905–14, *b*)

Jan. 1916 Sec. Lt., Spec. List. Min. of Mun. Lt. July 1917 Capt. wh. assisting Exptl. Off. Mentd. for valuable services Aug. 1918.

STEDEFORD, R. V. (1911–12, *b*)

1918 Inns of Court O.T.C.

STEELEY, G. L. E. (1909–11, *y*)

1914 L.-Cpl., R.E., T.F., 78 Field Coy. 1916 Sec. Lt., R.E., T.F. July 1918 Lt. France 1915, 1916, 1918. 1919 Cologne.

STEELEY, N. E. (1905–9, *y*)

1914 Pte., 14 R. War. R. Feb. 1915 Sec. Lt., R.F.A., T.F., 2/3 N. Mid. Bde. Adjt. July 1915 Actg. Lt. June 1916 Lt. Dec. 1917 Actg. Capt., Adjt., attd. 1 Lond. Bde. Wounded Oct. 1917. 1915, 1916, 1917 France ; 1918–19 Mesopotamia.

STEELEY, S. E. (1906–11, *y*)

1914 Pte., 14 R. War. R. Oct. 1915 Sec. Lt., 3 N. Staff. R., S.R. 1915 Lt. June 1918 to Feb. 1919 Actg. Capt. Wounded (1) Aug. 1917, (2) Nov. 1918. 1915 Ypres ; 1916 Somme ; 1917 Ypres ; 1918 Lens, Cambrai ; 1919 Tournai.

STEWART, C. R. H. (1901–6, *r*)

1914 Tpr., Kg. Edward's Horse. France, with 1 Can. Cav. Bde. Cpl. Feb. 1916 Flt. Sub-Lt., R.N.A.S. 1917 Otranto, Italy. Torpedoed on the Rewa. Flt. Lt. Capt. (A. and S.), R.A.F. (empd. as Lt.) till June 1919.

STEWART, J. H. (1903–7, *r*)

1914 Lt., 2 Can. Inf. Bn. Manitoba Dragoons, Canada.

STEWART, W. G. (1900–6, *b*)

Persia, through Russia, home. King's Messenger and Res. Off. 1914 Asst. Paymaster, R.N.R., H.M.S. Kent. Battle of Falkland Isles, sinking of the Nürnberg and the Dresden after a long chase up and down the Pacific, from the Horn to Peru, and back again as far as Juan Fernandez Is. 1916 Sec. Lt., R.F.C., S.R., France. Jan. 1917 Lt., attd. Seistan Levy Corps, Persia. Lt. (A.), R.A.F., till May 1919.

STIFF, C. L. (1881–6)

1914 Sgt., War. Yeo., T.F. June 1916 Sec. Lt., A.S.C., T.F., 3 S. Mid. Divl. Train. ~~July 1917 Lt.~~ Nov. 1917 Lt., T.F., Res. *France 1916-17.* *June 1916 Lt.* *Aug. 1916 attd. R.E. Dec. 1916 Actg. Capt. attd. G.H.Q.*

STINTON, T. (Asst. Master, 1914–19)

Capt. K.E.S., B'ham, O.T.C. Mar. 1915–Jan. 1919 Capt. 3/8 Worc. R. Feb.–Nov. 1917 France, 1/8 Bn., 48 Div. Mar. La Maisonnette (Somme), Péronne : May–June, Le Transloy area, near Mœuvres : July–Oct. 3 Battle of Ypres, Aug. 20 Maison du Huton, 27 Springfield Farm, Sept. 9 Stroombek Valley : Oct.–Nov. Vimy Ridge. Nov. 1917–Sept. 1918 Italy : to Mar. 1918 Padua–Vicenza area ; Mar. Piave ; Apr.–Sept. Asiago Plateau. Operations, June 15–16, Aug. 8–9, Aug. 30–1. Italian Bronze Medal for raid on suburbs of Asiago, Aug. 8–9. (Gazetted

T

Sept. 1918). Sept. France, 25 Div. Oct.–Dec. Senior Offrs.' Course, Aldershot. Apr. 1919 O.C. K.E.S., B'ham, O.T.C. to Aug. 10, 1919.

†STOCKDALE, F. (1908–10, *b*)

1914 Pte., 16 R. War. R. Jan. 1915 Sec. Lt. Jan. 1916 Lt. France. Wounded (1) 1916, (2) July 1917. Mentd. Jan. 1917. June 1917 secd. R. Welsh Fus. Oct. 1917 Capt. Salonica F. Killed Sept. 1918.

STOKES, J. S. B. (1899–1905, *b*)

July 1915 Lt., Army Pay Dept. May 1918 Capt., Spec. Appt. Dec. 1918 Paymaster. May 1919 Station Acct. Off., Oct. 1919 Cl. II.

STRANGEWAYS, L. R. (1893–8)

Dec. 1914 Sec. Lt., Nottingham High Sch. O.T.C. Oct. 1916 (May 1919) Lt.

STREET, A. W. (Asst. Master, 1912–)

Feb. 1914 Lt., K.E.S., Birmingham, O.T.C.

STUART, Murray (1896–1901)

Since 1907 engaged on Geological Survey in India : Asst. Supt. 1916 Sec. Lt. (Brit. Army), Poona Bn., I.D.F. 1915–17 N.W. Frontier. 1917–18, in unmapped country *c*. Long. 98° 0' E., Lat. 28° 0' N. Dec. 1917 Sen. Capt. May 1918 transfd. 44 Calcutta Scottish. Apr. 1914 Ootacamund.

†STUBBS, W. E. (1909–11, *b*)

1914 Pte., R. War. R. Reported missing, since presumed to have been killed, July 23, 1916.

†SUCKLING, C. V. (1897–9)

Sec. Lt., 5 R. War. R., T.F. Aug. 1914 Lt. May 1915 Actg. Capt. France. Killed July 17, 1916, in attack on Ovillers-la-Boiselle.

SUCKLING, W. S. (1908–13, *g*)

1913 Sec. Lt., 1 R. Berks. R., S.R. France. Dec. 1914 Lt., Comd. Dépôt. Apr. 1917 Res. Commn.

SUMMERFIELD, R. E. (1912–14, g)
1917 Cdt., R.F.C. Sec. Lt. 1918 Lt. (O.), R.A.F.

SURGEY, D. H. (1899–1903)
1914 Tpr., 15 Hussars.

SURGEY, R. A. (1900–2)
1917 Pte., 81 Prov. Bn., R. War. R.

SUTHERNS, H. D. (1900–2)
1915 Sgt., Durban L.I.

SWAYNE, F. G. (1873–83)
Lt., R.A.M.C. 1917 M.O., attd. A.S.C.

SWAYNE, W. C. (1872–8)
Jan. 1914 Maj., V.D., Unattd. List, O.T.C. 1915 attd. R.F.A.,
T.F., 3/1 S. Mid. Bde. (Gloucester). Maj., R.F.A., T.F. Res.,
3 S. Mid. Bde.

SWINGLEHURST, R. H. (1902–7, r)
1917 Pte., Essex R.

†TABBERNER, T. K. (1893–6)
1914 Pte., 14 R. War. R. Sept. 1915 Sec. Lt., 2/19 Lond. R., T.F.
July 1916 France. Salonica F. Egyptian E.F. Lt. Killed in
Palestine Dec. 8, 1917.

TAIT, W. H. (1906–11, r)
Aug. 7, 1914 Motor Cycl. D.R. : crossed to Belgium Aug. 12.
Cpl., R.E., Motor D.R., attd. G.H.Q., B.E.F. Retreat from Mons
Aisne, Flanders. Médaille Militaire. Feb. 1915 Sec. Lt., R.E.
Injured c. Sept. 1915. Invalided out Jan. 1916.

†TANFIELD, A. H. (1909–15, b)
Sept. 1915 Sec. Lt., 3 R. War. R., S.R. 1916 attd. R.F.C. Jan.
1917 Fl. Off. France. Missing, since presumed killed, Apr. 13,
1917.

TANNER, J. A. (1892–4)
Pte., A.S.C., M.T. France.

† TALBOT, E. F. (1893–7)
Mar. 1915 Pte., 26 R. Fus. (Bankers' Bn.) Apr. 1916 France.
Killed, nr. Flers (Somme), Sept. 16, 1916.

TANNER, W. H. L. (1889–94)
Pte., A.S.C., Clerks' Sectn., Havre.

†TART, C. J. (1906–7, *y*)
Sept. 1915 Sec. Lt., R.E., S.R., 219 Field Coy., France. July 1, 1916 killed by a shell in an attack on the German line, Thiepval Salient, near Albert.

TARTE, B. R. K. (1879–81)
Aug. 1902 Maj., R. of O., E. Kent. R. Aug. 1914 R.T.O. 1916 Lt.-Col., attd. M.G.C.

TASKER, T. J. (1896–1903)   O.B.E.
1915 Tpr., S. Prov. Mtd. Rif., Madras.

TAYLOR, A. G. (1914, *g*)
1914 Pte., R.A.M.C., T.F., 2 S. Mid. Bde.

TAYLOR, C. (1910–14, *g*)   1917 Pte., 11 Worc. R.

TAYLOR, E. A. (1913–15, *g*)
1916 Inns of Court O.T.C. 1916 Sec. Lt., 12 W. York. R., Lewis Gun Off. Dec. 1916 6 Dorset. R. France. Lt., June 1918. Wounded Aug. 1918.

TAYLOR, E. O. (1907–11, *g*)
Sept. 1914 Pte., 14 R. War. R. Dec. 1914 Sec. Lt., 13 R. War. R. Aug. 1915 Lt. July–Sept. 1916 attd. R.E. Signal Service. Sept. 1916–May 1917 attd. M.G.C. (Nov. 1916 Actg. Capt. and Asst. Instr. Sig. Sch.). May 1917–Mar. 1919 R.E. Signal Service. Nov. 1917 Gen. List. Palestine and Egypt : capture of Jerusalem, Jericho, &c.

TAYLOR, H. D. (1910–16, *g*)
1916 Pte., 28 R. Fus. 1917 D. of Corn. L.I., France. Invalided home, Mar. 1917. Command Dépôt.

TAYLOR, J. L. (1904–12, *g*)
1914 Pte., 14 R. War. R. 1914 Cpl., R.E., D.R., 20 Sig. Coy., France. 1916 Surg. Probr., R.N.V.R., H.M. t.b.d. Penn. Jan. 1919 Surg. Lt. Minesweeper.

TAYLOR, J. M. (1913–15, *g*)
July 1917 to Nov. 1918 Conducteur, Sect. Sanit., Croix Rouge Franç., Salonica F.

†TAYLOR, MARTIN B. (1907–10, *g*)
1918 Pte., 2/5 Hamps. R., T.F. Egyptian E.F. Khartum. Missing, in Palestine, 18 mls. N.E. of Jaffa, since officially reported killed, Apr. 10, 1918.

TAYLOR, R. C. (1909–14, *g*)
1914 Pte., 14 R. War. R. Apr. 1915 Sec. Lt., 3/6 R. War. R., T.F. 2/6 Bn. 1916 attd. R.F.C. Mar. 1917 Fl. Off. July 1917 Lt. France. (Sch. of Instn.) Nov. 6, 1917–Dec. 1918 Prisoner of War in Germany, Holzminden.

TAYLOR, T. E. (1910–12, *g*)
1914 Pte., 14 R. War. R., transfd. R.F.C. 1918 Sec. Lt. (O.), R.F.C. R.A.F.

TEBBIT, T. L. (1911–13, *y*)
Dec. 1915 enlisted. Jan. 1917 Sec. Lt., R.F.C., Pilot : 8 mths. flying in France. 18 mths. Defence of London (night flying). Lt., R.A.F. 37 H.P. Sqn., Biggin Hill, Kent.

TEBBUTT, C. W. (1904–10, *g*)
Apr. 1915 Sec. Lt., R.E. France. Severely wounded in many places, Sept. 11, 1916. Sept. 1917 Lt. Actg. Capt. Jan. 1918 Temp. Capt., Asst. Off., Record Office, R.E.

TERRY, M. (1913–15, *y*)
1917–18 Armoured Motor Cars, Russia. Invalided.

THOMAS, E. H. (1886–91)
May 1914 Lt., 7 R. War. R., T.F. Actg.-Capt., July 1915. June 1916 Capt. T.F. Res.

THOMAS, F. J. B. (1910–16, *y*)
Nov. 1917 Pte., H.A.C., 1 Res. Bn. L.-Cpl. Nov. 1918 Italian E.F. Imst, Austrian Tyrol.

THOMAS, L. K. (1885–90)
May 1915 Capt., R.A.M.C., T.F., 1 S. Gen. Hosp.

THOMPSON, A. M. (1895–7)
Dec. 1914 Sec. Lt., A.S.C., T.F., S. Mid. Divl. Train, H.Q. Coy. Early 1915 Lt., France. July 1915–Jan. 1919 Actg. Capt. 61 Div. Lt., Actg. Capt., R.A.S.C., T.F. Mentd. May 1918.

THOMPSON, B. J. DENTON, M.C. (1907–8, *y*)
1914 Pte., P. Sch. Bn. Sec. Lt., 11 Glouc. R. Transfd. 20 Manch. R. France. Mar. 1915 Lt. Wounded (1) July 1916. M.C. Aug. 1916.* Oct. 1917 Actg. Capt. Wounded (2) 1918. Empd. Min. of Lab.

THOMPSON, E. H. (1898–9)
1914 Pte., 6 R. War. R., T.F. Early 1915 Lt., 10 S. Staff. R. Dardanelles, attd. 8 Manch. R. Feb. 1916 Capt. Palestine. Invalided home. 1918 France. Invalided home, 3 Bn. Empd. Min. of Nat. Service.

THOMPSON, E. H. (1903–5, *r*)
Pte., 1/6 R. War. R., T.F. France. Invalided home, and, later, invalided out.

†THOMPSON, M. C. (1905–7, *b*)
1914 Pte., R.A.M.C., T.F., 1 S. Mid. Mtd. Bde. Apr. 1915 Egyptian E.F. Ras el Tin Hosp., Alexandria. Salonica F. (18 mths.). 1917 torpedoed in Mediterranean. Egyptian E.F. Nov. 1917 entry into Jerusalem. Damascus. Died of pneumonia at Homs (n. of Damascus), Oct. 25, 1918.

THORNTON, E. (1885–9)
1914 Maj., 16 Can. L.I. 1915 5 Can. Inf. France. Wounded.

THURMAN, R. C. (1914–15, *y*)
Sept. 1918 Sec. Lt., R. War. R.

TIERNAY, R. J. B. (1913–15, *g*)
Cdt., R.A.F. Apr. 1919 Sec. Lt. (Hon.).

TILDESLEY, T. E., M C. (1908–10, b)
B.U.O.T.C. Sept. 1914 Sec. Lt., 5 N. Staff. R., T.F. Dec. 1914 Lt.
France. Feb. 1916 Actg. Capt. June 1916 Capt. M.C. Feb.
1918.* Mar. 1918 Actg. Maj. Prisoner in Germany Mar. 21–Dec.
1918.

TIMINGS, F. H. (1897–9)
Sept. 1914 Capt., 15 R. War. R. Tr. Res.

TIPPER, B. C. C. (1911–14, g)
1914 Cdt., R.M.C., Sandhurst. Mar. 1915 Sec. Lt., 5 Worc. R.
Oct. 1915, attd. 2 Bn.. France. Jan. 1916 Lt. Wounded, High
Wood, July 15, 1916. 1916–19 5 Bn.

TOLKIEN, H. A. R. (1905–10, r)
1914 Pte., 16 R. War. R 1915–18 France.

TOLKIEN, J. R. R. (1903–11, r)
July 1915 Sec. Lt., 13 Lan. Fus. 1916 11 Bn., France. Beaumont
Hamel, Schwaben Redoubt. Sept. 1916 invalided home. July
1917 Lt., Signal Dépôt. Empd. Min. of Lab.

†TOMLINSON, H. L. (1907–12, y)
1914 Cpl., R.E., D.R. Gnr., R.F.A. France. Repd. missing:
killed by hostile aircraft in a hospital in France, June 23, 1918.

†TOMSON, J. W. (1893–8)
1914 Inns of Court O.T.C. Mar. 1915 Sec. Lt., 1/5 Leic. R., T.F.
Feb. 1915 France. Lt., Actg. Capt. Killed Sept. 24, 1918, shot
while dressing the wound of a Cpl. of his Coy. Mentd. Dec. 1918.

†TONGUE, J. W. C. (1909–10, g)
Feb. 1915 Lt., 10 Glouc. R. Capt. Killed 1917.

TONKS, A. E. (1897–1904, r)
1916 Artists Rif. O.T.C. Sec. Lt., 8 R. War. R., T.F. Dec. 1917
Lt. July 1917 Actg. Capt. Attd. 2/7 Bn. France, Italy.

TOSH, J. C. P., M.C. (1904–8, g)
July 1913 Sec. Lt., R.E. Aug. 20, 1914 France : works duties
on L. of C. Jan. 1, 1915 26 Fd. Coy. as Subaltern. June 1915 Lt.

Dec. 1915 to July 1917 Adjt. to C.R.E., 47 Lond. Div. M.C. June 1917. July–Nov. 1917 Instr., 2 Army Central Tr. Schools. Nov. 1917 Capt. Dec. 1917 to Jan. 1919 G.S.O. to C.R.E., 9 Corps, graded as Bde. Maj. The three retreats of 1918 on the Somme, the Lys, and the Aisne : right through the Great Advance from Sept. 8, into Germany. Dec. 1918 Actg. Maj., cdg. 459 Field Coy., T.F., Army of Occupn., Germany. Feb. 1919 Staff course, Chatham. Twice mentd.

TOWERS, L. T. (1912–18, g)

1918 Cdt.-Cand., R.G.A., Brighton. Jan. 1919 passed out 10th in Corps of R.E.

TOY, E. J. (1912–15, y)

To 1918 Spr., R.E., T.F., Lond. El. Eng., Searchlight Station, Windsor. 1918 Cdt., R.M.A., Woolwich. Jan. 1919 Sec. Lt., R.E.

TREDENNICK, G. H. P. P. (1911–18, r)

1918 Cdt., R.G.A., 1 O.C.S., Trowbridge. July 1918 Sec. Lt., R.G.A. Oct. 1918 France, 122 Siege By. (6-inch How.) Selle River. Educn. Off. of By. 1919 Opladen, nr. Cologne.

TREDENNICK, J. N. E. (1905–11, r)

Aug. 1914 Sec. Lt., 14 R. War. R. Jan. 1915 Lt. Nov., France. Attd. T.M.B. Severely wounded July 27, 1916. 1917–18 Gen. List, New Armies, for Min. of Nat. Service, Birmingham. Aug. 1918 Capt. Sept. 1918 Spec. Appt., Censor's Office, Rouen. Mar. 1919 Spec. Appt.

†TREGLOWN, R. C. (1899–1901)

1915 Pte., 14 R. War. R. Killed on the Somme, 1916.

TRIMBLE, C. D. (1904–11, y)

Sept. 1914 Pte., 10 S. Staff. R. Oct. 1914 Pte., 10 Linc. R. May 1915 Sec. Lt., 10 S. Staff. R. 3 Bn. June 1916 France, attd. 2/6 R. War. R., T.F. St. Quentin. May 1917 attd. 182 L.T.M. By. July 1917 Lt. Mar.–Oct. 1918 Actg. Capt., cdg. 182 L.T.M.B. 1916 Laventie, Albert, Ancre. 1917 German Retreat ; Chaulnes to St. Quentin ; Arras, Ypres, Cambrai. 1918 St. Quentin, Villers

Bretonneux, St. Venant, Armentières, Cambrai, Le Cateau, Mormal Forest.

†TRIMBLE, R. M. (1906–14, *y*)

1914 Pte., 14 R. War. R. 1915 Transpt. Off., R.A.M.C. Jan. 1916 Sec. Lt. 3/5 N. Staff. R., T.F. Dublin : mentd. for Distinguished Services. Feb. 1917 France. 2/5 N. Staff. R. Missing, believed killed, Mar. 21, 1918, near Bullecourt.

TROUGHT, TREVOR (1903–10, *r*)

Aug. 1914 Sec. Lt., 1/4 R.W. Kent R., T.F. India. June 1916 Capt. May 1918 G.S.O.$_3$, Northern Command, India : Rawal Pindi.

TUCKER, N. P. (1899–1904, *b*)

1913 Pte., Artists Rif., 28 City of Lond. R., T.F. Oct. 1914 Pte., 1 Bn., France. Jan. 1915 Sgt. Instr., M.G. School, St. Omer. May 1915 Sec. Lt., 2 Cam'n Highrs., 27 Div. Nov. 1915 Salonica F. Apr. 1916 Off. Instr. Army M.G. Sch. July 1916 Lt. Sept. 1916 Adjt., Q.-M. Mentd. July 1917. Aug. 1917 Capt.

TUCKER, P. A. (1898–1902)

Sept. 1914 Pte., 15 R. War. R. 18 mths'. training. 1916 Recalled for Govt. work.

TUNSTALL, W. J. C. (1907–13, *r*)

Sept. 1915 Sec. Lt., 10 The King's Own (R. Lanc. R.). Apr. 1916 France, 11 R. Innis. Fus., 36 Ulster Div. Invalided home. France (2) ; severely wounded (1) at Messines June 7, 1917. July 1917 Lt. France (3) : severely wounded (2) at the recapture of Armentières Oct. 1, 1918. Rel. commn. Sept. 1919.

TURNER, CRESSWELL, A.F.C. (1910–15, *b*)

Feb.–July 1915 Cdt., R.M.C., Sandhurst. Aug. 1915 Sec. Lt., 6 Worc. R. Dec. 1915–Feb. 1916 France, 1 Worc. R. Feb.–Sept. 1916 attd. R.F.C., 12 Sqn. (Obs.), France. Oct. 1916 Lt., Worc. R. Apr. to Oct. 1917 France (2), 32 Sqn. (Pilot). Oct. 1917–1919 Wireless Experimental Estabt., Biggin Hill, Kent. Dec. 1917 Capt., Flt.-Cdr., R.A.F. A.F.C. Feb. 1919.

U

TURNER, C. P. (1913–15, *y*)
1916 Artists Rif. O.T.C. May 1917 Sec. Lt., R.G.A.

TURNER, E. (1908, *b*)
Tpr., Yeo., T.F. May 1915 Sec. Lt., Res. Regt. Cav. July 1917 Lt., 6 D. Gds., S.R. Transfd. Ind. Army.

TURNER, E. L. (1898–1900)
1917 Inns of Court O.T.C. Cpl. Apr. 1918 Sec. Lt. R.E., T.F. R.E. Training Coll., Newark.

TURNER, E. R. (1893–1900)
1914 Sgt., 6 R. War. R., T.F. Apr. 1915 Sec. Lt., 2/6 Bn. France. Wounded. July 1917 Lt. 1918 Actg. Capt. Instr., Gas, 11 O.C.B., Pirbright, Surrey.

†TURNER, J. PERCIVAL (1894–7)
France Apr. 1915. Severely wounded. Sept. 1915 Sec. Lt., 3 R. War. R. France (2) Sept. 1916. Actg. Capt. Killed Nov. 26, 1917.

TURNER, J. W., M.C. (1883–91)
Apr. 1915 Lt., R.A.M.C. With Heavy Artillery, France. Apr. 1916 Capt. M.C. Nov. 1916.*

TURNER, J. W. CECIL, M.C. (1897–1906, *y*)
Sec. Lt., R.F.A., S.R. France. July 1917–Apr. 1919 Actg. Capt. M.C. Sept. 1917.* Mar. 1918 Lt. 505 By., 65 Bde.

TUTE, F. S. (1903–7, *y*)
Dec. 1915 Sec. Lt., 3/5 R. War. R., T.F. France. Wounded 1916. July 1917 Lt. Actg. Capt., S. Bn., Oct.–Nov. 1918.

†TWIGG, H. R. (1894–1900)
Oct. 1915 Pte., 14 Glouc. R. France. Killed Nov. 9, 1917.

TYE, C. H. (1902–10, *r*)
Aug. 1915 Sec. Lt., 14 Ches. R. Oct. 1915 attd., for Instl. duties, No. 5 (Scottish Cd.), T.F. Artillery Tr. School. July 1917 Lt.

Attd. 3/5 Lan. Fus., T.F. Prisoner in Germany (Mainz), Mar. 21, 1918.

TYE, E. H. S. (1911–14, r)
1918 P.F.O., R.N.A.S. Oct. 1918 Sec. Lt. (A.), R.A.F. Scilly Isles.

TYNDALL, Rev. E. D., M.C. and bar (1905–9, g)
Nov. 1915 C.F., 4th Cl. Aldershot. France, 12 E. York. R. M.G.C. 1918 11 E. York. R. M.C. Jan. 1918. Wounded. Bar to M.C. Aug. 1918.* May 1919 Army of the Rhine.

UMBERS, J. L., M.C. (1895–7)
1916 Sec. Lt., 10 North'd Fus., T.F. Jan. 1918 Lt. Italy. M.C. Oct. 1918.* 4 Bn., T.F., attd. H.Q., 69 Inf. Bde. Mentd. June 1919.

UNDERWOOD, M. J. F. (1907–13, y)
Salonica F.

UPTON, Rev. G. F. (1892–1900)
1914–1919 Actg. C.F., R.A.F., Coventry. Mentd. Sept. 1919 for valuable services.

USHER, J. M. (1893–1900)
Sgt., R.G.A. ½ W. Rid. H. By.

UTLEY, E. G. (1914–17, y)
1917 Cdt., R.M.C., Sandhurst. Dec. 1918 Sec. Lt., 2 R. Dub. Fus. Army of the Rhine.

†VARDY, A. T. (1900–2)
1914 Pte., 11 Midd'x R. (P. Sch.). Apr. 1915 Sec. Lt., 4 R. War. R., S.R. May 1916, attd. 2 Bn., France. Killed at Mametz Wood, July 4, 1916, while helping a wounded officer of his own battn.

VAUGHAN, C. H., M.C. (1903–6, r)
Aug. 1914–1919 Capt., Adjt., R.A.S.C., T.F., Welsh Divn. Active Service. M.C. Jan. 1918.

VAUGHAN, H. W. (1908–10, *g*)

Sept. 1914 Sec. Lt., 7 Queen's (R.W. Surr. R.). France. Wounded and prisoner, Feb. 27, 1917–Jan. 1918 at Ohrdruf, Saxony. Lt. Res. Commn. July 1918.

VAUGHTON, H. G. (1911–16, *b*)

July 1916 Driver H.A.C. 1/1 B By. Mar. 28, 1917 left England for Egyptian E.F. Joined S.S. Arcadian at Marseilles ; forced into Biserta, Gulf of Tunis : Malta, Mudros, Salonica ; torpedoed 5.50 p.m., Apr. 15 ; picked up by French destroyer, taken to Milo ; Crete ; Apr. 29 Alexandria. Palestine. Joined By. in the line at Khan Yanus ; attd. Impl. Mtd. Div. Oct. 28 commenced advance on Jerusalem, with Aust. mtd. troops : Beersheba, Sheria, Huj, Junction Station, Ludd, Ramleh : on left of Jerusalem when it fell on Oct. 9. Came out of the line Jan. 8, 1918. Apr. 28 till mid-Aug. in Jordan Valley ; 2nd Es Salt stunt (lost 1 gun). Sept. 19, 1918, 5 Cav. Div.—launch of last attack ; advanced up the coast, later cutting across to El Fule, Nazareth. Invalided. Rejoined at Tripoli (Syria) for 2 mths.

VAUGHTON, S. J. J. (1914, *b*) M.C.

1917 B.U.O.T.C. Nov. 1917 Sec. Lt., Tank Corps. France. May 1919 Lt. M.C. Nov. 1919 (Finland and Baltic States).

VICKERS, C. A. (1914–18, *b*)

1918 Cdt., Ind. Army. O.C.B., Catterick. Sept. 1918 R.M.C., Quetta. 1919 Sec. Lt., Unattd. List, Ind. Army.

VICKERS, G. K. (1913–16, *b*)

1916 Apprentice, Merc. Marine. Apr. 1918 Mid., R.N.R., H.M.S. Coventry.

VINCE, CHARLES (1899–1906, *r*)

Sept. 1915 Pte., 3/6 Cycl. Bn., R. Suss. R., T.F. Sec. Lt. July 1917 Lt., secd. War Office.

VINCE, F. H. (1907–9, *b*)

Aug. 1915 Sec. Lt., R.E., T.F., 4/1 N. Mid. Fd. Coy. France. Wounded, by mine, St. Eloi. Secd. for duty with Min. of Mun., Inspector, Woolwich Arsenal. July 1917 Lt.

†VINCE, W. L. (1901–9, *b*)

Aug. 1914 Sec. Lt., 14 R. War. R. Jan. 1915 Lt. France. Wounded, Somme, Sept. 3, 1916. Invalided home. France (2) Mar. 1917. Killed May 8, 1917, N. France.

VOKES, F. C. (1898–1902)

1914 Spr., R.E. Dec. 1914–1919 Sec. Lt., 12 R. War. R.

WACKRILL, W. F. (1910–12, *b*)

June 1915 Sec. Lt., 15 R. Fus. July 1917 Lt., R.E. May 1918 temp. Maj., Spec. Staff Appt. Croce di Guerra, Aug. 1919.

WADE, R. F. (1913–17, *r*)

Oct. 1918 Cdt., R.A.F.

WAITE, A. W. (1907–8, *g*)

1914 Cpl., R.A.M.C., 40 Fd. Amb. 1915 Sgt. Wounded, Gallipoli, 1915. Mesopotamia. Invalided 1916. 1917 India. 1917 Cdt., Sialkot, N. India. Mar. 1918 Sec. Lt., S. Lan. R., S. Bn.

WAITE, F. (1909–11, *y*)

1914 Cpl., 14 R. War. R. June 1915 Sec. Lt., 7 Dorset. R. Oct. 1915 attd. Army Cycl. C. France. Wounded, Somme, 1916. 1917 Palestine. July 1917 Lt. Empd., 6 Dorset R. Nov. 1918 Actg. Capt.

WAITE, W. I. (1902–3)

Feb. 1915 Spr., R.E. Sept., sailed for Dardanelles : Oct., Suvla Bay, Gallipoli : Dec., evacuation of Gallipoli ; to Egypt. Jan. 1916–Feb. 1917, on Suez Canal. Feb. 1917–Jan. 1918 Rafa, Gaza, Belah, Shellah, Karm. Jan. 1918–Jan. 1919 Southern Palestine, Ramleh, Jaffa, Jerusalem. Mar. 1919 left for England.

WALE, Rev. L. W. (1898–1904, *b*)

June 1913 Chaplain, R.N. H.M.S. Cochrane (Cruiser). Apr. 1919 H.M.S. Vivid for R.N. Barracks, Devonport.

WALFORD, J. O., M.C. and bar (1879–87)

Sept. 1914 Capt., 8 Worc. R., T.F. 1916 2/8 Bn. Italy 1/8 Bn. M.C. and bar, both gazetted May 2, 1919.*

WALKER, A. L. (1909–13, *r*)
Aug. 1915 Sec. Lt., 15 R. Fus. 11 Bn., France. Wounded Sept.
1916. July 1917 Lt. Transfd. R.F.C., Fl. Off. 1918 Lt. (A.),
R.A.F.

WALKER, E. (1892–5)
Nov. 1914 Sec. Lt., A.S.C., T.F., 2/2 N. Mid. Div. Train.
Warwick Bde. Coy. Feb. 1915 Actg. Lt. Aug. 1917 Lt.

WALKER, E. G. S. (1902–5, *b*) M.C.
Aug. 1914 Sec. Lt., 6 Bord. R. Jan. 1915 attd. R.F.C., Flying Off.
Lt., 16 Sqn. France. Wounded and Prisoner. Retd. from
Germany Dec. 1918. Lt., Hon. Capt. (A.), R.A.F. Oct. 1919
temp. Capt., Gen. List, Interpreter. Mentd., Dec. 1919, for
valuable services while a prisoner of war. M.C. Sept. 1920 *(S. Russia).*

WALKER, GILBERT (1902–4, *y*)
Pte., 5 Res. Bn., S. Staff. R., T.F.

WALKER, H. B. (1916–18, *b*)
1918 Cdt., Training Ship Worcester.

†WALKER, H. J. (1911, *r*)
1914 Pte., 14 R. War. R. 1916 15 Bn. France. Died of wounds,
received Aug. 4, 1916.

WALKER, L. H. (1905–7, *r*)
1915 Pte., 7 Can. Inf. France. Wounded and Prisoner.

WALKER, T. A. N. (1902–5, *r*)
1917 Sec. Lt., M.G.C. Injured. Mar. 1918 Lt. Sept. 1918 to Feb.
1919 Actg. Capt., 2nd in cd. of Coy., 46 Bn. Mentd. July 1919.

WALL, J. A. (1909–12, *b*)
1914 Pte., 16 R. War. R. Apr. 1915 Sec. Lt., 13 R. War. R.
France, 11 Bn. Wounded Sept. 1916. 1917 H.Q. Southern Command, Salisbury. Dec. 1917 R.T.O. June 1918 Capt., Gen. List
(at New St. Station, B'ham). May 1919 Lt., R. War. R., T.F.
(Sen. July 1917), Actg. Capt., Spec. empt.

WALLIS, H. B. (1896–1901)
1914 Sub-Lt., R.N.V.R. Oct. 1915 Capt., R.M. Wounded 1916.
Mentd. 1917 Capt., R. of O., R.M. Rel. Commn. Feb. 1919.

WALSH, F. NEWTON (1892–9)
Dec. 1915 Lt., R.A.M.C., T.F., attd. 1/8 R. War. R., T.F. France.
Wounded 1916.

WALSHE, R. S. E. (1905–7, g)
1917 Pte., 9 Can. Res. Bn. Apr. 1917 Sec. Lt., 5 R. War. R.,
T.F. 1918 Sec. Lt. (O.), R.A.F., 22 Sqn., France. Oct., Lt. No. 19
Tr. Sta., The Curragh.

WALTON, F. W. (1909–15, r)
1916 Sec. Lt., 3 R. War. R., S.R. 2 Bn., France. Wounded
(missing 3 days) at Ginchy, Sept. 3, 1916. July 1917 Lt., 1 Bn.,
France (2). Severely wounded (2) Nov. 20, 1917. Empd. Min. of
Labour.

WANSBROUGH, R. C. (1907–11, g)
Sept. 1914 Pte., 14 R. War. R. Dec. 1914 Sec. Lt., 9 S. Staff. R.
(Pioneer Bn.). Aug. 1915 10 Bn. Pioneer Dépôt. Dec. 1915
France, with 9 Bn. : Armentières, Bouvigny, Somme, &c. July
1915 transfd. 12 Sqn., R.F.C. (Obs.), Avesnes le Comte. Aug. 1915
England, Sqn. Recording Offr., No. 46 Sqn. Oct. 1916 France
(2), nr. Poperinghe, Rec. Offr., 46 Sqn. Apr. 1917 Rec. Offr.,
21 Sqn., Poperinghe. June 1917 Lt. Aug. 1917 Capt., Adjt.,
H.Q., 15 Wing, Poperinghe. Jan. 1918 England, Adjt., No. 3
Stores Dépôt. July 1918–Jan. 1919 Adjt., No. 8 Sch. of Aero-
nautics.

WANSBROUGH, R. F. (1905–7, g)
1914 Cpl., 7 Rif. Brig. Sgt., 5 Bn. France. Wounded 1915.
1918 Sec. Lt., Lab. Corps Mar. 1918 Actg. Capt., Chinese Lab.
Coy. July 1918 Lt. Jan. 1919 Capt.

†WANSBROUGH, W. E. (1907–11, g)
1914 Lt., 3 S. Staff. R., S.R. Aug. 1914 France, attd. 2 Bn. In
retreat from Mons. Wounded, Aisne, Oct. 11, 1914. Feb. 1915

Capt. Apr. 1916 France (2). Killed by a shell in Delville Wood July 27, 1916.

WARD, A. P. (1903–7, *r*)

1914 Pte., 2/6 R. War. R., T.F. 1916–17 France. In England, L.-Cpl., 3/7 Bn.

†WARD, W. A. B. K. (1903–4, *r*)

June 1914 Sec. Lt., R.E., T.F., Signals. Dec. 1914 attd. R.E., Sig. Coy., H.Q., 5 Corps, France. Mentd. 1915. Killed at Poperinghe 1915.

WARDEN, S. H. (1881–4)

Sept. 1914 Lt., A.O.D. (now R.A.O.C.). Inspr. of Ordnance Machinery. France. May 1916–Jan. 1917 Actg. Capt., Spec. Appt. Jan. 1917 Invalided home. I.O.M., Malta 1917–Aug. 1918. Invalided.   Oct.1917 I.P.M. Istce. , Maj.

WARDER, R. O., D.S.O. (1897–9)

Oct. 1914 Sec. Lt., R.F.A., S.R. Attd. 17 Div., France. Mentd. D.S.O.* (Hooge, gas attack) 1915. July 1915 Lt.   79 Bde. Wounded 1916. June 1918 Actg. Capt.

WARING, N. H. (1909 *r*)

Mar. 1915 Sec. Lt., 10 Bord. R. Feb. 1916 Civil empt. 1917 Lt. Gen. List. Min. of Mun.

†WARTH, E. F. (1900–5, *b*)

Spr., R.N. Div. Eng. Died of wounds June 25, 1915, at Alexandria.

†WARWOOD, F. J. D. (1903–6, *b*)   Delville Wd

1914 Pte., 14 R. War. R. France. Killed, Somme, July 30, 1916.
                                                              ^

WATHES, C. H. (1891–3)

1914 Sec. Lt., 6 R. War. R., T.F. Oct. 1914 Lt., 2/6 Bn. July 1915 Actg. Capt. June 1916 Capt. France. Secd. for duty as Bde. Trans. Off., Sept. 1918.

†WATHES, T. S. (1902–4, *r*)

1914 Sec. Lt., 6 R. War. R., T.F. Oct. 1914 Lt., 2/6 Bn. France. 1916 Capt. Killed July 19, 1916, while leading his men close up to the enemy trenches.

WATKIN, P. J., M.C. (1893–6)
Oct. 1914 Lt., R.A.M.C. Oct. 1915 Capt. Attd. Bedf. R. M.C.
July 18, 1917.*

WATKINS, V. G. B. (=909–13, b)
Sept. 1914 Pte., 15 R. War. R. Nov. 1915 France; Arras. July
1916 invalided. L.-Cpl., 3 Bn. Dec. 1916–Jan. 1917 France.
1 Bn. July 1917 Cdt., 19 O.C.B., Pirbright. Oct. 1917 Sec. Lt.,
2 R. War. R. Jan. 1918 France; attd. 2 Linc. R. Wounded
Mar. 21, 1918, Villers Guislain (bet. Gouzeaucourt and Epéhy).
Nov. 1918 France, attd. 8 N. Staff. R. Dec. 1918 to Mar. 1919
10 R. War. R

WAYNE, R. W. (1912–16, y)
1918 L.-Cpl., ∠ Notts. and Derby R., Bomber.

WEBB, J. G. (1901–5, g)
1917 Pte., 96 Res. Bn. *June 1918 Sec. Lt. 4 The Kings (Shrops. L.I.)*

WEBB, N. D. (1904, g)
1917 Artists Rif. O.T.C.

WEBBE, W. H. (1900–4, g) *C . B . E .*
1909–17 Sec. Lt., Unat?d. List, T.F. 1916 Sec. to Head of Dept.,
Min. of Mun. Promoted May 1918.

WEST, H. O. (1893–1900)
June 1917 Lt., R.A.M.C. July 1917–Jan. 1919 Salonica F., 64
Gen. Hosp.: O.C. 15 San. Sectn. and Specialist San. Off., 28 Div.
July 1918 Capt. 1919 Spec. San. Off. and Staff Off. to A.D.M.S.,
Grantham Dist.

WESTWOOD, P. A. (1910–11, b)
1914 Pte., 14 R. War. R. 1916 Able Seaman, R.N.V.R., H.M.S.
Sagitta; H.M.S. Britor. Apr. 1918 Sub-Lt., R.N.V.R., M.L.
175; Admiralty Trawler Gunner for special services; mine-
sweeping, H.M.S. Lewes.

WHEELOCK, H. J. (1897–9)
1916 Driver, A.S.C., 514 Coy. 1917 Sec. Lt., Welsh R. M.G.C.
Oct. 1918 Lt., M.G.C.

WATSON, E.E. (1912–5, g) M.M.
1917 Tr.Res. May 1918 Pte., 1/7 Lan.Fus., 42 Div. France;
Bucquoy–Achiet Sector. Aug. 23 — Final Advance of 3rd
Army — Sept 1918 Wounded, M.M.

WHEELOCK, PERCY (1896–9)
Aug.–Oct. 1914 Tpr., E. Afr. Mtd. Rif. Feb. 1916 L.-Cpl., 2 R.
War. R., France. Wounded Sept. 5, 1916. Discharged June
1917.

†WHITCOMBE, BERESFORD (1903–6, *y*)
1914 Pte., 14 R. War. R. France. L.-Cpl. Wounded July 1916.
Killed Sept. 3, 1916.

WHITCOMBE, DOUGLAS (1893–9)
1914 Pte., 14 R. War. R. Severely wounded July 1916. Discharged 1917.

WHITCOMBE, H. A. (1893–1901)
Lt., R.A.M.C., Liverpool.

WHITCOMBE, Rev. LEONARD (1896–1905, *r*)
1915 C.F., 4th Cl. Salonica F. 78 Bde., 9 Glouc. R. ; 7 R.
Berks. R. Mentd. June 1918.

WHITE, A. H. S. (1898–1906, *b*)
1917 Cdt., R.G.A., Uckfield. July 1917 Sec. Lt., R.G.A., S.R.
France, 70 Siege By. Dépôt, Field Survey Coy., G.H.Q. Oct.
1918 Sound-ranging Sectn.

WHITE, E. A. (1912–16, *b*)
B.U.O.T.C. Pte., Inf. Prelim. Course, M.G.C. Cdt., 1 M.G.C.
Cdt. Bn., Bisley Camp. Oct. 1917 Sec. Lt., M.G.C. 1918 France,
47 Div. Wounded, Bouzincourt, Apr. 5, 1918.

WHITEHILL, I. E. (1909–16, *y*)
2 O.C.B., Pemb. Coll., Cambridge. Sept. 1918 Sec. Lt., Garr. Bn.,
Worc. R. Transfd. 19 Garr. Bn., Hamps. R. France. Sept.
1918 Lt.

WHITEHILL, R. D. (1903–9, *y*)
Jan. 1914 Sec. Lt., 1/8 R. War. R., T.F. Dec. 1914 Lt. Adjt.
France. June 1915 Actg. Capt. June 1916 Capt. Invalided
home. 1918 secd. Ind. Army, attd. 121 Pioneers, Meerut. June
1918 Lt. Oct. 1918 Actg. Capt. May 1919 Capt., I.A.

WHITEHOUSE, A. G. R. (1908–16, *r*)
1916 Cdt., 4 O.C.B., Oxford. Mar. 1917 Sec. Lt., 3 R. War. R. :
4 Bn. India. Attd. 2/5 R. Suss. R. : attd. 9 R. War. R. Mesopot.
E.F. 100 miles above Baghdad. Invalided, Baghdad ; Bombay.
i/c Sign. Statn., Bombay Harbour. Dec. 1918 9 R. War. R.
Dépôt, Belgaum. A.-Q.-M., Poona. Sept. 1919 Lt.

WHITEHOUSE, ERIC (1900–5, *y*)
1917 Gnr., R.F.A.

WHITEHOUSE, F. R. B. (1900–3)
1916 Inns of Court O.T.C. Sec. Lt., R.E., T.F., 3/1 W. Riding Bde.
May 1918 resd. Commn.

†WHITEHOUSE, HERBERT (1909–11, *r*)
Sept. 1914 Lt., R.F.A., T.F., 3 S. Mid. Bde. Apr. 1915 France.
Early 1917 Actg. Capt. June 1916 Actg. Maj., for special services
rendered in the field. Killed Mar. 23, 1918.

WHITEHOUSE, S. (1907–11, *b*)
1916 Pte., 14 R. War. R.

WHITEHOUSE, S. C. (1904–5, *r*)
Oct. 1914 Sec. Lt., 14 R. War. R. Wounded 1916.

WHITEHURST, E. A. (1905–13, *r*)
July 1915 Sec. Lt., 14 W. York R. Wounded 1916. Jan. 1917
Lt. Aug. 1917 Actg. Capt., Adjt.

WHITMORE, C. J. R., M.C. (Asst. Master, 1911–19)
Nov. 1915 Sec. Lt., R.G.A., S.R. Dec. 1916 Actg. Capt., 264
Siege By. July 1917 Lt. May 1918 323 Siege By., Act. Maj.
1915 Forth Defences, Kinghorn. 1916 Ypres Salient : Somme
(Thiepval, Schwaben Redoubt, Beaumont Hamel). 1917 Somme
(Miraumont, Achiet-le-Petit, Achiet-le-Grand). Wounded and
M.C. (Gaz.* Mar. 1917) Feb. 28, Miraumont. Apr.–June Vimy
Ridge (O.C. 1 and 2 German Batteries, captured 8 in. Hows.) :
Messines : Ypres, to Passchendaele. 1918 Somme Retreat :
Lys Retreat : advance from Arras to Cambrai, Valenciennes,
Mons. 1919 Ath, nr. Brussels. Mentd. July 1919.

WHITWELL, E. J. (1911–18, *y*)
Mar. 1918 P.F.O., R.N.A.S. Sept. 1918 Sec. Lt. (A.), R.A.F. France, 213 Sqn. (Camels), Oct. 1918. Injured, aeroplane accident, Dunkirk, Oct. 30, 1918. 21 Tr. Sqn.

†WHITWORTH, E. S. (1908–9, *g*)
Sept. 1914 Sec. Lt., 10 R. War. R. France. 1915 Lt. Killed Dec. 20, 1915, by machine-gun fire, while in charge of a working party between the trenches.

†WICKHAM, T. S., D.S.O. (1893–4)
1914 Capt., W. Afr. Front. F. (Nigeria Regt.). D.S.O. Killed 1914.

WIEMANN, H. F. (1900–2)
June 1917 to Feb. 1919 Pte., R.A.S.C., M.T., 1010 Coy. E.E.F., Palestine.

WIGLEY, W. C. S. (1902–9, *r*)
1914 Cdt. Sgt., R.E., Res. Sig. Coy. Reserve, for work under Min. of Mun., Royal Aircraft Factory, S. Farnborough.

WILCOX, A. C. (1905–6, *y*)
1916 Pte., 1 Garr. Bn., Worc. R. 1917 Sec. Lt., Lab. Corps.

WILCOX, H. L. (1898–1902)
1917 Pte., Artists Rif. France.

WILCOX, R. C. (1900–3)
1917 Gnr., R.G.A. France.

WILES, J. W. (Asst. Master, 1905–13)
1915 Hon. Capt., Serbian Army. 1914–15 Interpreter, B'ham Medical Unit.

WILES, M. M. (1910–14, *y*)
1917 Pte., Orderly Room, Ballyvonare, Co. Cork.

WILLCOX, A. D. (1909–12, *y*)
Aug. 1914 Sec. Lt., 3/6 R. War. R., T.F. Lt. June 1916 Capt. Twice wounded, 1916 (severely), 1918.

WILLIAMS, H. C. (1912–13, *b*)
1914 Driver, A.S.C., T.F., S. Mid. Div. Train, Warwick Bde. Coy.

WILLIAMS, J. E. (1910–17, *b*)
Feb. 1917 to Mar. 1918 Pte., 6 Worc. R. Mar.–Nov. 1918 Cdt., 16 O.C.B.

WILLIAMS, J. L. (1913–14, *b*)
1916–19 1 Cl. Air Mech., R.N.A.S. R.N. Experimental Station, Stratford ; do. Dover. In Zeebrugge Raid, Apr. 1918.

WILLIAMS, R. H. (1907–10, *b*)
1914 Pte., 14 R. War. R. 1915 France. 1916 Sgt. Wounded, Somme, July 1916. June 1917 Discharged unfit. July 1917 Sec. Lt., R. War. R., S.R., for duty as Adjt. of Public Sec. Schools Camp.

WILLIAMS, R. N. (1908–11, *b*)
1914 Pte., 14 R. War. R. France. Wounded, Somme, July 1916. Italy. 1918 Cdt., O.C.B.

WILLIAMS, S. A. G. (1908–17, *b*)
Sept. 1917 Cdt., R.H. and R.F.A., No. 1 Sch., St. John's Wood. Mar. 1918 Sec. Lt., R.H. and R.F.A., S.R. June 1918–June 1919 France. June–Sept. 1918 Vimy Ridge ; Sept., Arras ; Oct.–Nov., Advance through Douai, St. Amand to Mons ; Dec. 1918–June 1919 Ath, Belgium. Sept. 1919 Lt.

WILLIAMS, W. B. (1895–8)
Sept. 1914 Lt., 8 S. Staff. R. Sept. 1915 Lt., 7 Bn. Oct. 1915 Actg. Capt., 1 Bn. May 1918 Capt., 7 Bn. Oct. 1915–Jan. 1916 Gallipoli. Jan.–Sept. 1916 Egypt. Sept. 1916 Invalided home. Mar. 1917–Mar. 1919 France.

WILSON, C. W., M.M. (1907–14, *y*)
1915 Pte., R.A.M.C., T.F., N. Mid. Mtd. Bde. France. M.M. for gallantry as stretcher-bearer, Sept. 20–3, 1917. Wounded 1917.

WILSON, E. F. (1913–17, *y*)
1917 Cdt., R.F.C., Upavon. Sec. Lt. 1918 France, night-bombing. Apr. 1918 Lt. (A.), R.A.F.

WILSON, F. C. (1898–1901)

Dec. 1914 Sec. Lt., 8 S. Staff. R. Nov. 1915 Sec. Lt., R.E. Sept. 1916 Lt., R.E.

WILSON, F. P. (1906–8, *y*)

Oct. 1914 to Mar. 1915, Oxf. Univ. O.T.C. Mar. 1915 Sec. Lt., 12 R. War. R. Apr. 1916 Lt., 14 R. War. R. May–June 1916, Arras. Severely wounded, Somme, before High Wood, Sept. 20, 1916. Resd. Commn. Jan. 1918. Apr. 1918–Mar. 1919, empld. at Min. of Food. The Bn., 14 R. War. R., went into the Somme line July 19, 1916 : 3 or 4 days later it was badly cut up in an attack on High Wood.

WILSON, G. G. (1907–10, *y*)

Sept. 1914 Pte., 14 R. War. R. June 1915 Sec. Lt., 3/8 R. War. R., T.F. Nov. 1915 Actg. Lt. July 1916 Lt. 1916–17 Actg. Capt. France May–July 1916. Wounded July 16, 1916. Sept. 1916 to July 1917 Min. of Munitions. Oct. 1917 to Nov. 1918 attd. 53 R. Fus.

†WILSON, J. S. (1908–14, *y*)

Camb. Univ. O.T.C. Mar. 1915 Sec. Lt., 11 S. Staff. R. July 1916, 8 Bn., France. Somme, Aisne. Wounded Feb. 1917. Mentd. Beaumont Hamel, Apr. 1917. May 1917 Lt. Intell. Offr., Asst. Adjt. Actg. Adjt. the 2 wks. before his last engagement. Wounded and missing, now presumed killed, at Ypres, Oct. 12, 1917.

†WILSON-BROWNE, R. M. (1912–15, *y*)

1915 Sec. Lt., R.F.C., Fl. Off. No. 2 Sqn., 1 Wing, France. Wounded and prisoner, died at German 5 Corps dressing station, July 21, 1916, buried at Vis en Artois, Pas de Calais, 8 mls. E. of Arras.

WINCER, E. C. H. (1905–7, *b*)

1914 Interpreter, Russian Army. 1917 Sec. Lt., 4 Oxf. and Bucks. L.I. France. Wounded Aug. 1917. June 1918 Lt. May 1918 secd. Spec. Appt. : learning Bulgarian. Jan. 1919 Spec. Appt., Interpreter.

WINCKLE, E. W. (1887–94)
1914 Cpl., R.E., D.R. R.A., H.Q., 3 Div., France.

WINN, W. (1907–10, *b*)
Pte., Worc. R.

WISEMAN, C. L. (1905–12, *r*)
Sept. 1915 Instr. Lt., R.N., H.M.S. Superb. Apr. 1918 H.M.S.
Monarch. Jan. 1919 Course of Instn., Cambridge Univ. May 1919
Instr.-Lt. H.M.S. King George V, Home Fleet.

WISEMAN, F. D. (1907–11, *r*)
1914 Sec. Lt., Interpreter attd. 7 Div. Amm. Col. Feb. 1917
Lt., A.S.C. Adjt. May 1918 Actg. Capt., R.A.S.C. Mentd. May
1918.

†WOOD, E. H. (Asst. Master, 1912–16)
Jan. 1916 Sec. Lt., 3 Hamps. R. France, 1 Bn. Missing, presumed killed, Oct. 23, 1916, *nr. Lesboeufs* .

WOOD, E. W., M.C. and bar (1904–6, *b*)
Sept. 1914 Sec. Lt., 8 S. Staff. R. M.C. and bar, 1916. Wounded
1916. 3 S. Staff. R. Capt.

WOOD, K. S. (1909–15, *r*)
1916 A.B. Seaman, R.N.V.R. Apr. 1917 P.F.O., R.N.A.S.
Vendôme, Cranwell, Killingholme, Calshott. Sept. 1917 injured
by collision in air, Yorkshire. 1917 Sub-Lt. Seaplanes, Southampton. Apr. 1918 Lt. (A.), R.A.F. Sept. 1918 sailed for Egypt.
Invalided at Faenza en route. Jan. 1919 near Genoa.

WOOD, T. S. (1910–11, *r*)
Mar. 1915, Sec. Lt., R.F.A., T.F., 2/3 S. Mid. Bde. June 1916 Lt.
1917 France, A/307 Bde. Aug.–Sept. 1917 ▬▬▬ Ypres. Sept.
1917 Gassed and wounded. Aug. 1918 at recapture of Merville.
Final Advance, Cambrai–Maubeuge.

WOODHOUSE, L. (1910–13, *b*)
1914 Pte., R. Fus. (P. Sch.). May 1915 Sec. Lt., 3 R. Berks. R.
July 1917 Lt. 8 Bn.

WOODHOUSE, S. C. (1910–13, *b*)

1915 R.A.M.C. 1916 Surg. Prob., R.N.V.R., H.M. t.b.d. Obdurate. Oct. 1918 Surg.-Lt., R.N., H.M.S. Birkenhead.

WOOD-WHITE, B. (1902–9, *b*)

1916 Lt., R.A.M.C. 36 Gen. Hosp., Salonica F. 1917 Capt. No. 1 Convalescent Dépôt, Narussa.

WORRALL, C. H. B. (1913–17, *r*)

1918 Air Mech., 3 Class, Eng., R.A.F., Orkney Isles.

WORTHINGTON, G. F. P., M.C. (1906–10, *g*)

May 1912 Sec. Lt., W.I.R., R. of O. Aug. 1914 Sec. Lt., attd. 3 N. Staff. R. Aug. 1915 Sec. Lt., W.I.R. Oct. 1915 Lt. Actg. Capt., York. R. Apr.–May 1918 Actg. Lt.-Col., cdg. 21 Midd'x R. M.C. Sept. 1918.* Oct. 1918 13 York R. N. Russia (Murman E.F.). Five times wounded.

WRIGHT, E. S. (1908–12, *r*)

Aug. 1915 Sec. Lt., 10 Bord. R. July 1917 Lt. 1919 Attd. Pris. of War Camp, Belbeis, Egypt.

WRIGHT, F. H. (1911–14, *r*)

R.N. Div. 1917 Cdt., Merchant Service, H.M.C.T. Chakrata 1853.

WRIGHT, S. C. (1897–1902)

May 1911 Q.-M., Hon. Lt., R.A.M.C., T.F., 1/2 S. Mid. Fd. Amb., 48 Div. Aug. 1914–Mar. 1915 Home Service. Mar. 1915–July 1917, Aug. to Dec. 1917 France. July 1917 Q.-M., Capt. Dec. 1917–July 1918 Italy. Mentd., Apr. 1918.

WRIGHT, T. (1907–9 *r*)

1916 Pte., R.A.M.C., T.F., S. Mid. Div., 1 S. Gen. Hosp. 1917 Sgt.

WYNNE, H. (1889–90)

July 1911 Capt., 8 Lond. R., T.F. (P.O. Rifles). 1915 Capt., Asst. Dir., A.P.S., cdg. R.E. Postal Section, H.Q., W. Frontier Force, Egypt. 1917 Sudan civil administration. T.F. Res. *Contr. ?*
Posts and Telegraphs, Khartum.

†YARDLEY, F. G. (1899–1906, g)

Aug. 4, 1914, 72 Sea. Highrs., 16 Can. Scottish. Jan. 1915 Sec. Lt., 8 N. Staff. R. Five weeks in France. Died of wounds (received Aug. 22, 1915, nr. Neuve Chapelle) in Calais Hospital, Sept. 17, 1915 : buried at Calais. He was shot by a stray bullet while superintending trench-digging operations.

†YATES, G. H. (1901–2)

Nov. 1915 Pte., 26 R. Fus. (Bankers' Bn.). Aug. 1916 France, on the Somme. 1916 partly buried. Belgian front, wounded. Aug. 1917 attd. Army Pay Corps. 1917 transfd., Cpl., A.P.C., Boulogne. Dec. 1918 Lt., A.P.C., under the Field Cashier, H.Q., 4th Army. Died of pneumonia, following influenza, 14 Gen. Hosp., Wimereux, Feb. 15, 1919.

YATES, R. W. (1898–9)

July 1915 Pte., H.A.C. Dec. 1915 transfd. R.F.C. 1917 Cdt., R.E., Newark. Feb. 1918 Sec. Lt., R.E., 290 A.T. Coy., France.

†YEANDLE, W. H. (1899–1902)

1914 Pte., 14 R. War. R. 1917 Cpl. Killed May 20, 1917.

YEOMAN, E. W. (1892–6)

1916 Sec. Lt., The King's (L'pool R.). July 1917 Lt. Apr. 1918 Actg. Capt., Spec. List, Garr. Phys. and Bayt. Trng. Supervising Off.

ROLL OF HONOUR

A LIST OF THE FALLEN

Arthur William Hamilton Adams.
Joseph Adams.
Ralph Adams.
Frederic Clifford Alabaster.
Frank Reginald Allen.
Wilfred Samson Allkins.
Sydney Anderton.
Gavin Campbell Arbuthnot.
David William Arnott.
Thomas Leslie Astbury.
Harold Godfrey Bache.
Frank Farmer Baker.
John Howard Banks.
Godfrey Barker.
Holroyd Birkett Barker.
Thomas Kenneth Barnsley.
Wilfred Roy Bartley.
Percival Baron Bayliss.
Edmund William Beech.
Hugh Randolph Ryan Bell.
Harold Beresford.
Norrys Aubrey Best.
Arthur Vanderkiste Bisseker.
John Wallis Bisseker.
John Henry Blewitt.
Ralph Thomas Boddington.
Augustine Bonner.
Leslie Harold Bowen.
Victor Henry Thompson Boyton.
John Randolph Brame.

Richard Balfour Bourne

Arthur Joseph Brearley.
Norman Blackburn Brearley.
Herbert Harry Weston Brown.
Horace Newland Brown.
Eric William Busby.
Vernon Erle George Busby.
Leigh Streetley Latham Butler.
Edward Lascelles Cashmore.   John Henry Cardew
Reginald Percy Chantrill.
Raymond Russell Cheshire.
Charles Cam Thackwell Clayton.
Langdon Sacheverell Coke.
Arden Cotterell Coldicott.
Frederick Henry Douglas Collier.
Ernest Stanley Collins.
Desmond George Conaty.
Alfred Thomas Cond.
George Frederick Cottrell.
Harold William Cottrell.
Frank Neville Cowper.
Donald Leslie Langford Craig.
Alexander Basil Crawford.
Gerald Edgecumbe Crichton.
John Drummond Crichton.
Ronald Crichton.
Frank Alan Cross.
Keith Saxby Curtis.
Fred Daniels.
Eric Powell Davies.
Trevor Arthur Manning Davies.
Hatton Bertram St. John De Vine.
Francis Devis.
Harry Dickinson.
Percy Groves Dingley.   Frederic Lynn Disturnal
Ferdinand Eglington.
John Albert Ehrhardt.

       William Hereward Ehrhardt

Frank Dudley Evans.
Frank Aldridge Fawcett.
Alfred George Fawdry.
William Davies Featherstone.
Hubert Ratcliffe Felton.
Benjamin John Morton Field.
Sydney Fink.
Philip Henry Burt Fitch.
Harold Egbert Foizey.
William Alfred Foley.
Frederick Cecil Franklin.
Cyril Charles Frost.
Beaumont Edward Gammell.
Harold Wheale Garratt.
Eric Thomas Gaunt.
William Gordon Gething.
Robert Quilter Gilson.
George Harold Goodison.
Douglas Edward Gosling.
Keith Forster Graham.
Harold Samuel Griffin.
Philip Forrest Groves.
Cyril Vernon Hadley.
Howard Hallam.
William John Hardwidge.
Joseph Cecil Harris.
Philip Dawson Harris.
Edward Rainsford Harrison.
Alan Pat Harrower.
William Ernest Hartley.
Walter Herbert Harvey.
Wilfrid Hawkes.
Alfred Norman Headley.
Edward Grafton Herbert.
Bertram Gilbert Hill.
Norman Hipkins.

Maurice William Hobson.
John Othic Holroyd.
Frederick Julian Horner.
John William Willoughby Hudson.
William Barton Hughes.
Frederic Harry Humby.
Leslie Glendower Humphries.
Howard John Hutchinson.
Conrade William Jacot.
George Clift Jenkins.
John Richard Jenkins.
Arthur Cyril Jervis.
John Cedric Jervis.
Arthur Edgar Johnson.
Frank Cecil Johnson.
Frank Isaac Jonas.
Frederick Wigan Jones.
Noel Edward Jones.
Richard John Keates.
Robert George Kekewich.
Malcolm Keys.
Norman Toynbee King.
Sydney Clifford Lamplugh.
James Norman Lancaster.
Sydney Henry Lane.
John Colin Larkins.
Leslie Sydney Last.
Francis Matt Lawledge.
Rudolph Russell Lawrence.
Richard Frederick Leacroft.
Ivo Frank Lewis.
Benjamin Charles Line.
Frederick William Lister.
Matthew William Lister.
Victor Alfred Manley Lory.
Edward Lovekin.

Jeffery Wentworth Lythgoe.
Donald McBean.
Felix Desmond Macswiney.
Hubert Franklin Madders.
Edward Francis Malins.
Horace Mann.
Charles Paul Mansell.
Walter Reynolds Mansell.
Isador David Marks.
Philip Spencer Marshall.
John Mason.
Philip Granville Mason.
Henry James Matthews.
Neville Miller   Herbert Ward Milligan.
William Millner.
Brian John Millward.
Thomas Ewart Mitton.
Charles Frederick Moore.
Geoffrey William Broadbent Moore.
Eric Simpson Morrison.
John Woodley Morrison.
Charles William Mould.
Oswald James Nicholl   Granville Murray-Browne.
Thomas Leslie Nichols.
William Leslie Onions.
Geoffrey Ewing Orton-Smith.
Raymond Gascoyne Ottey.
Cecil William Hannington Parker.
Beresford Frank Parsons.
Alec John Partridge.
George Patterson.
Ralph Stuart Payton.
Frank Shakespeare Pearson.
Harry Pearson.
Sydney Whitelock Pepper.
Cecil Howard Perkins.

Richard Hill Phillips.
David Archibald Pipe.
Percy Pountney.
Harry Stanyer Powell.
Brian Christopher Power.
Arthur Poynting.
Lawrence Jack Preedy.
Beryl James Pretious.
William Charles Richards.
Francis Henry Richardson.
Llewellyn Isaac Hilton Roberts.
Percy Arden Rogers.
Leslie Norton Rolason.
Reginald Vincent Rose.
Lewis Henry Salaman.
William Worthington Sanby.
George Ernest Sanders.
Thomas Frederick Proctor Sanders.
Leslie Kelham Sands.
William Spencer FitzRobert Saundby.
Leslie Sayer.
William Harold Scorer.
Frank Trevolla Secker.
Gordon Oliver Seers.
Henry Lynn Shaw.
Ralph Shaw.
Harold Welford Sheffield.
Edwin Guy Silk.
Eric Douglas Smart.
Alfred Percy Smith.
Geoffrey Bache Smith.
George Barker Smith.
George Morley Smith.
Roger Smith.
Hugh Russell Somerville.
Charles Eric Wakefield Speller.

Charles William Schwaben

Eliot Spencer.
Frank Stockdale.
William Ernest Stubbs.
Cornelius Vincent Suckling.
Edgar Francis Talbt Thomas Kemp Tabberner.
Arthur Horace Tanfield.
Cyril James Tart.
Martin Bartley Taylor.
Maurice Cecil Thompson.
Herbert Leslie Tomlinson.
James Wyndham Tomson.
Robert Cecil Teeghorn John William Collis Tongue.
Robert Maxwell Trimble.
John Percival Turner.
Harold Reece Twigg.
Albert Theodore Vardy.
William Lang Vince.
Horace John Walker.
William Evelyn Wansbrough.
William Arthur Bayford Kirwan Ward.
Edwin Frederick Warth.
Frank Joseph Dalton Warwood.
Thomas Sidney Wathes.
Beresford Whitcombe.
Herbert Whitehouse.
Ernest Stanley Whitworth.
Thomas Strange Wickham.
John Soulsby Wilson.
Rowland Murray Wilson-Browne.
Eric Horace Wood.
Frederick George Yardley.
George Herbert Yates.
William Henry Yeandle.

HONOURS

C.M.G.

A. S. Langley.

D.S.O. *and bar*

J. R. C. Dent.
C. Lister.

D.S.O.

E. P. Argyle.
G. H. Ball.
W. A. J. Barker.
R. A. Broderick.
S. A. Davis.
H. C. Harrison.
A. C. Howard.
D. J. McGavin.
†P. G. Mason.
R. T. Pemberton.
E. S. Phipson.
H. J. Sanders.
†R. Shaw.
R. O. Warder.

O.B.E. (*Military Div.*)

C. H. Caldicott.
S. A. Davis.
H. M. Edwards.
Ernest Goodwin.
H. H. Humphreys.
A. T. A. Naylor.
F. Newey.
F. R. Phipps.

z

O.B.E. Military Div. (continued)

T. Slater Price.
J. E. H. Roberts.
H. H. Sampson.
Stanley Smith.

M.B.E. (Military Div.)

G. P. Achurch.
J. E. Catherall.
H. Clarke.
N. A. Haywood.
A. W. Ibbotson.
J. W. Landon.
D. E. Riddell.
N. F. Rose.

M.C. and Bar

†R. Adams.
F. J. Bywater.
E. L. Hopkins.
A. H. Sayer.
†L. Sayer.
E. D. Tyndall.
J. O. Walford.
E. W. Wood.

M.C.

A. S. Alabaster.
A. W. Allkins.
H. S. Astbury.
F. E. L. Bache.
G. H. Ball.
L. Ball.
E. A. Barker.
†H. Beresford.
O. Bird.
W. Bowater.

F. J. Breeden.
P. S. Brindley.
R. A. Broderick.
G. M. Chantrill.
F. Clarke.
G. Clarke.
-A. C. Coldicott.
W. Mundy Cox.
†D. L. L. Craig.
L. C. Crockford.
S. G. Cuxson.
C. A. I. Damon.
F. Daniels.
H. Davies.
J. R. C. Dent.
C. N. De Vine.
R. F. Diggle.
H. J. Dixon.
S. F. Dixon.
W. G. B. Edmonds.
N. T. Ellis.
J. W. Fawdry.
†W. D. Featherstone.
†P. H. B. Fitch.
H. Forrest.
A. S. Fowler.
M. F. K. Fraser.
C. F. L. Gibson.
H. D. Gibson.
R. J. Gittins.
L. L. Goold.
H. R. Guest.
E. C. R. Haddow.
L. L. Hadley.
N. H. Hartshorne.

† J. H. Cardew.

M.C. (continued)

H. Hawkes.
E. G. Herbert.
H. L. Higgins.
D. F. Holmes.
████████████
†F. J. Horner.
A. C. Howard.
H. H. Humphreys.
A. E. T. Hunt.
A. W. Ibbotson.
N. E. Jervis.
†R. J. Keates.
A. S. Keep.
E. T. Kerby.
J. J. Kino.
A. C. Lambourne.
A. A. Lees.
C. Lister.
†F. W. Lister.
C. W. Longley.
E. W. N. May.
C. E. Milner.
R. D. Moore.
C. R. Norman.
T. J. Orme.
J. S. Phillips.
†H. S. Powell.
T. H. Ravenhill.
W. C. Retallack.
A. B. P. Roberts.
A. S. Roberts.
J. K. A. Robertson.
S. H. Robinson.
F. H. Rogers.

B. A. Jervis

A. J. Round.
J. H. St. Johnston.
H. H. Sampson.
H. J. Sanders.
R. H. M. S. Saundby.
B. R. Saunders.
T. H. Searls.
W. J. Slim.
B. J. Denton Thompson.
T. E. Tildesley.
J. C. P. Tosh.
J. W. Turner.
J. W. C. Turner.
J. L. Umbers.
C. H. Vaughan.   *S. J. J. Vaughton*
P. J. Watkin.   *E. G. S. Walker*
C. J. R. Whitmore.
G. F. P. Worthington.

D.S.C.

A. B. F. Alcock.

D.F.C.

R. H. Rusby.

A.F.C.

J. Line.
R. H. M. S. Saundby.
Cresswell Turner.

Territorial Force Decoration (T.D.)

T. F. Goode.   *J. Barnsley*
W. H. Kimpton.

D.C.M.

H. A. Cutler.
J. W. Muncaster.

M.M.

R. J. Ryan Bell.
A. S. Fowler.
H. J. Irwin.
C. W. Longley.
L. Nathan.
G. C. Peart.
N. F. Spencer.
C. W. Wilson.

E. E. Watson

M.S.M.

E. H. P. Rawlins.

Brevet Lieut.-Col.

E. P. Argyle.

Brevet-Major

L. C. Crockford.
H. C. Harrison.
J. F. Leacroft.

FOREIGN HONOURS

Legion of Honour : Croix de Chevalier

J. d'E. Fitz E. Coke.
J. H. Godfrey.
J. V. V. Magrane.
†P. G. Mason.

Croix de Guerre

E. P. Argyle.
W. A. J. Barker.

G. M. Chantrill.
G. H. B. Crossland.
J. R. C. Dent (Silver Cross).
A. C. Howard.
C. R. Norman.
A. J. Round (with palm).

Médaille d'Argent de l'Assistance Publique
J. K. Gaunt (twice).

Médaille Militaire
W. H. Tait.

Belgian Croix de Guerre
E. C. R. Haddow.
E. W. Jones.

Greece : M.C., 3ʳᵈ Cl.
K. W. Grant.

Italian Bronze Medal
A. Allen.
T. Stinton.

Croce di Guerra
A. S. Alabaster.
G. E. G. Assinder.
R. A. Broderick.
L. C. Crockford.
J. W. Fawdry.
W. F. Wackrill.

Serbia : *Order of St. Sava*
C. Y. Flewitt.
T. H. Ravenhill.

Serbia : *Cross of Serbian Red Cross*
E. B. Alabaster.
F. Newey.

Officer of the Crown of Roumania
H. M. Edwards.

Egypt : *Order of the Nile*
J. H. Godfrey.
P. S. Brindley (4th.)

MENTIONED IN DISPATCHES
J. Adams.
†R. Adams.
E. B. Alabaster.
A. B. F. Alcock.
A. Allen.
E. P. Argyle (3).
G. E. G. Assinder.
R. H. Astbury (2).
G. H. Ball (3).
L. Ball.
E. A. Barker.
W. A. J. Barker.
†T. K. Barnsley.
†P. B. Bayliss.
†H. R. Ryan Bell.
T. W. Bladon.
†J. H. Blewitt.
E. J. Boome.
C. S. Booth.
J. C. Boulger.
P. S. Brindley.
R. A. Broderick (3).
L. G. Burleigh.
E. de G. Carr.
G. M. Chantrill.
R. G. B. Chase.
S. W. Clift (2).
J. d'E. FitzE. Coke.

E. W. C. Bradfield

H. D. Coleman

†J. D. Crichton.
L. C. Crockford.
A. C. Curle.
H. Davies.
S. A. Davis.
J. R. C. Dent (3).
C. N. de Vine.
H. J. Dixon.
P. Docker.
W. G. B. Edmonds.
E. Edmonds-Smith.
F. M. Edwards.
W. H. Ennals.
J. W. Fawdry.
C. Y. Flewitt (3).
R. O. Gatheral.
J. K. Gaunt.
C. F. L. Gibson.
H. D. Gibson.
F. Goodman (2).
E. C. R. Haddow.
†E. R. Harrison.
H. C. Harrison (3).
W. Harriss.
H. Hawkes.
D. J. R. Hawkins.
N. A. Haywood. (2)
F. J. Hemming.
R. B. Henderson.
†N. Hipkins.
M. E. Holdsworth.
A. C. Howard (3).
W. Hughes.
H. H. Humphreys.
G. L. Hyde.

A a

MENTIONED IN DISPATCHES (continued)

E. T. Kerby.
J. J. Kino.
†S. H. Lane (5).
A. S. Langley.
F. H. Lee.
C. Lister (5).
C. V. L. Lycett.
S. N. McKenzie.
J. V. V. Magrane.
†H. Mann.
†P. G. Mason.
E. J. Mitton (3).
A. T. A. Naylor (2).
F. Newey (2).
J. D. d'A. Northwood.
D. H. Parry.
G. C. Peart.
R. T. Pemberton.
J. S. Phillips.
A. B. Phillp (2).
E. S. Phipson.
J. R. Pickmere.
C. K. K. Prosser.
T. H. Ravenhill.
W. C. Retallack.
A. S. Roberts.
J. E. H. Roberts.
S. A. Roberts.
S. H. Robinson.
J. F. Roe.
C. F. Rowe.
R. A. Rowse.
H. J. Sanders.
W. H. Scorer.

J . R . Phillip .

†R. Shaw.
C. F. V. Smout.
N. F. Spencer.
A. G. Stanbury.
†F. Stockdale.
A. M. Thompson.
B. J. Denton Thompson.
†J. W. Tomson.
J. C. P. Tosh (2).
†R. M. Trimble.
N. P. Tucker.
J. L. Umbers.
T. A. N. Walker.
H. B. Wallis.
†W. A. B. K. Ward.
R. O. Warder.
L. Whitcombe.
C. J. R. Whitmore.
†J. S. Wilson.
F. D. Wiseman.
S. C. Wright.

Distinguished War Services

J. & E. FitzE. Coke (2).   *V. Curle.*
G. W. Craig.
F. le N. Foster.
E. Goodwin.
L. C. Hayes.
R. M. Trimble.
G. F. Upton.

Valuable War Services

T. R. Groom.
J. Hall-Edwards (2).
H. C. Harrison.
E. H. Stansbie.

DEEDS OF GALLANTRY
FOR WHICH HONOURS WERE AWARDED
From the *London Gazette*

N.B.—The ranks and units are as given in the *Gazette* at the time.

†ADAMS, R., Lt., M.C., 8 R. War. R., T.F.—*Bar to M.C.* (Sept. 1916).

For conspicuous gallantry in leading a raid on the enemy's trenches during the night of March 22 and 23 (1916). Under close fire he cut the enemy's wire with torpedoes. He then bombed his way along the enemy's trench, killing three of the enemy himself, and held a barricade until reinforced.

ALABASTER, A. S., Capt., 1–5 R. War. R., T.F.—*M.C.* (Oct. 20, 1916).

For conspicuous gallantry in action. He led his company in the attack with great dash, capturing many prisoners and two machine guns. He held on to the position won for thirty-six hours, until relieved, and beat off several counter-attacks.

ALCOCK, A. B. F., Actg. Lt., R.M.L.I., Portsmouth Bn.— *D.S.C.* (Sept. 13, 1915).

For gallantry and good service near Gaba Tepe between April 28 and May 1, 1915. Accompanied by Lt. Empson, of the same regiment, with two platoons, numbering in all sixty men, he defended an isolated trench against overwhelming odds. Lt. Empson was wounded early in the day of April 30, and was killed on May 1, and Lt. Alcock was finally compelled to withdraw, after having held this ground for four nights and three days. During this time no food or water could be conveyed to the trench, and at one time ammunition was reduced to about fifteen rounds per man.

ALLKINS, A. W., Lt., M.G.C.—*M.C.* (Mar. 7, 1918).

When the section on his left hand had sustained several casualties, he dressed their wounds and got them to a place of safety, and organized stretcher-bearers. On another occasion he went out at great risk and brought in two wounded men.

BACHE, F. E. L., Capt., S. Staff. R., T.F.—*M.C.* (July 26, 1918).

For conspicuous gallantry and devotion to duty in command of his company and later of the battalion, when his C.O. became a casualty. He made a personal reconnaissance, when the situation was obscure, getting within 15 yards of the enemy, and later extricated his battalion from a difficult position without loss.

BALL, G. H., Capt., 1/5 S. Staff. R., T.F.—*D.S.O.* (Mar. 8, Oct. 4, 1919).

On September 27-8, 1918, north of Bellenglise, he by a counter-attack ejected the enemy, who had bombed their way into newly captured trenches. Later, being short of ammunition and bombs, he was forced to fall back, showing great courage and stubbornness, and inflicting heavy casualties on the enemy. Next day he made a reconnaissance with a small patrol, and with two men went forward and captured sixteen enemy and two machine guns. He did fine work.

BALL, G. H., Capt., D.S.O., 1/5 S. Staff. R., T.F.—*M.C.* (Mar. 8, Oct. 4, 1919).

On October 12, 1918, east of Bohain, he led an attack on the south-west edge of Riqueval Wood. The enemy barrage disorganized the attack, and drove it back temporarily. He reorganized his company, and with the help of part of another company he again attacked, gaining the edge of the wood and occupying a line some 200 yards into the wood. His great gallantry and devotion to duty won the admiration of his men.

†BERESFORD, H., Lt., R.F.A.—*M.C.* (Sept. 16, 1918).

For conspicuous gallantry and devotion to duty when forward observation officer. He remained at his post until his communications were cut and he was nearly surrounded. He eventually brought in very useful information. He subsequently displayed great coolness and gallantry while temporarily in command of his battery.

BREEDEN, F. J., Capt., 5 R. War. R., T.F.—*M.C.* (Apr. 6, 1918).

For conspicuous gallantry and devotion to duty when in command of a successful raid. He captured twelve prisoners and demolished a dug-out, afterwards withdrawing his party without loss.

BYWATER, F. J., Lt., temp. Major, M.C., R.E., T.F., 47 Div. —*Bar to M.C.* (July 28, 1918).

For conspicuous gallantry and devotion to duty while superintending the destruction of river and canal bridges. Owing to the complicated nature of some of the bridges, which necessitated placing additional charges after the original charges had been fired, he remained to see the work thoroughly completed, in spite of the fact that the enemy were close upon him. He set a splendid example of courage and skill to all ranks.

CHANTRILL, G. M., Sec. Lt., Gen. List (N. Russia).—*M.C.* (Feb. 1, 1919).

For conspicuous gallantry and devotion to duty. He personally guided the infantry to their objective at V.P. 455 on October 14, 1918. He had previously reconnoitred the position four times. This work necessitated his passing behind the enemy lines to a depth of four miles. He has been with the attacking forces since the landing on Modyuski Island, and his reconnaissances have been of the greatest value.

CLARKE, G., Lt., Actg. Capt., N. Staff. R., S.R.—*M.C.* (Apr. 22, 1918).

During a reconnaissance his party was suddenly fired on by the enemy, and one of his men was found to be missing. He at once returned and found the man lying wounded close to the enemy's position. He reached the man under fire from the enemy, and was severely wounded in doing so. He showed the greatest courage and self-sacrifice.

†COLDICOTT, A. C., Sec. Lt., 15 R. War. R., S.R.—*M.C.* (Jan. 8, 1918).

For conspicuous gallantry when commanding a raiding party. Although the original scheme had to be altered at a moment's notice, his resource and skilful leadership saved any confusion. During the raid he accounted for two of the enemy himself, and afterwards withdrew his party in good order, and brought them safely and skilfully through an intense hostile barrage back to our own lines. His enthusiasm and personal example kept his men in high fettle throughout, and contributed greatly to the success of the raid.

†CRAIG, D. L. L., Lt., R.F.A.—*M.C.* (Jan. 8, 1918).

For conspicuous gallantry and devotion to duty when under heavy and continuous shell fire for five hours with his battery. During the shelling a dump of charges caught fire, and he, with others, succeeded in removing a large pile of neighbouring shells, which was all the time in danger of an explosion. His prompt action and gallantry saved a large amount of ammunition and material, and probably many lives.

CROCKFORD, Lt., temp. Capt., 1/5 R. War. R., T.F.— *M.C.* (Oct. 20, 1916).

He did fine work during a night attack ; and, in conjunction with a bombing attack fired over the ' stop ' at the enemy's machine-gunners, while two men handed him ammunition. Finally he consolidated the position won.

CUTLER, H. A., Mtr. Cycl.-Sgt., 1 Div. Sig. Coy., R.E.—
D.C.M. (Sept. 5, 1919).

For consistent gallantry and devotion to duty. He has seen pro-
longed service with the 1 Div. Sig. Coy., and has repeatedly
during the last six months daringly reconnoitred forward roads
for his dispatch riders to follow. He has on many occasions himself taken forward important dispatches under most trying
circumstances. His services have been noteworthy, especially
near Festubert in April 1918, and near Eterpigny, near Arras,
and Naissemy in August and September 1918.

CUXSON, S. G., Lt., Actg. Capt., 9 attd. 1 S. Staff. R.—
M.C. (Sept. 16, 1918).

For conspicuous gallantry and devotion to duty when in command of three platoons. He led them with skill and determination,
and played a leading part in overcoming the enemy's resistance.
He shot one of the enemy dead with his revolver. Both before
and during the operation his example infused his men with keen-
ness and courage.

DAMON, C. A. I., Lt., Actg. Capt., Glouc. R., attd. 1/5 Bedf.
R., T.F. (Egypt).—M.C. (Mar. 8, Oct. 4, 1919).

On September 19, 1918, at Kefr Kasim, under heavy enemy
barrages, he, commanding the leading company of the battalion,
showed the utmost coolness and gallantry. It was largely
due to his leadership that his company suffered low casualties,
and his action was of the greatest value to his battalion commander.

†DANIELS, Fred, C.S.M., 2/5 R. War. R., T.F.—M.C.
(July 28, 1916), for July 1, on the Somme.

For conspicuous gallantry throughout an intense bombardment.
He moved about utterly regardless of danger, encouraging his
men after all his officers had become casualties.

DAVIES, HERBERT, Capt., 1/8 R. War. R., T.F.—*M.C.* (1915).

For conspicuous gallantry and resource on many occasions when on patrol duty in front of the trenches, notably on the night of June 20–1, 1915, when he carried out a very daring reconnaissance close to the River Douve. From his knowledge of German he obtained very valuable information from the enemy's conversation after passing over ground lit by flares and constantly swept by machine-gun fire.

DAVIS, SIDNEY ALFRED, Sec. Lt., temp. Lt., Gen. List, Cdg. T.M.B.—*D.S.O.* (Sept. 22, 1916).

For conspicuous gallantry in action. He worked his guns with great skill and courage, repelling three counter-attacks. Finally he carried his wounded to the dressing station under heavy fire.

DENT, J. R. C., Capt., Actg. Lt.-Col., M.C., 1 R. Innis. Fus.—*D.S.O.* (Mar. 8, Oct. 4, 1919).

For conspicuous gallantry and good leadership in command of his battalion during operations from October 14–16, 1918, in the Moorseele–Gulleghem–Heule Sector. His skilful leading enabled the battalion to reach its final objective in face of determined resistance and over difficult ground. After making a personal reconnaissance he again led his leading companies, and cleared the ground to the Heule area. He did good work.

DIGGLE, Rev. R. F., C.F., 4th Cl.—*M.C.* (Dec. 2, 1918).

During several days' hard fighting he attended to the wounded under heavy machine-gun fire. He was frequently in the advanced posts, bringing little creature comforts to the men, to whom his cheerful and composed demeanour and perfect disregard of danger were a great encouragement.

EDMONDS, W. G. B., Lt., 1 R. War. R., S.R.—*M.C.* (July 26, 1918).

For conspicuous gallantry and devotion to duty in action. When the troops on the right were forced to withdraw, exposing the

B b

flank, he led a party of about sixty men from various units and counter-attacked. He obtained a footing on the high ground, when our artillery put down a heavy barrage, and he was forced to withdraw owing to casualties among his men. He showed great dash in taking the ridge.

†FEATHERSTONE, W. D., Sec. Lt., R.F.A.—*M.C.* (Jan. 8, 1918).

For conspicuous gallantry and devotion to duty on two separate occasions under heavy shell fire, during which he showed extreme courage in putting out fires which had broken out in his gun-pits.

†FITCH, P. H. B., Sec. Lt., R.F.A.—*M.C.* (Aug. 16, 1917).

For conspicuous gallantry and devotion to duty in accompanying another officer and a sergeant into a gun emplacement in which a serious explosion had taken place, bringing out the killed and wounded and extinguishing a fire caused by the explosion among the ammunition.

FOWLER, A. S., Sec. Lt., M.M., R.F.A.—*M.C.* (Nov. 11, 1918).

For conspicuous gallantry and devotion to duty. With the assistance of two men he tore down the camouflage of a gun which had been set on fire by the bomb from an enemy aeroplane, and extinguished the flames, though there was no water available and the heat was so intense that the ammunition in the pit was liable to explode at any moment. The position was being heavily shelled at the time. By his courage and presence of mind he averted an explosion which would have caused heavy casualties.

FRASER, M. F. K., Sec. Lt., York and Lanc. R.—*M.C.* (Aug. 16, 1917).

For conspicuous gallantry and devotion to duty. As intelligence officer during our offensive he carried out his work with the greatest ability and courage. By his untiring energy under heavy shell fire, touch was kept day and night between the different units, under very difficult conditions ; and he personally led with great success a party against a strong point which had for some time been holding us back from the final objective. His example throughout the whole of the operations was magnificent.

GIBSON, C. F. L., Capt., R. War. R., T.F.—*M.C.* (July 26, 1918).

Whilst acting as brigade major, he rallied a large body of men and led them back to the trenches, where he remained until the line was re-established and properly organized. For the next several days he arranged all the details connected with the defence, ammunition, and food of this mixed force. His personal example was of exceptional value.

GIBSON, H. D., Sec. Lt., Actg. Lt., N. Staff. R., secd. M.G.C. —*M.C.* (July 26, 1917).

For conspicuous gallantry and devotion to duty when in command of mortars during an attack upon enemy trenches. His forward guns were completely buried by hostile shelling, but he succeeded in bringing them back ready to fire again, although a terrific barrage was going on at the time. He also took charge of a party of infantry who were left without an officer, and led them forward and established bombing posts. He set a very fine example to all ranks.

GOOLD, L. L., Sec. Lt., Worc. R., S.R.—*M.C.* (July 26, 1917).

He kept his machine gun in action amidst an intense hostile barrage, personally observing and inflicting heavy loss upon an enemy counter-attack. He was exposed to view all the time, and his courage and coolness were magnificent. On previous occasions he has done excellent work of a similar nature.

GUEST, H. R., Sec. Lt., Oxf. and Bucks. L.I., T.F.—*M.C.* (Mar. 7, 1918).

In an advance against the enemy position, when his company officers became casualties, he sited and consolidated a position on reaching the objective, arranging a defensive flank. He organized a resistance to counter-attack, and by his example and courage he inspired his men to hold the position.

HADDOW, E. C. R., Capt., R.F.A., T.F., D.T.M.O., 41 Div. —*M.C.* (Feb. 1, 1919).

For conspicuous gallantry and devotion to duty on Sept. 23, 1918, near Pilkem. While reconnoitring positions for trench-mortar batteries close to the front line, the officer with him was hit by machine-gun fire, which was continuous in the area. In spite of this, after careful reconnaissance, he got up the mortars and ammunition by night. He set a fine example under constant shell and machine-gun fire.

HARRISON, H. C., Lt., temp. Capt., R.M.A., attd. S.A.A., temp. Maj.—*D.S.O.* (Aug. 25, 1916).

For conspicuous gallantry during operations. He carried out two dangerous reconnaissances far in front of our foremost line, and brought back valuable reports. On both occasions he was under heavy shell and rifle fire. He had previously been observing from a tree when it was struck by a direct hit from an enemy gun.

†HERBERT, E. G., Sec. Lt., temp. Lt. and Actg. Capt., R. War. R., attd. 121 M.G.C. (France).—*M.C.* (Sept. 16, 1918).

When the commander of the company had been killed, this officer took command. Under very heavy fire he showed himself regardless of personal safety, visiting his sections, some of which were almost surrounded. It was largely owing to his exertions that six successive attacks by the enemy on our positions were annihilated by our fire. The skill with which he handled his company, his courage, and his initiative were admirable.

HIGGINS, H. L., Sec. Lt., R. War. R.—*M.C.* (Nov. 25, 1916).

He went forward under very heavy fire to ascertain the situation. Later, on three occasions, he carried out most valuable reconnaissances. He was severely wounded.

HOLMES, D. F., Lt., Actg. Capt., 46 Divl. Train., R.A.S.C., T.F., attd. 4 N. Staff. R.—*M.C.* (Mar. 8, Oct. 4, 1919).

Near Sweveghem, on October 20, 1918, he showed marked gallantry and ability when in command of his company. The enemy put up a stubborn resistance during the whole of the attack ; but, in spite of heavy machine-gun and shell fire, he, by his skilful handling of his men, forced the enemy to give ground, and eventually, after hard fighting, reached his objective.

HOPKINS, E. L., Sec. Lt., 2 Worc. R., S.R.—*M.C.* (Apr. 17, 1917).

For conspicuous gallantry and devotion to duty during a raid on the enemy's trenches. He handled his men with marked ability, and himself accounted for two of the enemy. Later, he effected a skilful withdrawal and brought all his party safely back.

HOPKINS, E. L., Lt., Actg. Capt., 6 attd. 2 Worc. R.— *Bar to M.C.* (Mar. 8, Oct. 4, 1919).

During the operations, October 22–3, 1918, up to the capture of Englefontaine, he commanded the leading company with great skill and daring, maintained communication with units of another division on his flank, and kept his commanding officer informed of the situation. Although shaken by the near explosion of a gas shell, he remained at duty, led his company in the attack, killed several of the enemy with his revolver, and supervised the consolidation and establishment of communication when the village had been captured.

HUNT, A. E. T., Sec. Lt., R.F.A., S.R.—*M.C.* (Apr. 25, 1918).

While the battery was being moved up to a forward position under exceptionally difficult circumstances, three officers became casualties. He, though much shaken by a shell bursting near him, took charge and, with the greatest gallantry and resource, com-

pleted the advance into action. He commanded the battery for
a considerable period under very trying conditions, and has done
much good work in the forward area, obtaining a great deal of
valuable information.

JERVIS, N. E., Sec. Lt., R. War. R.—*M.C.* (Sept. 17, 1917).
  During and after an assault upon enemy trenches, he led his
  company with great dash and skill, capturing both his objectives.
  Though hit in the head immediately afterwards, and in considerable pain, he insisted in carrying on with the consolidation,
  remaining with his company for two days until sent to the dressing
  station, much against his wish. His pluck and determination set
  a magnificent example to his men. He has previously done consistently good work.

†KEATES, R. J., Sec. Lt., R.G.A., S.R.—*M.C.* (Mar. 18,
  1918).
  During a heavy gas-shell bombardment a dug-out was hit by a gas
  shell and a man was buried. He at once went to the dug-out,
  which was full of gas, and extricated the wounded man. Owing
  to the darkness he had to remove his respirator in the dug-out.
  Though suffering from gas, he superintended the removal of the
  wounded man under the most intense fire. His courageous action
  undoubtedly saved the man's life.

KEEP, A. S., Lt., Gen. List, attd. R.A.F.—*M.C.* (Sept. 16,
  1918).
  For conspicuous gallantry and devotion to duty on long-distance
  bombing raids. He showed great skill and determination while
  raiding enemy towns. One day, with his oil-feed pipe broken, he
  reached his objective, and disposed of an enemy machine on his
  way back. His work was splendid.

LISTER, Cecil, Capt., temp. Lt.-Col., M.C., North'n R.,
  attd. 1/6 S. Staff. R., T.F.—*D.S.O.* (Mar. 8,
  Oct. 4, 1919).
  His battalion was allotted the difficult task of storming the
  St. Quentin Canal and capturing the village of Bellenglise on the

further bank. Amongst the defences he had to attack was a tunnel system. On September 29, 1918, he achieved a complete success with slight casualties, and this was in great measure due to his careful preparation of the attack and the determination with which he personally inspired all ranks serving under him during the action.

†LISTER, F. W., Capt., = Bn., Tank Corps (Lt., Worc. R.).—
    M.C. (Dec. 2, 1918).

For conspicuous gallantry and devotion to duty. He led his tanks into action and directed them personally to their objectives up to the moment of their engaging the enemy. Throughout two actions he was on foot with his tanks, and showed an absolute disregard for personal safety.

LONGLEY, C. W., Sec. Lt., M.M., R.F.A.—M.C. (Jan. 8, 1918).

For conspicuous gallantry and devotion to duty as Forward Observing Officer. Having got into touch with the attacking infantry he continued throughout the day to send back most useful information, although the whole time exposed to heavy machine-gun and shell fire, displaying splendid resolution and courage under the most trying circumstances.

MOORE, R. D., Capt., R.A.M.C.—M.C. (Feb. 18, 1918).

He worked continuously for eight days attending to the wounded at an advanced dressing station, often under shell fire. His organization of the work was excellent, and by his courage and cheerfulness he inspired all ranks with confidence, which assisted them materially in the performance of their duties.

NORMAN, C. R., Lt., Actg. Capt., R.E., T.F. (Russia).—
    M.C. (Feb. 1, 1919).

This officer has done consistently good work under fire during the operations of Force ' C ' on the River Dvina, as the only engineer officer with the expedition. He has also, without any staff or assistance, carried out efficiently and well the additional duties of Ordnance Officer, Artillery Officer, Officer in charge of wireless and signals. At Pontchonga and elsewhere he has shown special zeal in the landing and re-embarking of stores, guns, and wireless gear under very difficult circumstances, and his energy and devotion to duty have been of great assistance to the force.

ORME, T. J., Sec. Lt., M.G.C.—*M.C.* (Apr. 6, 1918).
He took his guns forward during an action in a most courageous manner in spite of numerous casualties from enemy snipers. He held his position under the heaviest shell fire, and materially helped to beat off strong counter-attacks by his skilful handling of his own and captured enemy machine guns.

†POWELL, H. S., Sec. Lt., temp. Capt., R. War. R., T.F.— *M.C.* (Mar. 22, 1918).
His company being enfiladed by the enemy, he led a party and captured the position under heavy machine-gun fire. He then reorganized his company and continued the original advance.

RAVENHILL, T. H., Capt., R.A.M.C.—*M.C.* (Aug. 16, 1917).
For conspicuous gallantry and devotion to duty in collecting and evacuating wounded under heavy shell fire, notably during a gas attack, when his coolness and judgement saved very many casualties.

ROBERTSON, J. K. A., Sec. Lt., 8 R. High'rs.—*M.C.* (Apr. 23, 1918).
For conspicuous gallantry and devotion to duty when in command of his company. When all the other officers became casualties, he consolidated a line of shell holes, gaining touch with the troops on his right and left. Though wounded during the advance, he remained on duty and brought his company out of action on the relief.

ROUND, A. J., Lt., attd. 7 S. Wales Bord. (Salonica).—*M.C.*
(Feb. 1, 1919).

In the attack on Grand Couronne on September 18, 1918, Lt. Round was commanding a company. Though wounded early in the day he continued to lead his men to the assault of the final position, when he was again hit and carried out of action. The fine example set by his bold and fearless leading helped to inspire all ranks under his command. As Brigade Bombing Officer for about ten months, Lt. Round has shown great zeal and initiative, and his efforts have contributed largely to the fighting efficiency of the battalions.

ST. JOHNSTON, J. H., Lt., 98 Fd. Coy., R.E.—*M.C.*

During the operations on October 23, 1918, he displayed conspicuous gallantry and devotion to duty in command of his section. Under heavy shell fire he reconnoitred sites for, and constructed five infantry crossings over the Harpies Brook in the vicinity of Vendegies-au-Bois, and rendered harmless two bridges over the stream.

SANDERS, H. J., Sec. Lt., 1/24 Lond. R., T.F.—*M.C.*
(Nov. 14, 1916).

He showed great courage and resource in consolidating a line of shell holes, and in resisting the enemy's counter-attacks. His courage and endurance, under very trying circumstances, assisted very materially in maintaining the position.

SANDERS, H. J., Lt., Actg. Capt., M.C., 1/24 Lond. R., T.F.
—*D.S.O.* (Feb. 1, 1919).

At Le Forêt and St. Pierre Vaast Wood, August 30 and September 2, 1918, this officer led his company in the attack, and succeeded in capturing the objective and 60 prisoners, seven machine guns, and two 77 mm. guns. When the position on Hill 150, near Raucourt, was obscure, he went forward several times under very heavy shell and machine-gun fire to clear up the situation. Throughout the operations he displayed great courage and ability.

c c

SAUNDBY, R. H. M. S., Capt., R. War. R., T.F., and R.F.C.
  For conspicuous gallantry in attacking and destroying an enemy airship.—*M.C.* (July 1, 1917).
At about 2 a.m. two airships came a short distance inland, one
crossing the East Anglian coast . . . made an attack on a coast
town of East Anglia at about 2.30 a.m. She was heavily shelled
by the guns of the anti-aircraft defences, and was driven off. . . .
Shortly afterwards this raider, after dropping a number of bombs
in open places, was engaged and brought down in flames by
a pilot of the Royal Flying Corps. The airship was destroyed.
No casualties or damage were caused in East Anglia.

SAUNDERS, B. R., Lt., Actg. Capt., 2/6 R. War. R., T.F.—
Oct .1 .1917   *M.C.* (Mar. 7, 1918).
For conspicuous gallantry and devotion to duty in leading his
company into the enemy's position and remaining there for over
an hour. The machine-gun fire met with was most intense, but
he was able gradually to withdraw his company after heavy
casualties.

†SAYER, L., Capt., M.C., 16 R. War. R.—*Bar to M.C.* (Dec. 2,
  1918).
During an attack this officer led his company to the final objective
with magnificent courage and ability. When a withdrawal
became necessary he saw a gap on the right flank, and at once
took his company and established touch with the flanks. He did
splendid work re-organizing and consolidating the position under
very heavy machine-gun fire.

SEARLS, T. H., Lt., S. Staff. R.—*M.C.* (Sept. 16, 1918).
For conspicuous gallantry and devotion to duty when in command
of a platoon. He successfully completed an enveloping movement,
with the result that none of the enemy garrison escaped death or
capture. He showed conspicuous courage in hand-to-hand fighting, and personally inflicted several casualties on the enemy. He
captured several prisoners single-handed.

†SHAW, RALPH, Sec. Lt., temp. Lt., 11 R. War. R., S.R.—
  D.S.O. (July 18, 1917).
For conspicuous gallantry and ability in action. When all the
senior officers of the brigade had become casualties he assumed
charge of the whole line, and showed great courage and judgement
under very heavy fire in organizing the consolidation.

THOMPSON, B. J. DENTON, Lt., 10 Manch. R.—*M.C.*
  (Aug. 19, 1916).
For conspicuous gallantry and determination during operations.
When completely surrounded and with only eight men, he held
his own by rapid fire for over a quarter of an hour. Though
wounded in the head, he finally succeeded in getting along the
trench and establishing communication.

TILDESLEY, T. E., Capt., 5 N. Staff. R.—*M.C.* (July 5,
  1918).
For conspicuous gallantry and devotion to duty in superintending
the defence of the sector held by his company during an enemy
counter-attack. He visited the series of disconnected posts held
by his company in broad daylight, and in full view of the enemy,
who could be seen massing for attack, and under heavy fire. By
his excellent behaviour and cheerfulness under fire he inspired all
ranks with a determination to hold on.

TURNER, J. W., Capt., R.A.M.C.—*M.C.* (Nov. 25, 1916).
He worked incessantly by day and night, bringing in wounded
from shell-holes and attending them in dug-outs. He displayed
great determination and a total disregard of personal safety
throughout.

TURNER, J. W. C., Sec. Lt., Actg. Capt., R.F.A., S.R.—
  M.C. (Jan. 8, 1918).
During an intense hostile bombardment of his battery position, he,
accompanied by another man, went back to the position after his
battery had taken cover to a flank, and worked for half-an-hour

under continual shell fire, extricating an N.C.O. who had been severely wounded and half buried in the ruins of a house. No praise can be too great for this gallant act of devotion.

TYNDALL, Rev. E. D., C.F., 4th Cl.—*Bar to M.C.* (Oct. 15, 1918).
During an important engagement the services rendered by this officer in organizing parties who cleared up the battlefield and brought in large numbers of wounded under heavy fire were most valuable. He worked with unremitting devotion to duty for 48 hours, and his cheerfulness and endurance were a fine example to every one.

UMBERS, J. L., Lt., North'd Fus.—*M.C.* (Oct. 15, 1918).
For conspicuous gallantry and devotion to duty during an enemy attack. He was responsible for obtaining much valuable information concerning the enemy's movements throughout the day under heavy shell fire, and thus enabled the various situations to be dealt with rapidly and successfully. He did valuable service.

WALFORD, J.O.
p. 198

WARDER, R. O., Lt., R.F.A.—*D.S.O.* (1915).
For gallantry at Hooge during the gas attack, when he was the last officer left with the guns.

WATKIN, P. J., Capt., R.A.M.C., attd. Bedf. R.—*M.C.* (July 18, 1917).
For two days he dressed wounded under heavy shell fire, and, when the captured trenches had been cleared, he commenced to search the shell holes in ' No Man's Land ', under heavy sniping fire, until ordered to desist.

WHITMORE, C. J. R., Sec. Lt., Actg. Capt., R.G.A., S.R.—*M.C.* (Apr. 17, 1917).
Although wounded, he continued to observe for his battery, in spite of heavy hostile fire. He has on many previous occasions done fine work.

WALKER, E.G.S., Capt., Gen. List. — M.C. (Sept. 27 1920, S. Russia).
For gallantry at Ushun on the 8th and 10th March 1920. He attached himself to the Pelici Regt. and rem⁴. with them throughout the 2 days' counter-attacks, during wh. they sustⁱ. heavy casualties. By his personal example & coolness, under heavy m.g. fire, he was largely resp. for the decisive success

WORTHINGTON, G. F. P., Lt., temp. Capt., W.I.R., attd. Midd'x R.—*M.C.* (Sept. 16, 1918), for Mar. 1918.

For conspicuous gallantry and devotion to duty. When the enemy broke through the line, this officer, with a portion of his company, was surrounded, but he succeeded in fighting his way out. On the following day, during a rearguard action, he superintended the withdrawal of his men, under heavy shell fire, with coolness and skill.

RECEIVED AFTER GOING TO PRESS

FORREST, H., Capt., 7 S. Staff. R.—*M.C.* (Apr. 2, Dec. 10, 1919).

On the night of October 6, 1918, near Fressies, information was received that the enemy had withdrawn from the railway. He was ordered to send out a strong patrol at once to take up a position commanding the railway. This he succeeded in accomplishing under heavy fire. On October 9, during the advance through Abancourt, he led his company with marked skill and dash, and eventually took up a forward position under difficult circumstances.

WALFORD, J. O., Capt., 1/8 Worc. R.—*M.C.* (Apr. 2, Dec. 10, 1919).

In the attack on Bazuel on October 18, 1918, he commanded a company in the leading wave with conspicuous courage and skill. When the advance was held up by heavy machine-gun fire, he made a personal reconnaissance, and gaining touch with a company on the left, he gave orders to the remainder of the line to advance, gaining the objective with few casualties. His company captured a complete battery of 4·2-inch howitzers.

5,

WALFORD, J. O., Capt., M.C., 1/8 Worc. R.—*Bar to M.C.* (Apr. 2, Dec. 10, 1919).

In the attack on Landrecies on November 4, 1918, he displayed marked gallantry and determination in forcing the passage of the canal under heavy artillery and machine-gun fire. Dashing to the top of the canal bank, he personally assisted in launching the rafts and pulling them to and fro. Then he reorganized his company and led them forward to their objective.

SUMMARY

Total serving 1,403

CASUALTIES

Killed in Action or Died of Wounds (of whom 2 are known to
    have died in German hands) 226
Died in Performance of Duty 17
Wounded, exclusive of fatal wounds (259 persons) . . . 321
Injured 21
Prisoners of War (of whom 2 died in captivity) . . . 34

       Total 619

HONOURS

C.M.G.	1
D.S.O. and Bar	2
D.S.O.	14
O.B.E. (Mil.)	12
M.B.E. (Mil.)	8
M.C. and Bar	8
M.C.	97
D.S.C.	1
D.F.C.	1
A.F.C.	3
T.D.	2
Bt. Lt.-Col.	1
Bt.-Maj.	3
D.C.M.	2
M.M.	8
M.S.M.	1

Foreign Honours :

French : Legion of Honour, Croix de Chevalier	. . .	3
Croix de Guerre	. . . . . .	8
Silver Medal, Assistance Publique	. . . .	2
Médaille Militaire	. . . . . .	1
Belgian : Croix de Guerre	. . . . . .	2
Italian : Bronze Medal	. . . . . .	2
Croce di Guerra	. . . . . .	6
Serbian : Order of St. Sava	. . . . .	2
Red Cross	. . . . . .	2
Officer of the Crown of Roumania	. . . .	1
Egyptian : Order of the Nile	. . . . .	1
Total	. . . .	194

Mentioned in Dispatches	. . . . . .	150
(number mentioned = 118)		
Mentioned for Distinguished War Services	. . . .	7
Mentioned for Valuable War Services	. . . .	5
(number mentioned = 4)		
Total	. . . .	162
Combined Total	. . . .	356

www.ingramcontent.com/pod-product-compliance
Lightning Source LLC
Chambersburg PA
CBHW030933150426
42812CB00064B/2838/J